Cambridge International AS and A Level

Business

Revision Guide
Second edition

Peter Stimpson and Peter Joyce

CAMBRIDGE
UNIVERSITY PRESS

CAMBRIDGE
UNIVERSITY PRESS

University Printing House, Cambridge CB2 8BS, United Kingdom

One Liberty Plaza, 20th Floor, New York, NY 10006, USA

477 Williamstown Road, Port Melbourne, VIC 3207, Australia

4843/24, 2nd Floor, Ansari Road, Daryaganj, Delhi – 110002, India

79 Anson Road, #06–04/06, Singapore 079906

Cambridge University Press is part of the University of Cambridge.

It furthers the University's mission by disseminating knowledge in the pursuit of education, learning and research at the highest international levels of excellence.

Information on this title: www.cambridge.org/9781316611708

First published 2013
Second edition 2017

20 19 18 17 16 15 14 13 12 11 10 9 8 7 6 5 4 3 2

Printed in Malaysia by Vivar Printing

A catalogue record for this publication is available from the British Library

ISBN 978-1-316-61170-8 Paperback

....

Table of contents

How to use this book

Learning summary – a summary list of key topics and concepts that you will be looking at in this chapter, to help with navigation through the book and give a reminder of what's important about each topic for your revision.

Terms – clear and straightforward explanations are provided for the most important words in each topic.

Tip – quick suggestions to remind you about key facts and highlight important points.

Progress check – check your own knowledge and see how well you are getting on by answering regular questions.

Exam-style question

Paper 1 (short answer question)

1 Explain briefly the rights of two of a supermarket's stakeholders. [3]

Student's answer

A supermarket will have many stakeholders, e.g. workers and local communities in which the shops operate. These are just two of the groups interested in the decisions and activities of a supermarket.

Workers have legal rights and these would include a contract of employment and working conditions that meet health and safety standards.

Local communities have the right to be asked if the supermarket is planning a large expansion of its shop. Members of the community might be worried about the extra traffic and deliveries by large truck. The community, e.g. local government, might have some control over planning rules.

Authors' comments

This answer is just the right length. It is important not to write too much for the short answer questions as a detailed essay question also needs to be answered on Paper 1.

The answer is clear, concise and accurate – an excellent answer.

Additional exam-style questions

Paper 1 Section A

1 a Explain the term 'sole-trader business'. [3]

   b Explain why a sole-trader might take on a partner. [3]

Section B

2 a Explain why the concept of limited liability is important to both shareholders and limited companies. [8]

   b Discuss whether a retailing business that plans to set up operations for the first time in a foreign country should establish a joint venture with a retailing company in that country. [12]

Paper 2

Spanish Minerals Ltd. (SML)

'I do not see how we are going to compete with ROC Incorporated', said Joe Sainz, the managing director and main shareholder of SML. This is a private limited company that extracts minerals from three quarries in Spain. 'As one of the largest public limited mining companies in the world, ROC Inc's decision to start up operations in Spain by opening a huge new quarry could force us out of business! We operate in the private sector and have no government support.'

'We have capital saved from retained profits and we could consider conversion to a public limited company', said the other main shareholder of SML Pablo Massa. 'With the capital raised we could aim to become a highly mechanised and efficient supplier of high grade minerals. If the sale of shares was successful, we could also become very rich!'

'Perhaps', Joe replied, 'we should focus on our cement factory which uses some of the minerals we extract. If we concentrated on processing minerals rather than mining them, we could use ROC as one of our suppliers or even form a joint venture with the company'.

3 a i Define the term 'private limited company'. [2]

      ii Briefly explain the term 'private sector'. [3]

   b Using examples from the text, explain the difference between primary sector activity and secondary sector activity. [6]

   c Analyse the reasons why SML might gain from forming a joint venture with ROC. [8]

   d Evaluate whether Joe and Pablo should convert SML into a public limited company. [11]

Exam-style questions/Additional exam-style questions – these questions enable you to test your knowledge and understanding at the end of each chapter. The answers are provided at the back of the book.

Chapter levels – chapters have been colour-coded as either AS or A Level in order to help guide you through the book's content, with AS chapters coloured orange and A Level chapters coloured green.

Introduction

Purpose of this revision guide

Cambridge International AS and A Level Business Revision Guide has been written to support students working towards these important qualification. The guide follows exactly the order of topics contained in the current Cambridge International AS and A Level Business syllabus produced by Cambridge International Examinations and the endorsed textbook *Cambridge International AS and A Level Business Coursebook* published by Cambridge University Press (Stimpson/Farquharson ISBN 9781107677364). The guide is so comprehensive that it will also prove to be invaluable to students following other similar courses such as AQA A Level and IB Business and Management.

The Revision Guide has four main objectives:

1 To explain important subject content, concepts and techniques using easily remembered approaches.
2 To give a clear understanding to students of the key skills that each type of examination question requires.
3 To allow for practice at planning and answering examination-style questions.
4 To encourage students to avoid the most common errors in their answers but include the most relevant points of analysis and evaluation.

What makes this book different?

- It is written by two experienced examiners with many years of teaching and examining experience in Business.
- It does not just focus on subject content – it is not designed to be a textbook – but also gives clear guidance on how students can improve skills so that they can do better and achieve high grades by preparing appropriate answers.
- It contains example student answers and answer plans to 40 exam-style questions – with invaluable comments and advice from the authors on these.
- It uses a variety of different presentational styles to make it easier to revise and learn important material and essential Business concepts.
- The student answers to the exam-style questions and the outline answers at the end of the book have been written by the authors.

Note

Cambridge International Examinations bears no responsibility for these answers or for the comments offered. Inevitably, discursive style questions can have a variety of possible answers – in Business there are often no 'right' or 'wrong' answers. The suggested answers provided should be seen as only one possibility, designed to illustrate the approach rather than the answer itself.

The style of each chapter follows the same format and the key features are:

Chapter section	Purpose of each section	How to use each section
Learning summary	Outline the key objectives to be reached as you work through the chapter.	These objectives serve as a checklist of your progress through each chapter.
Bullet points and diagrams of important subject content	Key subject knowledge that is presented in an easy to recall style.	Use these as summaries of the important subject knowledge covered by the main textbook.
Notes with key definitions, formulae and common errors to avoid	Summarise the main terms and formulae in AS and A Level Business and the common mistakes to avoid.	Test your knowledge against these definitions and formulae and make sure you avoid the common mistakes!
Progress check questions	Test your understanding of the subject content covered by each topic.	If in doubt about any of these go back and re-read the topic or the textbook.
Exam-style questions	Allow practice at answering typical examination questions.	Authors' comments allow you to see what is important and compare your own answers against sample answers.

Explanation of the features in each chapter

Each chapter title is drawn from the headings used in the specification.

> **TIP**
>
> Obtain a copy of the syllabus (you are studying), and example papers/mark schemes and keep them in your Business file.

Tips on how to revise

Different people revise in different ways and the aim of this section is not to make you change the way you revise – if it works well for you and you get the results you are capable of then stay with that!

However, there are some important steps that anyone can take to improve the effectiveness of the revision period.

Place

- Find a quiet place to study – but sometimes, testing yourself with friends can be a useful checking process and can lead to discussion of important ideas and common problems.
- Make sure you are sitting comfortably – perhaps, at a well-lit desk.
- Avoid studying in an area where there will be distractions – such as television!

Planning

- This is very important as it is so easy to waste valuable revision time.
- Allow plenty of time for revision – especially if you are taking more than one AS or A Level subject.
- List all of your exam subjects and the amount of time you think you will need for each one.
- Divide each subject into major topic areas (use your copy of the syllabus to help you) and allocate sufficient time to revise each one – allow more time for the topics you find most difficult.

- Vary your revision plan – do not revise one topic or even one subject for a whole day but include other subject areas to avoid becoming bored with just one.
- Build 'time off' into your plan – allow five or ten minutes' break each hour and go out of the room you are in and take some exercise.
- Write up your plan, display it somewhere visible and do your best to stick to it!

Methods of revising

- Reading notes and textbook are important but rarely enough by themselves – this is rather passive revision.
- Make definition lists, bullet points of key factors; write out a summary of existing notes, make spider or mind map diagrams, test yourself using e-versions of multiple choice questions, test yourself with a friend revising for the same subject – these are all active forms of revision.
- Use the 'look, cover, write and check' technique for learning important topics. This involves:

1 study the topic for a few minutes
2 cover up the book and notes
3 write down all you can recall about the topic
4 check what you have written against the book and notes.

  - Study your past test and mock examination scripts to identify what went wrong – things to avoid – but also what went right – things to repeat and build upon during the 'real' exam.
  - Practise writing answers to past examination questions – or questions in this book – and either ask your teacher to mark them or check them against the student's answers with authors' comments at the end of each chapter.

Last minute tips

- Don't leave all your revision to the last minute!
- Use your summary notes, checklists, definitions sheets, spider diagrams etc., to check final facts and understanding.
- Sleep well – do not stay up all night trying to cram in yet more knowledge! It's more important to get a good night's sleep before any examination.

TIP Use the Student CD-ROM in the *Cambridge International AS and A Level Business Coursebook* published by Cambridge University Press (Stimpson/Farquharson ISBN 9781107677364) as it has many multiple choice questions and mind maps to aid your revision.

Examination skills

How can you use the skills and knowledge you have been building to perform to your best abilities in examination?

The answer to this question is: show the key examination skills in your answer that are relevant to the question set.

What is meant by 'examination skills'?

They are also known as 'assessment objectives' which means the ways in which an examiner will assess or mark your answer. Your answers need to demonstrate the following:

Knowledge with understanding

This means, does your answer contain accurate and relevant Business subject knowledge which shows understanding of the part of the course that is being examined? **All** of your answers must contain evidence of relevant knowledge. One way of showing knowledge is to accurately define the Business term used in the question. So, if the question asks: 'What is meant by the term "price skimming"?' then a full and accurate definition of this term will help.

Even if the question is a more challenging A Level question, for example as found on the Cambridge Paper 3 Case Study, then a definition can be an excellent way to start an answer – and demonstrate knowledge in the first sentence! For example: 'Evaluate a marketing plan for the successful launch of Product X in your country'.

A definition of 'marketing plan' would help you show good subject knowledge and it would also direct you to what factors to include in the rest of the answer! However, the most effective way to show knowledge is through its appropriate use.

Application

This skill requires you to make a clear link between your answer and the business in the case study (Example: Cambridge Papers 2 or 3) or in the stem of the question (Example: Cambridge Paper 1). A 'clear link' does not just mean mentioning the name of the business or the names of the owners/directors of the business. True application of an answer means that, for example, your knowledge and understanding are being used to analyse the problems **this** business may be facing or how an important decision will impact on **this** particular business.

For example, if the question is: 'Analyse the advantages and disadvantages of the piece rate system of payment for cooks in Jamie's restaurant', then an example of part of an answer which is **not** applied would be: 'The piece rate system encourages faster working by employees and this may reduce the quality of the finished product'. This argument could apply to **any** business, not just a restaurant.

Here is an example of part of an answer that **is** applied:

> 'If cooks are paid piece rate then they may concentrate on preparing meals too quickly so food may not be cooked properly causing customers to complain'.

Application is a very important skill to demonstrate in Business examinations as different businesses will respond in different ways to problems or ways of resolving them or be affected in different ways by external events. Without demonstrating this skill of application you will lose about 25 per cent of the total marks but, in addition, you are likely to lose more marks because the skill of evaluation can usually only be shown by answering in the context of the business.

Analysis

This skill requires that answers contain more than just knowledge. Analysis can be demonstrated in several different ways in answers to Business questions. For example:

- Using the theoretical concepts and techniques included in the Business course to explain the advantages and disadvantages of a business decision, or to develop consequences of that decision.
- Examining the impact on a business of information provided, for example, economic data or information about competitors' actions.

- Selecting information presented in different forms, such as graphs, tables and charts, and identifying trends and changes and explaining their impact on a business.

- Drawing together ideas and information.

If the question is: 'Analyse the likely impact on Business B's profits of an increase in its selling prices' then an example of one part of an analytical response would be:

'An increase in prices means that the gross profit margin on each unit sold will be higher, assuming that the costs of making it did not increase too. If the business sells the same amount as before, then total gross profits will rise'. However, this is not contextual yet.

Evaluation

This skill requires students to draw conclusions from the arguments used, make judgements which are supported or make recommendations that are justified by preceding analysis. To be effective – and to earn the marks – the evaluation must be rooted in the context of the business featured in the data or case study – which means the judgement made must be applied to the business.

Before evaluation can be effectively demonstrated, the answer must show evidence of knowledge, application and analysis. Evaluation cannot just 'appear' in an answer without the building up of relevant and applied arguments, based on subject knowledge, to support it. Many examples of questions that require evaluation – and students' answers to them – are contained in this book.

How will I know which skills are being examined?

The 'command words' are the important word or words that appear in a question that indicate to students which skills are being examined. It is very important that you understand these command words so that you do not:

✓ waste time developing an answer with examination skills that **are not** being examined in a question

✗ throw away marks by not showing evidence of the skills that **are** being examined.

TIP

Questions consist of:

'**Command word**' + **Topic** being examined + **Context** (for example, case study).

Spend time thinking about what each question is asking before writing answers!

These are the main command words that will be used on Business AS and A Level examination papers:

Command words	Skills being examined
State List Define What is meant by…	Knowledge
Calculate for this business… Explain how this business… From the data outline…	Knowledge Application
Analyse Explain why… Explain the advantages and disadvantages of…	Knowledge Application Analysis
Evaluate Discuss Assess Recommend and justify… Do you agree…	Knowledge Application Analysis Evaluation

TIP

Spend time analysing questions to decide which is the best way to demonstrate evaluation in an answer. For example: 'Recommend' requires a justified recommendation, 'Evaluate the factors' requires a prioritisation of factors, 'Discuss' requires a balancing of arguments and so on.

Understanding mark schemes

Have you seen examples of mark schemes for the Business examination papers?

 TIP Ask your teacher for examples of mark schemes from past Cambridge examination papers.

Mark schemes are the documents used by examiners to guide their assessment of examination scripts. Although the schemes contain details of the subject knowledge that students are expected to show in their answers, this is not their only purpose. They also give details of the number of marks available for each examination skill – and these are normally divided into 'levels' that denote the quality of the answer. It's demonstration of skills that gets the marks – the higher the skill, the higher the mark!

Keys to examination success – the day of the examination

Assuming you have done your very best during the Business course and that you have followed the revision tips above, what are the best ways to prepare for the examination day itself?

- Check the time of the examination and leave for the exam in plenty of time.
- Take all of the necessary equipment with you – for Business, two black pens (one could run out of ink!), a calculator and a ruler should be sufficient. Your exam centre will want these in a 'see through' plastic case.

- When the exam starts, read the instructions carefully and ask the invigilator if any of these instructions are unclear before you start writing.
- Read through case study material very carefully – do this again after you have read the questions because a hurried start in answering the first question nearly always leads to poor marks if the case study material is not understood and key points from it are not incorporated in your answer.
- Look at the marks available for each question and the 'command' word – these will indicate to you which of the examination skills are being tested. They will also give you an indication of how long to spend on answering each question.
- Divide the total time up – you may need to make a note of this – between the questions in proportion to the marks each one carries.
- Write as neatly as you can. It is recommended that you leave a line between each paragraph and at least two lines between each separate answer.
- Plan answers to the longer questions.
- Answer the question that has been set, not necessarily the one that you want to answer!
- Allow ten minutes at the end to read through answers to correct any glaring errors or to add a key point that has been missed out.

Now that you have read this introduction you are well prepared with important advice on how to face your examinations! However, first, you have to actually do the revision and the remainder of this book will, we hope, make your revision more effective and will help you gain the final grade that you deserve. Good luck in your examinations!

Peter Stimpson

Peter Joyce

Unit 1
BUSINESS AND ITS ENVIRONMENT

Enterprise

1.1 Business activity

Businesses aim to meet the needs of customers by using resources to make goods and services that they will buy. These products can be either for final consumers or capital and intermediate goods for business customers. Which resources (factors of production) do businesses need?

- Labour: human effort to produce goods or provide services to customers
- Capital: equipment and machinery
- Land: a location to operate the business from
- Enterprise: risk taking and decision making undertaken by an entrepreneur.

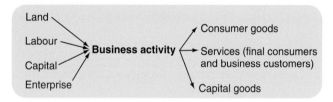

Figure 1.1 Business activity – resources and products

1.2 Opportunity cost

Opportunity cost is an important concept in business activity and business decisions. When a decision is made to purchase one item – for example, a new machine – other items have to be 'given up' as resources are scarce. The loss of benefit that would have been gained from the 'next best' item is called opportunity cost. This applies to decisions made by consumers and governments too.

TERMS

Consumer products (goods and services): bought by 'final' consumers who will benefit from them and not use them to produce other products.

Capital and intermediate goods: goods bought by industry to be used in the production of other products.

Opportunity cost: the benefit of the next most desired option that is given up.

1.3 Added value

Business activity aims to increase added value. Increasing 'added value' has many benefits – the key one being that it could lead to higher profits for the owners of the business.

TERMS

Added value: the difference between the cost of purchasing raw materials and the price of the finished good.

Creating value: increasing the difference between the cost of bought in materials and the price finished goods are sold for.

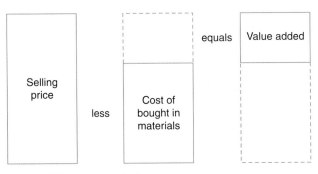

Figure 1.2 Valued added

Ways of adding more value to raw materials include:

1 Raising the selling price but keeping the raw material costs constant **but** will customers still buy?
2 Purchasing cheaper raw materials but keeping selling prices the same **but** will customers notice a reduction in quality?
3 Using raw materials more efficiently so the cost per item falls **but** this might need more accurate machines or more highly trained staff.

1.4 Entrepreneurs

The role and characteristics of successful entrepreneurs

Entrepreneurs are people who are determined to create their own business – not work as an employee for another firm. This means they must have:

- a business idea
- some savings to invest
- willingness to take risks and accept responsibilities.

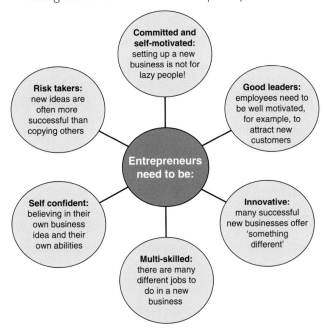

Figure 1.3 Characteristics of successful entrepreneurs

Progress check A

1 What capital equipment would a hairdressing business need?
2 Where is an entrepreneur likely to locate a new shop selling mobile (cell) phones?
3 What types of workers would an entrepreneur operating a road transport business most probably need to employ?
4 A business making clothes has managed to use ten per cent less material on each item of clothing by using a new cutting machine. Explain what will happen to the 'value created' by this business.
5 Explain how a computer could either be sold as a 'consumer good' or a 'capital good'.

1.5 What do businesses need to succeed and why do many new businesses fail?

Business success requires:

- Adequate factors of production
- Customers
- Suppliers
- Government – to provide a legal framework, infrastructure and education.

These are the most common reasons for new enterprises not succeeding:

1 Lack of finance or working capital – often difficult to encourage people or banks to invest in new business ideas.
2 Lack of record keeping – not having sufficient information to operate the business.
3 Poor management skills – even the hardest working and most enthusiastic entrepreneur needs basic management skills, for example, communication and leadership skills.

4 Competition – most new enterprises are small and compete against larger rivals who may try to 'squeeze them out of business'.

5 A dynamic business environment – economic or technological changes can be a serious problem for new small businesses as they often do not have the resources to respond to them effectively.

Progress check B

1 Why are leadership skills important to an entrepreneur?

2 Why is it often important for an entrepreneur to be prepared to be a 'risk taker'?

3 Why might an 'entrepreneur's innovation' be important for the success of a new business?

4 Explain why a new business might fail even though the entrepreneur who set it up has all of the 'key characteristics' listed above.

1.6 Benefits for the entrepreneurs' countries

Entrepreneurs' new businesses give economic benefits to a country. These include:

- Reduce unemployment.
- Increase national output – some could be exported to earn foreign currency.
- Create additional competition for existing firms.
- Increase government tax revenue.
- Innovate and accept technological change.
- May develop and expand into huge corporations!

1.7 Social enterprises

It is wrong to assume that 'all businesses want is to make profits'. This is too simple – as Chapter 4 shows. Good examples of business organisations that try to achieve non-profit based objectives are 'social enterprises'. Many cooperative organisations are operated as social enterprises (see Chapter 2).

The 'triple bottom line' of social enterprises means that they aim to achieve:

1 Economic objectives – making profits to reinvest.

2 Social objectives – supporting disadvantaged groups such as providing work for disabled workers or providing support for refugee groups.

3 Environmental objectives – managing the business in an environmentally sustainable way.

TERM

Social enterprise: business with mainly social objectives that reinvests most of its profits into benefiting society rather than maximising returns to owners.

TIP

Do not confuse social enterprises with charities – social enterprises will aim to make a profit but will try to do so in an environmentally and socially responsible way.

Progress check C

1 Explain **two** reasons why most countries' governments are trying to increase the number of new enterprises in the economy.

2 Why might a social enterprise find it easy to recruit well motivated staff?

3 Does a social enterprise need profits?

4 What other objectives might a social enterprise have apart from making a financial return?

TIP

When a question asks you to 'discuss' you must make sure that you weigh up several possibilities and draw a conclusion in your answer – this will demonstrate the skill of evaluation.

Exam-style questions

Paper 1 Section B

1 a Explain the importance of business activity to a country. [8]

   b Discuss the characteristics an entrepreneur needs to set up a successful new retail business. [12]

Student's answer to 1(b)

An entrepreneur is a person who is prepared to take risks in setting up and managing a business, often with their own savings or capital.

Such a person needs to have several personal characteristics if they are going to set up a successful business. They will have to be prepared to work hard as there will be so much to do. Plans will have to be made, a location needs to be arranged, inventory bought and, if the shop is going to be big enough, workers will have to be employed. If an entrepreneur is lazy the retail business is unlikely to succeed.

The entrepreneur will need to be good at making decisions. As there are already so many shops the entrepreneur will need to make the new retail store 'stand out'. Perhaps unusual products will be sold to attract customers or the location of the shop might be really important. If it was a shop selling sandwiches and drinks then locating it near where many people work would be a good idea. If the entrepreneur is not good at making decisions, the shop will fail.

The entrepreneur will need people skills too. This means they will need to be able to get on well with customers and workers. If they are bad leaders and shout at workers in front of customers in the shop then this will lead to customers leaving. If they cannot talk to customers to find out what they really want then the shop may end up selling the wrong products.

Perhaps the most important characteristic that the entrepreneur must have is to be multi-skilled. They will have to be good at numbers to do the accounting and check the inventory. They need to know about the product they are selling. They will need to know about displays and presentation. As the business is new and small the owner will not be able to afford to employ people to do all of these things which is why multi-skilling is so important.

So, a successful entrepreneur must have many characteristics to succeed in retailing. However, even all of these might not be enough to make sure the business is successful if there is a recession or if customer tastes change quickly.

Authors' comments

This is an excellent answer. It demonstrates knowledge as entrepreneur is defined and good awareness of personal characteristics is shown. Can you also see that the answer is applied to retailing? This is very important – the student tries to make points that are particularly relevant to setting up and running a shop. The points made are well explained or analysed and there is good judgement or evaluation. The evaluation is strong in two ways. The student suggests and justifies the 'most important characteristic' and also looks briefly at other factors, apart from the entrepreneur, that could affect the success of a shop.

Additional exam-style questions

Paper 1 Section A

1 Explain the term 'creating value'. [3]

2 Explain why opportunity cost results from the decision by a business to purchase a new vehicle. [3]

Paper 1 Section B (essay)

3 a Explain the main features of social enterprises. [8]

   b Discuss the most likely reasons why some new enterprises fail in the first year of operation. [12]

Paper 2

Linda's Pottery

4 Linda decided three months ago to set up her own business. She has been told that she has enough enterprise to make a success of her new business idea – a pottery making plates and bowls. After leaving her office job she spent

→

some of her savings to obtain essential factors of production. In the first three months of trading she recorded the following figures:

Plates sold, 50 – average price $4
Bowls sold, 120 – average price $3
Cost of bought in materials used – $280

Linda wants to create more value. She is planning either to increase prices by ten per cent or cut the cost of the materials she buys in – mainly clay and paints.

There are several pottery businesses in her region and some of them claim to sell the best quality plates and bowls.

Although Linda is a skilled potter she has never gained any management experience. She is prepared to spend a lot of time learning how to operate her business successfully.

a   i   Define the term 'enterprise'.   [2]

    ii Briefly explain the term 'factors of production'.   [3]

b   i   Calculate the added value of Linda's business in the first three months.   [3]

    ii Explain one reason why 'added value' is important to Linda.   [3]

c   Analyse **two** of the characteristics that Linda will need to reduce the chance of her new business failing.   [8]

d   Recommend to Linda which method of creating added value she should choose. Justify your answer.   [11]

Business structure

Learning summary

After you have studied this chapter you should be able to:

- understand the different levels of business (economic) activity and the difference between private sector and public sector

- understand limited liability and its importance

- understand legal forms of business organisation and their main differences

- assess the factors that influence the most appropriate form of business organisation

- understand the problems of changing from one legal structure to another.

2.1 Economic activity

It is common to divide business activity into three sectors. The relative importance (as a percentage of total national output) of these varies greatly between countries. Generally, it is true that in high income developed economies, such as France, the tertiary sector is the most important. In middle income emerging economies such as Brazil and China, the secondary sector tends to be the most important. In low income developing economies the primary sector is often the most significant. This helps to explain the low average incomes in these countries – the value added by the primary sector is usually much lower than that of the other two.

TERMS

Primary sector: businesses involved in farming, fishing and extracting natural resources.

Secondary sector: businesses involved in manufacturing products from primary goods.

Tertiary sector: businesses involved in providing services to consumers and other businesses.

2.2 Private sector and public sector

Private sector businesses are often operated with the objective of earning profits. Public sector organisations – such as police force, schools, universities and hospitals –

have other objectives. These could include social aims, such as caring for the elderly, or keeping law and order.

Nearly all economies have a 'mixture' of these two sectors and are referred to as mixed economies. If there was no public sector activity it would be called a free-market economy. If there was no private sector, it would be called a command or a planned economy.

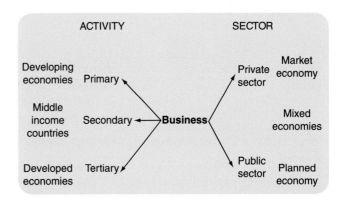

Figure 2.1 Economic activities and economic systems

TERMS

Private sector: comprises businesses owned and controlled by individuals or groups of people.

Public sector: comprises organisations owned by, accountable to and controlled by the state.

Limited liability: investors/shareholders are only liable (can only lose) for their original investment in a company.

Progress check A

1   Research (using the internet) the share of the total economy accounted for by the private sector in any two countries of your choice.

2   Would you classify a business that roasts and grinds coffee beans as being in the primary or secondary sector of industry?

3   Explain one reason why the tertiary sector is often much more important in developed economies than in developing economies.

4   Is the private sector more or less important than the public sector in your economy?

    Use employment or output data to help you answer.

2.3 Legal forms of business organisation

	Sole trader	Partnership	Private limited company	Public limited company
	A business owned and controlled by one person	A business owned by two or more people sharing investment and responsibilities	A business owned by shareholders, often family members, which cannot sell shares to general public	A business, owned by shareholders, which has the right to sell shares to general public
Ownership	One person	Shared between partners	Shareholders (but shares not available publicly)	Shareholders (general public or investment/ pension funds)
Senior managers	The owner	One or more of the partners	Usually one of the main shareholders but can be a professional manager	Professional directors elected by shareholders – CEO appointed by Board of Directors
Financial liability	The owner	Shared by the partners – except in case of limited partnership	Limited to the amount invested by shareholders	Limited to the amount invested by shareholders
Main capital sources	Owner's savings Bank loans	Partners' savings Bank loans	Capital from sale of shares Retained profits Bank loans	Capital from sale of shares Retained profits Bank loans
Common problems	Lack of management skills Lack of capital for expansion Unlimited liability	Some partners may be more competent or harder working than others Unlimited liability Profits shared	Some loss of control/ ownership when the original owner sells shares to friends/business contacts Cannot sell shares to general public Legal formalities Some disclosure of accounts	Further loss of control/ ownership by original owners Divorce between ownership and control Full disclosure of accounts as legally required

	Sole trader	Partnership	Private limited company	Public limited company
	A business owned and controlled by one person	A business owned by two or more people sharing investment and responsibilities	A business owned by shareholders, often family members, which cannot sell shares to general public	A business, owned by shareholders, which has the right to sell shares to general public
Common benefits	Owner keeps all profits Owner takes all decisions – no need to consult with others which can be time – consuming	More capital invested by partners Sharing of responsibilities Often partners have different skills and experience	Limited liability for shareholders Less disclosure of accounts than public limited company Continuity	Limited liability for shareholders – this makes it easier to attract new shareholders who can now include the general public Access to more capital through sale of shares via Stock Market Continuity
Most likely to be appropriate for	One person business owned by an entrepreneur wanting to keep control and not expand the business	The owner wants to expand business by taking on partner with capital – able to share responsibilities	Owners want the security of limited liability, want to raise funds by sale of shares and status of separate legal entity	Owners want to raise large sums of capital for substantial business growth Prepared to risk some loss of control

Table 2.1 Types of business organisation

> **TIP**
>
> There is no one correct or appropriate form of legal structure or business organisation – it depends on the size and nature of the business and the objectives of the owners.

2.4 Other business structures

Cooperatives

These can offer the opportunity for members to gain from bulk buying and the incentive to operate the cooperative efficiently as all will benefit from higher profit.

Decision making can be slow if all members have to be consulted.

> **TERM**
>
> Cooperatives: all members/owners can contribute to the running of the organisation and profits are shared between them.

Franchise

An entrepreneur might decide to take out a franchise of an existing successful business to reduce risks, to receive advice and training, to gain a reliable source of supplies and benefit from a well-established brand. However, this business model will reduce the entrepreneur's independence and there will be franchise fees to pay plus, probably, a share of the sales or profits to the franchisor.

> **TERM**
>
> Franchise: a business that uses the name, logo and trading systems of an existing business.

Joint venture

This structure is particularly common when expanding abroad as local knowledge can be gained through a joint venture with a firm based in the country.

Different leadership/management styles and clashes of culture can lead to problems with these ventures.

TERM

Joint venture: two or more businesses agreeing to work together on a particular project. This allows risk and costs to be shared although it might lead to disputes over leadership.

2.5 Problems of changing legal structure

- Cost – it can be expensive to create a limited company or to arrange the public sale of shares to convert a private company into a public limited company.
- Loss of control – taking on a partner, selling shares to new shareholders or converting a private company into a public limited company all involve some loss of control over business decision making.
- Sharing of profits – by taking on additional owners, profits have to be shared between more people.

Progress check B

1 List **two** types of business organisation that do not give their owners limited liability.

2 Why is 'shareholders' limited liability' important to a public limited company when it advertises its shares for sale?

3 Why might a sole trader decide **not** to take a partner into the business?

4 Why might the directors of a private limited company decide **not** to convert the business into a public limited company?

5 Differentiate between a joint venture and a franchise.

6 Explain why the managers of a retailing business might choose to expand the business through franchising.

7 Explain why a business planning to operate in a foreign country for the first time might decide to establish a joint venture there.

8 Why is limited liability important to someone planning to invest in a business?

9 Explain **two** problems to the owners of a private limited company of converting the business to a public limited company.

Exam-style questions

Paper 1 Section A

1 Discuss whether a new entrepreneur who wishes to set up her own café should take out a franchise with a well-established international café company. [20]

Student's answer

A franchise means that the business buys a licence from a franchisor to operate the business under the name of the franchisor. The franchisee would use the logo/brand name of the franchisor and would usually sell all of the products/services supplied by this business too.

The question states that this is a new entrepreneur which means that she might not have much business experience. Operating as a franchise means the franchisor will provide training, advertising, advice on products and pricing and other issues which means that the new entrepreneur has a greater chance of avoiding important mistakes. Also, using the name of a well-established business means that customers of the café will already know the name, products and image of the business, making the launch of the new enterprise less risky. The food and drinks sold by the franchisee will already be 'tried and tested' and the entrepreneur will not have to make decisions about these products.

New entrepreneurs do not usually have much finance so the cost of the franchise licence may be too expensive and leave too little money for employing workers or for buying or leasing the premises. This could be the most important reason why the new entrepreneur might decide to just set up her own café under her own name. Also, she probably wants to be independent – this is an important reason why many people set up their own business. The franchisor will insist on taking many decisions and will also demand a share of revenue or profits. For an independent minded person this level of control might be too much.

There are many factors for the new entrepreneur to consider before making this important decision. Operating a café is not as difficult as, say, setting up a car factory and the machinery and materials used are relatively easy to work with. The brand name of a large franchisor could also be damaged, e.g. by a food poisoning scare in another café. For this reason,

I think most new entrepreneurs planning to start a new café would not take out a franchise – but much will depend on how much capital they have and how much risk they are prepared to take.

Authors' comments

This is a well-planned and clearly written answer. Can you see the clear references to 'new entrepreneur' and 'café'? – these help to apply the answer firmly in the context given by the question. There is some good analysis of both the advantages and disadvantages of franchising. There is clear evaluation – not only in the final paragraph but also when the student assesses the 'important reasons' and explains these well.

Additional exam-style questions

Paper 1 Section A

1 a Explain the term 'sole-trader business'. [3]

   b Explain why a sole-trader might take on a partner. [3]

Section B

2 a Explain why the concept of limited liability is important to both shareholders and limited companies. [8]

   b Discuss whether a retailing business that plans to set up operations for the first time in a foreign country should establish a joint venture with a retailing company in that country. [12]

Paper 2

Spanish Minerals Ltd. (SML)

'I do not see how we are going to compete with ROC Incorporated', said Joe Sainz, the managing director and main shareholder of SML. This is a private limited company that extracts minerals from three quarries in Spain. 'As one of the largest public limited mining companies in the world, ROC Inc's decision to start up operations in Spain by opening a huge new quarry could force us out of business! We operate in the private sector and have no government support.'

'We have capital saved from retained profits and we could consider conversion to a public limited company', said the other main shareholder of SML Pablo Massa. 'With the capital raised we could aim to become a highly mechanised and efficient supplier of high grade minerals. If the sale of shares was successful, we could also become very rich!'

'Perhaps', Joe replied, 'we should focus on our cement factory which uses some of the minerals we extract. If we concentrated on processing minerals rather than mining them, we could use ROC as one of our suppliers or even form a joint venture with the company'.

3 a i Define the term 'private limited company'. [2]

      ii Briefly explain the term 'private sector'. [3]

   b Using examples from the text, explain the difference between primary sector activity and secondary sector activity. [6]

   c Analyse the reasons why SML might gain from forming a joint venture with ROC. [8]

   d Evaluate whether Joe and Pablo should convert SML into a public limited company. [11]

Size of business

3.1 Measuring business size

Why is it important to know 'how big' a business is or 'how many' small businesses there are in a country? Business managers and governments are interested in measuring business size. For example:

- Managers want to know if their business is becoming relatively larger than others in the industry.
- Governments want to know if national businesses are becoming larger compared to those of other countries – and whether the number of small businesses is increasing.

None of the measures of business size is perfect. In some cases they can give rather misleading indications of business size – which is why it is common to use more than one measure to make comparisons between businesses.

Some of the problems include:

- **Market capitalisation:** would exclude IKEA, Virgin and other large private limited companies. The market capitalisation values can also change greatly with a Stock Market 'boom' or 'slump'.
- **Employment:** this would make a nuclear power company – with relatively few employees but huge capital investments – appear quite small.
- **Capital employed:** this would make a labour intensive industry – such as a postal service – appear quite small compared to the large number of people it employs.
- **Sales value:** although useful for making comparisons between firms in the same industry, it is of limited value in making inter-industry comparisons.
- **Market share:** useful for making comparisons between the relative importance of firms in

the same industry, it is of no use in making size comparisons between firms in completely different industries.

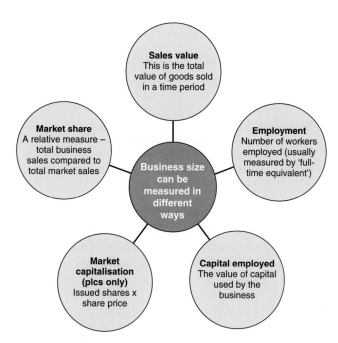

Figure 3.1 Measuring business size

Progress check A

1   Company A is a construction business employing 100 part-time workers who, on average, work 20 hours per week. Company B is a construction business employing 30 full-time workers (40 hours per week, on average). Which company is larger (using the employment measure)?

2   Why would it be misleading to compare the size of an electricity generating business with that of an office cleaning business using the 'capital employed' measure?

3   Why would it be impossible to compare the size of two sole trader businesses by using the 'market capitalisation' measure?

4   Explain whether 'sales value' is a good way of measuring the size of two car manufacturing businesses.

3.2 Small firms can benefit an economy

Most governments are willing to offer special support for small businesses because of the economic benefits they offer.

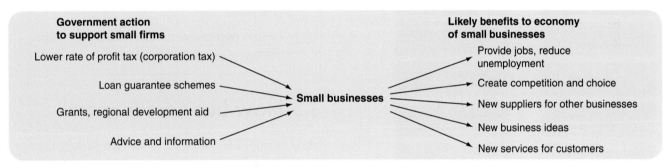

Figure 3.2 Small businesses – government support and economic benefits

3.3 Common strengths and weaknesses of family businesses

Feature of family business	Common strengths	Common weaknesses
Structure	Informal, flexible, entrepreneurial, innovative.	Resistant to change, lack of management development, no organisation charts – unclear structure.
Roles	Family members often play multiple roles, flexible, quick decision making.	Role confusion, jobs do not get done, family favouritism can lead to unqualified family members in jobs.
Leadership	Creative, ambitious, informal authority, entrepreneurial.	Autocratic, resistant to new ideas, avoids delegation.
Employees including family members	Employees often committed and loyal, shared values and culture.	Cannot keep family issues out of business, inability to balance family's and business's needs, inward looking, can't separate work and family, family rivalries.

Feature of family business	Common strengths	Common weaknesses
Succession	Training successors can begin early, can choose when to leave.	Family issues get in way, unwillingness to let go, unwilling to choose a successor.
Ownership/control	Closely held, family owned, high degree of control, earnings are motivators.	May sacrifice growth for control, often no outside directors, need for privacy.
Culture	Innovative, informal, flexible, creative, adaptable, common language, efficient communications.	Founder's role can stifle innovation, inefficient, emotional, resistant to change, high risk of conflicts.

Table 3.1 Family businesses – strengths and weaknesses

3.4 The relative advantages and disadvantages of small and large businesses

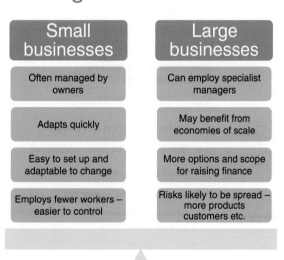

Figure 3.3 Advantages of small businesses compared with advantages of large business

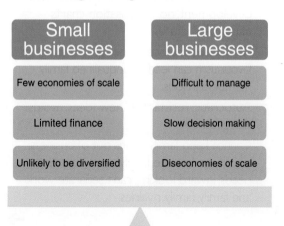

Figure 3.4 Disadvantages of small businesses compared with disadvantages of large businesses

Progress check B

1 Research the support given by the government in your country to small businesses.

2 Explain **two** problems often faced by small businesses.

3 Explain **two** problems that often result from managing a large business.

3.5 How businesses grow

Many owners and managers of businesses want their firm to expand. Some do not – and the reasons for different business objectives are considered in Chapter 4.

Business expansion can take place in two ways:

1 Internal growth (or organic growth) through expanding existing operations and opening new ones e.g. Apple developing new products or ZARA opening more shops.
2 External growth through integration with another business (see Chapter 7).

TERM

Internal growth: expansion of a business by means of increasing sales and opening new branches, shops or factories – also known as organic growth.

TIP

Remember that internal growth is often easier to manage than sudden external growth.

Exam-style question

Paper 1 Section A

1   Define the term 'internal growth'. [2]

Expansion of a business that comes from increasing sales due to opening new branches/shops/factories.

Author comment

This is a good answer to this question.

Additional exam-style questions

Paper 1 Section A

1   a   State **two** ways in which business size can be measured and compared. [2]

　 b   Explain one reason why small businesses are commonly found in the hairdressing industry. [3]

Section B

2   Analyse the possible weaknesses of family businesses. [8]

3   Discuss the importance of small firms to the economy of a country. [12]

Paper 2 (part question)

Joe Trading (JT)

Joe started JT 25 years ago with capital of $1000. JT's accountant now values the capital employed at $12.5m. Joe believes that JT is now one of the largest retailers of sports equipment in the country. JT operates 35 shops, all leased from property companies at very competitive rents. Joe thinks the main reasons for JT's success are his commitment to the business and low prices. 2 years ago Joe passed overall control of the business to Liam, his son. He had just graduated from university with a Business degree. Some JT workers have recently left the business because of Liam's different approach to management, compared with Joe. Liam has appointed his sister as Marketing Director. She is keen to do well but admitted to a friend that she was not really interested in sport.

4   Analyse two benefits to JT from being 'one of the largest retailers of sports equipment in the country'. [8]

5   Discuss whether the future success of JT will depend mainly on it remaining a family business. [11]

Business objectives

4.1 Why should businesses set objectives?

An objective is an aim or target for the future. If businesses do not have objectives then:

- there is no sense of direction or focus for the management team or employees
- employees in the organisation do not know what they are aiming to achieve
- there is no way of assessing 'success' or 'failure'
- investors will not be keen to invest in the business as it is unlikely to have a clear future strategy – because there is no clear objective.

Having set objectives, senior management must communicate them to stakeholders for them to have any impact on employees, investors, customers and other groups.

4.2 Why should objectives be SMART?

Consider this statement by a company Managing Director:

'Our company should aim to become bigger in the future and dominate the market we sell our products in'.

Is this a clear and effective corporate objective?

TERMS

Strategies: long-term plans to achieve objectives.

Corporate objectives: specific goals set for the business to achieve.

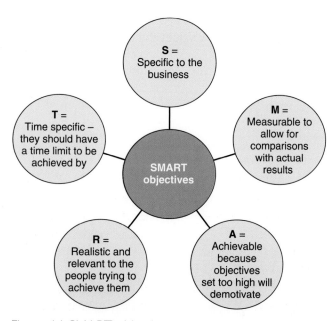

Figure 4.1 SMART objectives

S = Specific to the business

M = Measurable to allow for comparisons with actual results

A = Achievable because objectives set too high will demotivate

R = Realistic and relevant to the people trying to achieve them

T = Time specific – they should have a time limit to be achieved by

SMART objectives

Progress check A

1 Explain why the objective: 'Our company should aim to become bigger in the future and dominate the market we sell our products in', is not SMART.

2 Explain **two** benefits to an entrepreneur of setting clear objectives for a newly formed business.

3 Give an example of a SMART objective that a large business might set.

4 Explain **two** benefits to this business of the objective being 'measurable'.

5 Explain how the workers in a business might react if the firm had no clear objectives.

6 Give an example of an 'unrealistic objective' for a small shop selling food and drinks.

4.3 Linking mission statements, objectives and strategies

Figure 4.2 Hierarchy of objectives

Advantages	Disadvantages
• Tells stakeholders what the business 'is about'.	• It can be very general and just 'wishful thinking'.
• The process of creating a mission statement can help bring managers together.	• It does not provide SMART objectives for use within the business.
• It provides a sense of purpose to managers and workers.	• It may need to be revised frequently if the nature of the business changes.

Table 4.1. Mission statements - advantages and disadvantages

TERMS

Corporate aim: long-term goal of the business.

Mission statement: statement of the business's core aims and purpose.

Divisional/departmental objectives: the specific objectives of each division or department of the business, based on the corporate aim and objectives.

TIP

Remember, without a clear objective, developing effective plans of action or taking strategic decisions will become almost impossible.

Further points:

1 Once a corporate objective(s) has been established the senior management of a business will then focus on developing strategies to achieve this objective.

2 Corporate objectives should not be 'set in stone'. They may need to be adapted or changed completely over time. For example:
   i   Once a newly established firm has 'survived' the first crucial few months of operation the owner may seek to expand the business or aim to achieve high profits.
   ii Major changes to the external environment – such as an economic recession – might result in objectives for business growth being changed to aiming for survival.

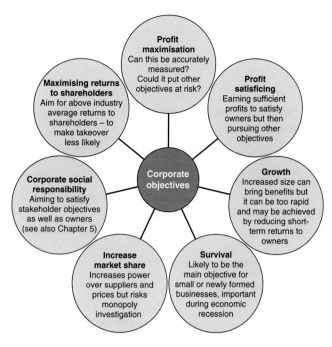

Figure 4.3 Corporate objectives

Progress check B

1 'We intend to make our products the best known computers in the world'. Do you think this is an objective or a mission statement? Explain your answer.

2 Explain why the objectives set for the marketing and finance departments of a car manufacturing business should be based on the company's overall objectives.

3 Would you advise an entrepreneur to spend time on developing a well thought out mission statement? Explain your answer.

4 Explain one reason why a business might change its objectives over time.

4.4 Objectives and decision making

Clear objectives are essential for effective business decision making. Objectives should be at the centre of the decision-making process (see Fig 4.3).

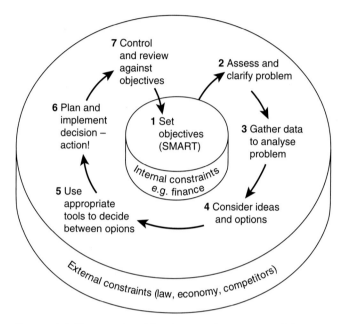

Figure 4.4 Corporate objectives at the centre of the decision-making cycle

4.5 Factors influencing corporate objectives

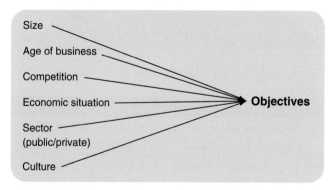

Figure 4.5 Influences on business objectives

4.6 Potential conflicts between objectives

Conflicts can occur in a number of different ways:

1. Maximum sales growth might conflict with a profit objective – selling **more** does not necessarily mean **higher** profits.
2. Between short-term objectives and long-term objectives – investing capital for long-term expansion may conflict with short-term profit objectives.
3. Stakeholders objectives often conflict (see Chapter 5).

4.7 Ethics – should business objectives reflect ethical standards?

Should business decisions be influenced by just profit calculations – or should moral issues be considered too? This is one of the big debates in global business today. Should managers be allowed to:

- advertise directly to children?
- employ very young workers?
- pay workers as little as possible?
- pollute the environment if it is not illegal to do so?
- pay bribes to gain extra orders?

The arguments for and against ethical decisions are:

For

- May give business positive publicity
- Attracts customers who are ethically minded
- Attracts employees who want to work for an ethical business
- Avoids breaking laws and the consequences of this.

Against

- May add to business costs, for example, paying workers above 'poverty wages'.
- May make the business uncompetitive if other firms in the industry are not acting ethically.
- Sales may be lost if bribes are not paid.
- Most customers want low prices and are not worried about how products are made or how workers are treated.

Most businesses have an ethical code. This can be used as a guide to all employees as to what behaviour is and is not acceptable in that business. However, if workers or managers are paid large bonuses for 'outstanding sales or profits', might they be tempted to break the ethical code to try to cut costs or increase sales?

TIP

When discussing a question about ethical issues do not just state your opinion without explaining the business arguments for and against a particular decision.

TERMS

Ethics: moral guidelines that influence decision making.

Ethical code: a document detailing the rules and guidelines on staff behaviour that must be followed by all employees of an organisation.

Progress check C

1. Explain why the objectives of a business might change if it was a private limited company but is converted to a public limited company.

2. Explain how the economic cycle of boom and recession might influence business objectives.

3. Explain why some business analysts think that advertising products directly to children is unethical.

4. Suggest **three** statements that might be included in the ethical code of a large oil company.

Exam-style questions

Paper 1 Section B

1 a Analyse how the objectives of a social enterprise are likely to differ from those of a privately owned manufacturing company. [8]

Student's answer

An objective is an aim to work towards. Social enterprises are managed by people who want to do good for society and help the environment. For example, they might want to operate a bus service for disabled people. This would help people who would find it difficult to travel. Bus services are more environmentally friendly than other forms of transport. However, social enterprises cannot operate without some income or profit so they also aim to make a financial surplus. So disabled people might be charged for the bus service – or government might provide a payment for each person transported by bus. Usually, any profit made by social enterprises is put back into the organisation to improve services in the future. Profit, people, environment – this is sometimes called the 'triple bottom line' meaning there is more than one objective for social enterprises.

Privately owned companies are often only interested in profit. They may not have any social or environmental aims as often the only 'bottom line' they are interested in is making money for the owners. This depends on the views and culture of the owners – shareholders of companies – and senior managers. If a manufacturing business has owners and managers who are only aiming for high profit, then it will produce in ways that damage the environment in order to make higher profits. Not all non-social enterprises operate like this. Some may have owners and managers to accept some social responsibility. They will not want to damage the environment or endanger their workers even if it means raising costs and reducing short-term profits. Some analysts argue that if a privately owned business acts socially responsibly it could result in higher long-term profits.

Authors' comments

This answer starts off really well. Objectives are defined. There is a very good understanding of social enterprises and their objectives. The student then analyses and compares the objectives of social enterprises with those of a privately owned manufacturing business. This shows good understanding of some of the key differences – and possibly similarities – between these organisations. This is a good essay and time has not been wasted 'showing evaluation' as the command word 'analyse' does not require this skill to be demonstrated.

Additional exam-style questions

Paper 1 Section A

1 a What is meant by a 'SMART objective'? [2]

b Explain briefly why ethics might influence the objectives of a business. [3]

Paper 1 Section B

2 a Explain the relationship between mission statement, objectives and strategy. [8]

b Discuss the extent to which setting clear business objectives will ensure that a book retailing business is successful. [12]

Paper 2 (part question)

Read again the Paper 2 case study in the Additional exam-style questions in Chapter 3.

Liam plans to make JT even more profitable. He has told all workers that making the highest levels of profit will benefit the business and make their jobs more secure. Liam has told his purchasing manager to insist that all suppliers of sports equipment – especially the smaller one who depend greatly on JT's orders – cut the cost of their supplies to JT by 15% or risk losing contracts. He also insists that all new employees should be put on a 12 month trial period before their job is confirmed. Liam has recently met with the country's Sports Minister and told her that "I will make whatever payments are necessary to secure the contract to supply the country's Olympic sports teams".

3 Analyse the benefits to JT of having a clear long term objective. [8]

4 Discuss whether Liam's recent decisions are examples of unethical business practices. [11]

Stakeholders in a business

5.1 Stakeholders and the stakeholder concept

Most organisations accept, in some degree, the stakeholder concept and have moved away from the view that all business decisions must be taken with only shareholders' interests in mind. Why this change?

- Stricter legal controls over business decisions, for example, pollution levels, wage levels, product standards.
- Increasing recognition that business activity should operate in wider interests of society.
- Extensive negative publicity for companies and senior managers who are seen not to be acting in society's interests – and the impact this can have on long run profitability too.

TIP

Careful! Shareholders own shares in limited companies but the term 'stakeholders' has a much wider meaning.

Do not confuse these two terms – and do not forget that shareholders are just one of the many stakeholder groups.

TERMS

Stakeholder: people or groups of people who can be affected by, and have an interest in, any action by an organisation.

Stakeholder concept: the idea that businesses and their managers have responsibilities to many groups, not just shareholders (business owners).

5.2 How stakeholders are affected by business decisions and activities

Businesses have responsibilities to stakeholders. For example:

- Customers – good value, safe products, fair competition
- Workers – fair pay, job security, safe working conditions
- Suppliers – payment on time
- Local community – pollution kept to minimum, support for local groups.

Business decisions can affect different stakeholders in different ways. An example of an important strategic business decision that affected many stakeholders was the decision by Burberry clothing to relocate some production from the UK to factories in China. How were stakeholder groups affected? Did Burberry meet stakeholders' objectives?

Progress check A

1   What do you think the 'stakeholder concept' of operating a business means?

2   Why might the local community be both positively and negatively affected by the opening of a new tyre making factory?

3   Under what circumstances could some customers be prepared to accept products of slightly lower quality?

Figure 5.1 Impact on stakeholder groups of Burberry's decision

5.3 Roles, rights and responsibilities of important stakeholders

Stakeholder group and role	Rights	Commonly accepted responsibilities
Customers – buying products provides revenue for business.	• Receive goods and services that meet national legal standards. • To be offered replacements, repairs, compensation in the event of failure of the product or service.	• To be honest – to pay for goods bought or services received when requested. • Not to steal. • Not to make false claims about poor service, under performing goods or failed items.
Suppliers – deliver agreed quantity and quality of resources to business.	• To be paid on time – as laid down either by law or by the service agreement agreed between the business and suppliers. • To be treated fairly by the purchasing business, for example, not to be threatened with losing big contracts from much more powerful customer businesses.	• Supply goods and services ordered by the business in the time and condition as laid down by the purchase contract or 'suppliers service agreements'.
Employees – work according to agreed conditions of employment.	• To be paid at least the national minimum wage. • To be given an employment contract with reasonable terms and conditions. • In most countries, to be allowed to join a trade union if desired. • Increasingly, workers expect to be involved in business activities and to be given opportunities to participate.	• To be honest. • Meet the conditions and requirements of the employment contract. • To cooperate with management in all reasonable requests.

→

Stakeholder group and role	Rights	Commonly accepted responsibilities
Local community – provide local facilities to business.	• To be consulted about major changes that affect it, for example, expansion or rationalisation (closure) plans. • Not have lives of local residents very badly affected by the businesses' activities, for example, pollution or excessive truck movements.	• To cooperate with the business, where reasonable to do so, on expansion and other plans. • To meet reasonable requests from business for local services such as public transport (for example, to allow staff to get to work) and waste disposal.
Government – control business activity and provide secure and stable economic/political/legal environment.	• Businesses have the duty to government to meet all legal constraints such as producing only legal goods, and to pay taxes on time.	• Treat businesses equally under the law. • Prevent unfair competition which could damage business survival chances. • Establish good trading links with other countries to allow international trade.

Table 5.1 Stakeholders - roles, rights, responsibilities

5.4 Conflicting stakeholder objectives

Shareholders' objectives often conflict. It is often impossible for a business to satisfy all stakeholders all of the time. Two examples are given in Table 5.2.

All important business decisions must involve some stakeholders gaining and some losing and therefore a compromise might be necessary. Business managers will have to prioritise – which stakeholder groups are more important in this decision – and which ones might have to accept a negative impact? Can the business do anything to reduce the size of this negative impact?

For example:

• Pay substantial redundancy payments to workers who are losing their jobs.
• Support local community groups if some residents have to move for a new coal mine.
• Plant many trees to support an environmental group to counteract the carbon emissions of a new factory.

> **TIP**
> If you are asked to discuss a business decision it is often useful to consider the stakeholder groups likely to benefit and those likely to lose from it.

Decision	Stakeholders that benefit	Stakeholders that lose
Supermarket – expand the business operation by building a new warehouse.	**Workers** – more jobs. **Customers** – more reliable deliveries and wider choice of stock. **Government** – increased economic activity and tax revenues. **Suppliers** – likely to be more orders.	**Local community** – additional transport of goods, for example, more trucks on roads. **Environmental groups** – building of warehouse uses 'greenfield' site and extra truck movements create more pollution.
Café chain – purchase more coffee supplies from 'fair trade' producers, paying above market prices.	**Suppliers** – offered 'fair trade' prices above the market price. **Local community (of the suppliers)** – higher local incomes will increase spending. **Customers** – those who want to buy 'ethical' products.	**Customers** – those who want lowest possible prices – they might rise to pay for the higher cost of 'ethical' supplies. **Non – fair trade suppliers and their workers** – fewer orders may lead to businesses failing and job losses.

Table 5.2 Two business decisions and possible stakeholder impact

5.5 Changing business objectives and impact on stakeholders

Stakeholders can be affected by changes in business objectives. Here are two examples:

1 Economic recession forces a business to change objective from growth to survival – workers may lose jobs or have pay reduced.

2 Private limited manufacturing company converts to a public limited company and the business changes the objective from retaining control to rapid growth – more employment opportunities for workers; higher government tax revenue **but** pressure groups might be worried by environmental impact of increased industrial output.

Progress check B

1 Explain **two** responsibilities that a business has to its employees.

2 Explain **two** responsibilities that employees have to their employer.

3 Research a major decision recently taken by a business in your country. Explain how this decision might lead to conflicts between the business's stakeholders.

4 Assume that a privately financed school changes its structure and objectives from those of a social enterprise to a privately limited company owned by profit seeking shareholders. Explain how any **two** stakeholder groups are likely to be affected by these changes.

Exam-style question

Paper 1 (short answer question)

1 Explain briefly the rights of two of a supermarket's stakeholders. [3]

Student's answer

A supermarket will have many stakeholders, e.g. workers and local communities in which the shops operate. These are just two of the groups interested in the decisions and activities of a supermarket.

Workers have legal rights and these would include a contract of employment and working conditions that meet health and safety standards.

Local communities have the right to be asked if the supermarket is planning a large expansion of its shop. Members of the community might be worried about the extra traffic and deliveries by large truck. The community, e.g. local government, might have some control over planning rules.

Authors' comments

This answer is just the right length. It is important not to write too much for the short answer questions as a detailed essay question also needs to be answered on Paper 1.

The answer is clear, concise and accurate – an excellent answer.

Additional exam-style questions

Paper 1 (essay)

1 a Analyse why many businesses attempt to satisfy the objectives of stakeholder groups other than shareholders. [8]

b Discuss whether it is possible for a steel making business to satisfy the objectives of all of its stakeholders. [12]

Paper 2 (part question)

NMR Mining Group

'The opening of the new open-cast copper mine in this country will benefit all stakeholder groups.'

This was a recent headline in a company's internal newspaper. The NMR Mining Group is suggesting that its investment in Country A, a developing country, would be for the good of everyone.

The company plan was to use a large area for open-cast copper mining. Few people live in this area. A new road would be built from the capital city to transport the copper. The world price of copper is very high. It is needed by electronics industries in industrialised countries.

2 a Explain how any **two** stakeholder groups might be adversely affected by this decision.

[4]

   b Evaluate the extent to which business decisions such as this lead to a conflict of stakeholder objectives.

[11]

Business structure

6.1 Local, national and multinational businesses

Local businesses have operations in just one location or region.

National businesses have operations in several locations or regions of a country but do not operate in other countries.

Multinational businesses operate in more than one country and these are termed 'multinationals'.

6.2 Multinational trading links

Trading links between nations are increasing rapidly and this is a major feature of globalisation. The main reasons for this growth are:

- Cheaper transport – especially when huge container ships are used.
- Fewer trade restrictions – free trade agreements have reduced the number of tariffs and quotas and other restrictions on trade in goods and services
- Internet – has increased the quantity of information about goods and services available in other countries.

The main impacts of growing multinational trading links are:

- More opportunities for businesses to sell in other countries – but it also creates more competition in local and national markets.
- Greater flows of capital around the world which is often controlled by multinational companies – but these flows can be quickly reversed causing instability and profits from capital investment are usually sent abroad.
- More choice for domestic consumers and prices are often lower as a result of importing goods and services.

TERM

Globalisation: the increasing freedom of movement of goods, capital and people around the world.

Progress check A

1   State one example from your own country of each of: local business; national business; multinational business.

2   List **three** goods that your country imports and **three** goods that your country exports.

3   Give examples from your own experience of how globalisation and multinational trade have increased consumer choice.

6.3 Multinational businesses

The recent growth of multinational companies can be explained by:

- Increased free trade and reduction in barriers makes it easier for businesses to start up operations in other countries (globalisation)

- Potential cost savings made by operating in a low-cost country
- Foreign operations might be closer to important markets – goods can be exported more easily
- Access to local resources that might not be available in 'home' country.

TERM

Multinational company (or corporation): businesses with headquarters in one country but with operating branches or factories in other countries. Commonly known as MNCs.

TIP

Be prepared to examine the impact of the growth of multinational corporations on your country's economy.

The impact of multinationals

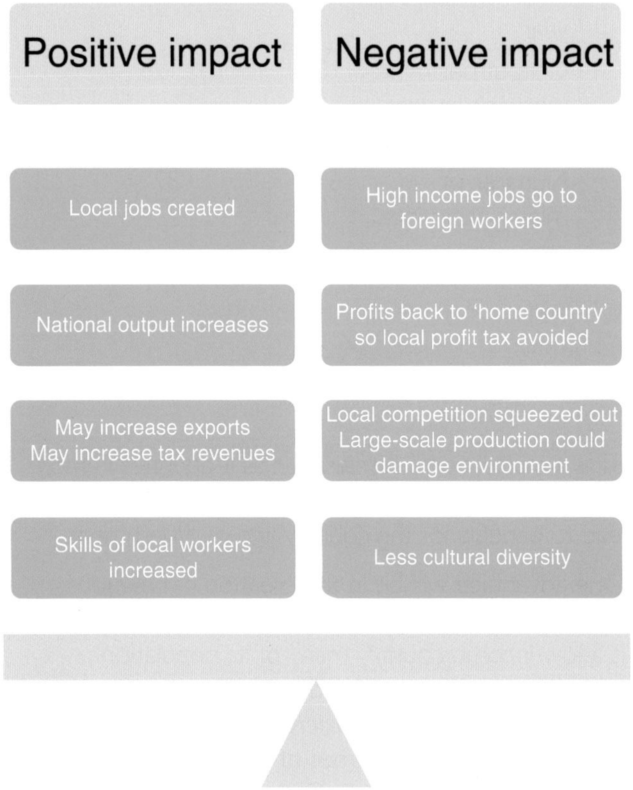

Positive impact
Negative impact
Local jobs created
High income jobs go to foreign workers
National output increases
Profits back to 'home country' so local profit tax avoided
May increase exports May increase tax revenues
Local competition squeezed out Large-scale production could damage environment
Skills of local workers increased
Less cultural diversity

Figure 6.1 Advantages and disadvantages of multinational corporations to the countries they operate in

The relationship between multinationals and the states they operate in can be a close one – with the company helping governments meet their economic objectives and, commonly, governments providing financial incentives to the company to invest in their country. The issues to be considered when considering the impact of MNCs include:

6.4 Privatisation

Privatisation has been used by many governments in recent years. The reasons for this include:

- Raises finance for government
- Businesses can now operate without political control/interference
- Private owners will expect profits from their investment so the business will have to be operated efficiently
- Without government financial support the business will be subject to market forces – to be successful it will have to produce what customers are prepared to pay for
- It could lead to increased competition as other businesses enter the industry, forcing existing businesses to increase efficiency and possibly reducing prices for consumers.

TERM

Privatisation: selling state owned organisations to investors in the private sector.

Some economists and politicians are opposed to privatisation claiming that:

- some important public services may now be cut back if they are not profitable
- job losses are inevitable when the private owners attempt to improve efficiency to increase profits
- some industries are too important to be operated by private investors
- if a state controlled monopoly is replaced by a private owned monopoly then customers may be exploited with higher prices.

Progress check B

1 What factors are important in deciding whether the water supply industry in your country should operate in the public sector or the private sector?

2 Name **four** multinational businesses operating in your country.

3 Suggest reasons why each of these multinationals is operating in your country.

4 Suggest **three** benefits to your country from the operation of these multinationals.

5 Suggest **three** possible limitations to your country from the operation of these multinationals.

Exam-style question

Paper 3 (using an abbreviated case study)

National Minerals Ltd. (NML)

'I do not see how we are going to compete with ST Incorporated,' said Joe Chavez the managing director of NML at a meeting with government officials. This company extracts minerals from three quarries in Country X, a low income Country in South America. NML was set up three years ago when the government privatised all of the state owned mining businesses. 'ST is one of the largest multinational mineral producing and exporting companies in the world. It operates in 35 countries. ST Inc's decision to double the size of its operations in Country X by opening a huge new quarry could force us out of business. We will have to cut costs and become even more efficient – but even this might not be enough to survive.'

The government officials understood Joe's point but suggested that: 'Perhaps your business could aim to provide specialist knowledge and materials to ST Inc rather than try to compete with them head-on. ST's new quarry will provide jobs in a depressed region of the country and it will pay tax on its profits. ST has claimed that 50 per cent of the quarry's output will be sold abroad. The government is confident that the newly privatised mining businesses will be able to compete with new foreign rivals.'

1 Analyse **two** possible benefits to the economy of Country X from ST's increased operations there. [10]

	Before privatisation	After privatisation
Total profit made by mine industry	$25 m	$65 m
Numbers employed	35 000	23 000
Number of mines operating	23	16
Capital invested in new mines per year	$5 m	$21 m
Output per mine worker per year (2012 = 100)	102	125
Number of mining accidents per year	6	32

Table 6.1 Country X mining industry – before and after privatisation

Student's answer

ST is a multinational organisation as it operates in more than one country. Operating mines in Country X can lead to benefits for the country and its government.

One advantage will be in the creation of new jobs which will pay workers an income. As Country X is a low income country many of its population might either be unemployed or be in low income employment. The new jobs created by ST's expansion should increase the incomes of the workers employed. This will benefit Country X's economy and especially the local shops. Workers will spend much of the income earned from their jobs at ST and this spending will create more jobs for other workers. This will help to raise incomes in Country X.

A second advantage is that ST competes with existing Country X businesses. This will force them to become more efficient and fewer resources will be wasted. If National Minerals are to survive after STs expansion, Joe Chavez accepts that the business will have to become more efficient. If it does not, its prices will be too high and ST will take customers away from National Minerals. So, MNCs can force local businesses to increase efficiency and

this will help to keep prices low for customers – an important point in a low income country.

Authors' comments

This is a well-structured answer. A definition is given to a relevant term. There are then two paragraphs – one for each of the benefits that the student has chosen to analyse. Both points are relevant and the context of ST and Country X is used effectively. Each benefit is not just 'stated' but explained – in other words the student has analysed why the point being made is a clear benefit to Country X. A very good answer.

Additional exam-style question

Paper 3 Section A

1 Based on the case study above, evaluate the success of the government's decision to privatise the mining industry. Refer to Table 6.1 and other relevant information. [16]

Size of business

7.1 External growth

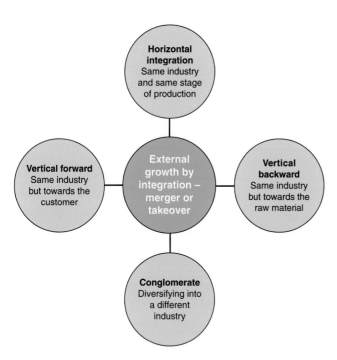

Figure 7.1 Types of external growth

TERM

External growth: occurs when two or more businesses join together into one larger business.

7.2 Business integration – do all stakeholders benefit?

A 'friendly' merger of two businesses or a 'hostile' takeover of one by another is a good example of a business decision that can cause 'stakeholder conflict'. This means some stakeholders will benefit more than others – and some, in fact, may lose out.

TIP

Discussing stakeholder conflict can be an effective way of showing evaluation when judging the impact of a merger or takeover.

Type of integration	Possible impact on business	Impact on stakeholders – advantages and disadvantages
Horizontal	• Higher market share. • More control over market, for example, in setting prices. • Opportunities for economies of scale. • Opportunities for cost cutting, e.g. rationalising production onto one site. • Greater bargaining power over suppliers. • Greater influence on government policy.	• Customers – prices could be reduced because the larger business can cut unit costs **but** less choice and prices could rise as the business now has more market share/power. • Suppliers – able to supply higher quantities to the larger business **but** forced to cut cost of supplies as the larger business puts more pressure on suppliers. • Workers/managers – more opportunities for promotion within larger business **but** some jobs lost through rationalisation and some managers, posts now duplicated.
Vertical forward	• Control over next stage of production. • Control over marketing strategy, for example, if manufacturer takes over chain of shops. • Obtains a secure outlet for the firm's products.	• Customers – retailers dedicated to selling just one manufacturer's products **but** less product choice in the manufacturer's own shops. • Senior managers – may have problems controlling a business in another sector of industry **but** workers and managers have opportunities to gain experience in different part of industry.
Vertical backward	• Control over supplier. • Able to monitor quality of supplies more easily. • Able to control costs of supplies. • Joint research into improved materials or components more likely.	• Customers – product quality may improve as firm now has control over suppliers **but** the expanded business may refuse to supply materials or components to other manufacturers, limiting product choice. • Senior managers – may have problems controlling a business in another sector of industry **but** workers and managers have opportunities to gain experience in different part of industry.
Conglomerate	• Diversification of risks by moving into different products and markets. • These products/markets may offer opportunities for faster growth.	• Managers and workers – greater career opportunities **but** business may lack focus and sense of direction which may reduce motivation. • Shareholders might not benefit if lack of synergy results from the integration.

Table 7.1 Impact of different types of integration on business and stakeholders

7.3 Why external growth might not achieve its objectives

The overall benefits of integration depend on the level of synergy that results from the merger or takeover. There are several potential disadvantages of integration. These explain why integration often fails to achieve the benefits claimed for it – in other words, the synergy gains are less than expected. These reasons include:

• Clash of management styles and cultures between the two businesses.
• The motivation of the combined workforce may fall if redundancies are planned to save costs.
• The problems of managing a much bigger business outweigh the potential cost savings (see diseconomies of scale in Chapter 23).
• Customers seek alternative suppliers as they become concerned about increased market share and power of the expanded business.

Synergy: the idea that one larger integrated business should be more successful than the two original smaller and separate businesses.

Merger: shareholders/directors of two businesses agree to join them to form one larger business.

Takeover (or acquisition): company buys more than 50 per cent of shares in another company.

7.4 Joint ventures and strategic alliances

Joint ventures and strategic alliances allow companies with complementary skills to benefit from one another's strengths. They are most common in technology, manufacturing and when developing new markets. In a joint venture, the companies start and invest in a new business that is jointly owned by both of the parent companies. A strategic alliance is a legal agreement between two or more companies to share access to their technology, intangible assets and customer information. A strategic alliance does not create a new company.

The advantages and disadvantages of joint ventures and strategic alliances are shown in Fig 7.2:

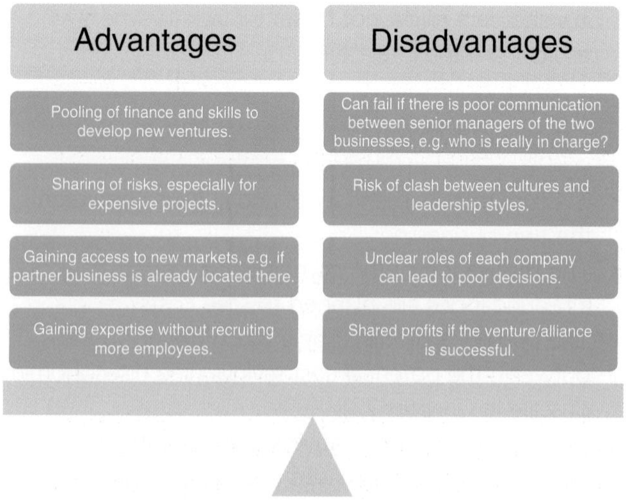

Advantages	Disadvantages
Pooling of finance and skills to develop new ventures.	Can fail if there is poor communication between senior managers of the two businesses, e.g. who is really in charge?
Sharing of risks, especially for expensive projects.	Risk of clash between cultures and leadership styles.
Gaining access to new markets, e.g. if partner business is already located there.	Unclear roles of each company can lead to poor decisions.
Gaining expertise without recruiting more employees.	Shared profits if the venture/alliance is successful.

Figure 7.2 Advantages and disadvantages of joint ventures and strategic alliances

Progress check A

1 If a car manufacturer takes over an airline business, why would this be called 'conglomerate integration'?

2 'If a farmer buys out a food shop in his local town, this is called backward vertical integration'. Explain why you would disagree with this statement.

3 Explain one benefit to the shareholders of two banking businesses if the banks merged their operations.

4 Would you expect the customers of these two banks to benefit from this merger? Explain your answer.

5 Assume that a recent merger between a Russian TV manufacturer and an Indian TV manufacturer has just been reversed (a 'demerger'). Explain one possible reason for this decision.

7.5 Rapid growth can cause problems as well as bring benefits

Businesses sometimes experience serious problems as a result of expanding too quickly:

- Lack of capital – expansion can be expensive. Additional fixed assets may be needed. The cost of a takeover may be very high. Additional inventories might be needed and finance required to give more customers credit to encourage sales. Running short of working capital during rapid expansion is sometimes called 'overtrading'.

  Possible solutions: sell additional shares (if limited company); raise adequate finance before expansion/takeover.

- Lack of management expertise – if growth is slow and 'manageable' then this problem is less likely to occur. Rapid growth, often achieved through integration, though, may put strains on existing managers and additional new managers may take time to understand how the business operates.

  Possible solutions: prepare management for rapid growth through training; appoint managers experienced in operating large businesses – although may have to offer high salaries and fringe benefits.

Progress check B

1 Explain the most important difference between a joint venture and a strategic alliance.

2 IBM (best known for producing computer systems used by industry) and Apple have recently announced a strategic alliance. Suggest possible reasons for this alliance.

3 BP Oil's strategic alliance with Russian oil company Rosneft recently broke up with both companies blaming each other for the failure. Suggest possible reasons for this strategic alliance failure.

4 Use the internet to find out **two** strategic alliances between businesses that operate in your country.

5 Groupon, a web-based deal-of-the-day recommendation service for consumers, experienced a rapid fall in its share price when analysts reported that the 'company had grown too quickly for its resources to cope'. Explain how a business can grow 'too quickly'.

Exam-style question

Paper 3 (using an abbreviated case study)

A failed takeover

LoCost Clothing merged with Exclusive Fashions two years ago. The managers of the two clothing manufacturing businesses expected the new firm, called Global Wear, to make much higher sales and profits than the two separate companies. The two original businesses used to sell clothes in different countries and in completely separate market segments. The corporate objective of LoCost Clothing had been to 'achieve maximum profitability from a low-cost strategy'. Exclusive Fashions had a corporate objective of: 'To be the best recognised clothing brand in the markets we operate in.'

Original hopes for the merger were high: 'We will now be able to produce clothes at a lower cost and with a greater variety of fashion designs than before', commented the two former managing directors when the news of the merger was first announced. Two years later, with falling profits, high labour turnover and increasing customer complaints, the directors of Global Wear have decided to split the business into two businesses – one specialising in low-priced clothing and the other specialising in fashionable, high-priced clothing.

1 Analyse **two** likely benefits to stakeholders that could have resulted from this merger. [10]

Student's answer

This is an example of horizontal integration as both businesses manufacture clothing – they operate at the same stage of production in the same industry.

Customers are a stakeholder group expected to benefit from this merger. Prices of clothing could fall if costs of production fall. Also, Global Wear should be able to offer a wider range of clothing to customers than either of the two separate businesses could before the merger. This could mean that in a clothing shop, customers have more choice than before the merger if the shop only used to sell items from one of the two separate companies. Also, higher profits for Global Wear could lead to more investment in research into new materials – warmer or more suited to hot conditions, for example – and this could mean that customers benefit from better quality clothing.

Shareholders would also be expected to benefit from this merger. Global Wear will be making a higher output than the two original businesses. This should mean that it gains from economies of scale, like buying in large quantities of material for clothes more cheaply. Lower costs per unit of clothing could mean that either the business lowers prices to customers which is likely to lead to higher sales and profits. Alternatively, the business could keep prices the same and benefit from higher profit margins on each item of clothing sold. Global Wear should be able to increase dividends to shareholders.

Authors' comments

This is a good answer because:

- the type of integration is clearly understood and two different stakeholder groups are referred to.

- the possible benefits to both groups are well applied to the clothing business.
- the benefits are analysed – the ways in which stakeholder groups are expected to benefit are well explained.

Additional exam-style question

Paper 3 (based on case study above)

1 Discuss the likely reasons why the merger that created Global Wear did not result in the benefits expected. [14]

External influences on business activity

8.1 Legal influences on business activity

Types of laws	Common requirements	Costs to business	Benefits to business
Consumer laws	• Product safety. • Consumer rights for refund or replacement. • Accurate weights and measures. • Advertising accuracy.	• Higher product development costs. • Higher quality/safer material costs. • Cost of refunds/replacements.	• Consumers more confident about product safety. • Consumer loyalty from improved products and services. • Consumer confidence in promotional and advertising campaigns.
Employment laws	• Minimum wage level. • Health and safety at work. • Employment conditions, for example, holidays/pensions. • Employment contracts. • Anti-discrimination in employment/recruitment. • Trade Union rights.	• Higher wage costs, may lead to relocation to low wage country. • Costs of improved safety equipment. • Costs of meeting legal requirements on conditions of employment. • Costs of monitoring employment and recruitment practices to avoid discrimination.	• More motivated staff. • Fewer accidents at work. • Less risk of bad publicity, for example, resulting from discrimination of workers. • More likely to sell products to ethical 'customers'.
Competition laws	• Not engaging in monopolistic and anti-competitive practices.	• Not able to 'fix' prices or engage in uncompetitive actions. • Limits to mergers and takeovers as monopolies may be illegal or investigated.	• Customers will prefer to deal with businesses that are thought to be competing fairly. • Less risk of smaller firms being forced out of business by dominant firms.

Types of laws	Common requirements	Costs to business	Benefits to business
Planning and environmental laws	• Restrictions on location of industry, for example, in towns/cities or in areas of natural beauty. • Control business developments that damage the environment.	• Cheapest sites may not be available for construction. • Additional costs of meeting planning laws, for example, waste disposal methods. • Applications for planning take time.	• Less risk of businesses being accused of damaging residents' health or damaging the environment. • Can promote the business as being 'environmentally friendly'.

Table 8.1 Laws that affect business activity

TIP Do not be too negative about legal constraints on business activity. They help to provide a framework in which responsible businesses can operate profitably whilst not exploiting workers, consumers or the environment.

TIP Be prepared to discuss the impact of laws on business activity in your own country – it is unlikely you will be expected to have specific knowledge of laws in any other country.

Progress check A

1 Would you advise a restaurant owner to try to cut costs by reducing the frequency of cleaning the kitchens? Explain your answer.

2 Explain **one** benefit to employees and **one** benefit to employers of having a formal contract of employment.

3 How might small businesses risk being forced out of business by anti-competitive practices of larger firms in the industry?

4 If some consumers are happy to pay very low prices for potentially dangerous products, why does the government prevent this with consumer laws?

5 Explain how a business might be affected by an increase in the country's minimum wage level.

8.2 Technological change – the opportunities and threats

Opportunities

- New product development Example: iPad
- Improved efficiency Example: CAM quicker design (CAD)
- More effective communication Example: email
- New marketing methods Example: online selling
- Efficient data processing Smarter market knowledge

Threats

- Costs:
  • Capital
  • Maintenance/updating
  • Training
- Reliability/security
- Need for adaptable workforce Effective management of change needed
- Data protection issues

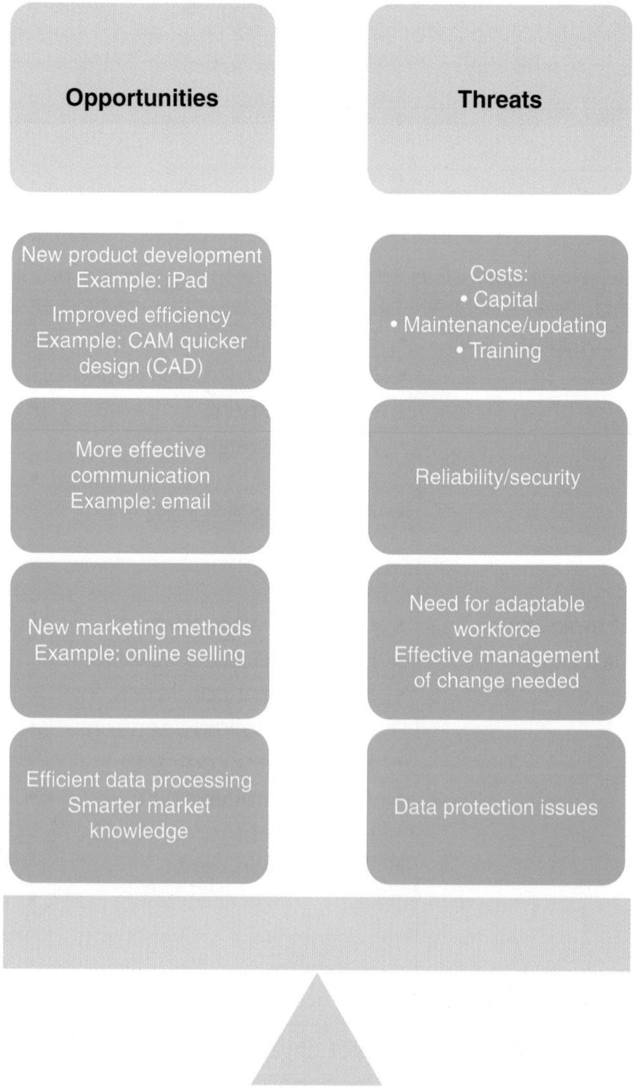

Figure 8.1 Opportunities and threats of technology

TERMS

Information technology (IT): the use of electronic technology to gather, store, process and communicate information.

Computer aided design (CAD): using computers and IT to assist in the designing of products.

Computer aided manufacturing (CAM): using computers and computer controlled machinery to speed up production processes and make them more flexible.

TIP

Nearly all businesses use modern technology to some degree. *But* remember that new technology does not solve all business problems of inefficiency or poor communication. It can create problems too – especially if not well implemented. Remember, too, employment issues are not necessarily negative, for example, if workers learn new skills in handling technology that make them more flexible and motivated.

Progress check B

1 A furniture making business adopts new computer controlled production methods. Explain which business costs might increase and which might reduce as a result of this decision.

2 Explain **two** uses of IT in a typical business office.

3 Explain **two** possible uses of IT by a marketing department of a business.

4 Explain **three** important stages in the successful implementation of a new technology production system.

5 Suggest one type of business that might employ very little IT.

6 Explain the importance of new technology product developments to a business of your choice.

8.3 Impact of social and demographic changes on business activity

In most countries there are significant changes occurring in the structure of society. The main ones are given in Table 8.2.

Social change	Potential positive business impact	Potential negative business impact
Rapidly increasing population	• Increased potential market. • Increased potential workforce.	• Increased demand for available land for expansion.
Ageing population	• Increased demand for 'old-age related' products. • Older workers often more loyal and experienced.	• Increased taxation as government has increased pension and other costs. • More difficult to recruit younger workers. • Older workers may be more resistant to change.
Increased numbers of women in workforce	• Greater potential workforce. • Higher family incomes created. • Potential for increased demand for some products.	• Increased levels of maternity leave/pay.

→

Social change	Potential positive business impact	Potential negative business impact
Increased multi-culturalism, for example, through migration	• Increased demand potential for culturally specific products. • Potential workforce increases if there is net immigration. • Foreign workers may be prepared to accept lower wages. • New ideas, new products.	• Existing products may need to be adapted to suit cultural differences. • Cultural differences may need to be reflected in HR policy, for example, different religious holidays may require careful staff planning. • Possible friction with existing workers if foreign workers accept lower pay.

Table 8.2 Impact of some social changes on business

Progress check C

1 What do you understand by an 'ageing population'?

2 Suggest **two** ways in which a business could respond to the impact of an ageing population.

3 Research the average age of the population in your country. How has this average changed over the last ten years?

4 Explain the likely impact of increased immigration on a retail business's strategies.

8.4 Corporate social responsibility

(See also Chapter 4.)

CSR issues include:

• Business decisions that impact on the environment – should businesses protect the environment for future generations even if this substantially adds to costs and reduces short-term profits?
• Social and environmental auditing – should businesses report on their social and environmental impacts even though these reports might contain some negative factors, such as levels of waste?
• Accurate financial accounting (see Chapter 30) – is it acceptable to 'window dress accounts'?
• Not paying incentives to gain contracts – this will help ensure fair prices are paid by customers but may lead to some contracts being lost to 'unethical businesses'. This issue clearly links with 'ethics' covered in Chapter 4.

TERM

Corporate social responsibility (CSR): the concept that accepts that business should consider society's interests in its activities and decisions.

8.5 Environmental audits

Environmental audits are part of a business's Corporate Social Responsibility report. They are usually part of a company's social audit – reporting on the overall impact of a business's activity on society.

Benefits of environmental audits

• Highlights the efforts made by the business to reduce negative environmental impact, for example, using less energy, producing less waste, reducing 'carbon footprint', using renewable resources.
• Informs stakeholders of the progress the business is making to reduce negative environmental impact. This could reduce pressure group activity.
• Gives future targets for improvements in environmental impact.

Limitations

• Not a legal requirement in most countries – should time and resources be spent on producing it?
• It will contain details of current energy use and waste production levels. Even if these are improving, many companies will still be huge users of energy or of non-renewable resources. This might increase pressure group activity.
• It must reflect a truthful record of what the company is doing – if there is evidence of 'window dressing' or 'greenwash' then will result in bad publicity.

8.6 Influences on environmental policies of business

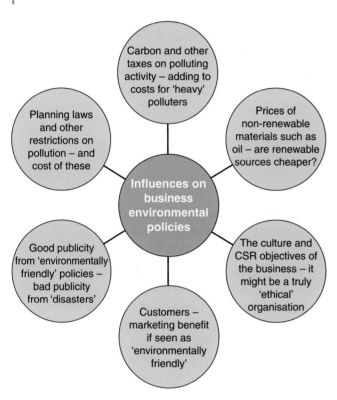

Figure 8.1 Influences on the environmental policies of a business

8.7 Pressure groups

The power of pressure groups increases when:

- they have many members and can organise an effective consumer boycott
- they have influence over government through lobbying and having popular objectives
- they are well organised and well financed, for example, to pay for media campaigns
- the company the pressure group is targeting is short of resources, for example, cash; wants to avoid bad publicity and will lose profits quickly from consumer boycotts or other direct action.

TIP

Remember that in the short term a business might cut costs and increase profits by using environmentally damaging methods.

For example, dumping waste cheaply in a river. You might be asked to consider whether this could damage its long-term reputation and profitability.

Other businesses may seem to use 'environmentally friendly' tactics as part of marketing and you might be asked to consider the ethics of this.

Progress check D

1 Explain why a business might produce a social or environmental audit even if the government does not demand it.

2 Why might an increase in the price of oil encourage a business to become more 'environmentally friendly'?

3 Explain the marketing benefits that might result from introducing systems and machinery that cause little damage to the environment.

4 Should a business in a competitive industry undertake its production in a less developed country with few environmental controls? Explain your answer.

5 Explain why the impact on profits of a new machine that uses less energy might be difficult to calculate.

6 Explain **two** reasons why a business might decide to adopt a policy of 'corporate social responsibility'.

7 Explain **two** factors that might encourage a business to agree to changes in its activities resulting from pressure group activity.

Exam-style question

Paper 3 (using an abbreviated case study)

AMG

AMG manufactures cars that are sold at low prices. It is profitable but the profit margin on cars is falling. The cars have a reputation for reliability but they are not very attractively designed and they use old fashioned engines. They are painted in a very limited range of colours. Due to the equipment and production methods not having changed for 20 years, the cars are standard models with very few variations allowed for customer needs.

The cars have much less safety equipment than models produced by other manufacturers. Some consumers do not worry about this as they just want cheap cars. Some sales have been lost, however, because of the safety issues – some potential buyers lack confidence in AMG cars. The government is planning a new consumer law to make it illegal to produce cars without the latest safety equipment.

AMG workers perform boring, repetitive flow-line production jobs. They are paid production bonuses but most of them earn just enough to buy food and other essentials for their families. Some workers want to join a trade union but AMG management are opposed to this. Most workers are told that if they do not work hard they could be sacked yet few of them have written employment contracts – it is not yet a legal requirement in the country in which AMG operates. Labour efficiency levels are low by international standards.

1   Evaluate the extent to which AMG might increase its profits from adopting production methods using new technology.   [14]

Student's answer

Technology has changed production methods greatly in recent years. Computer aided design allows new designs of products, such as new car models, to be designed and amended by computer. This saves a great deal of time compared to old 'pen and paper'

methods and could help AMG develop new models quickly to be more competitive. Customers often want to buy cars with the latest designs and features and CAD could give AMG a competitive advantage if the company used it effectively.

Computer aided manufacturing, such as the use of robots, could transform AMG's low labour efficiency as well as making car production more flexible. Robots could do many of the more boring, repetitive tasks in car manufacturing and would greatly increase car production per day. This high efficiency level will help AMG to keep production costs down which will help the business maintain its low price strategy. Increasing flexibility of production allowed by modern computer controlled machines means that different models, colours and specifications of cars could all be produced on the same production line. This would make AMG's products more appealing to customers, increasing sales and profits. So, using the latest technology could help increase profits for AMG.

However, there will be high costs too. Buying or leasing the new technology will increase fixed costs. New employees with IT skills may need to be employed or existing workers expensively retrained. Even the latest IT equipment will need to be maintained and updated regularly – so these additional costs will have to be compared with the cost savings from using IT.

Although the cost savings are likely to outweigh the additional costs, it is doubtful that AMG will benefit from using new technology if the company does not change its existing HR strategy. IT and computer based technology requires well motivated, flexible and well trained employees for most effective application. AMG's HR strategy does not give employees the security or motivation needed to accept or work with new technology. If AMG offers employment contracts, good training opportunities and adopts a participative style of management to encourage feedback then adopting new technology is most likely to lead to higher profits. If there is no change in HR strategy, then even extensive use of technology is likely to lead to lower profits.

Authors' comments

This is a well written and well balanced answer. The student clearly understands some important uses of new technology and applies these clearly to car production. The costs and cost savings of new technology are well analysed in context. The evaluation is a particular strength as the student combines knowledge of IT with an understanding of the importance of HR strategy to making IT work effectively. There is a clear overall conclusion. An excellent answer.

Additional exam-style question

Paper 3 (based on case study above)

1   Analyse how changes in consumer protection laws and employees' rights laws could affect AMG.   [10]

Chapter 9

External economic influences on business behaviour

9.1 Government economic objectives

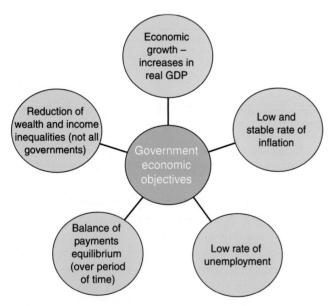

Figure 9.1 Economic objectives of governments

In practice, achieving all objectives at the same time is difficult. There are conflicts.

For example:

- Rapid economic growth can help to reduce unemployment – but inflation might rise.
- Economic growth, by increasing peoples' living standards and their ability to buy imports, often leads to a Balance of Payments (Current Account) deficit.

Also, the main economic objective might change over time.

For example:

- Rising prices caused by external factors could mean that the government prioritises the reduction of inflation not the reduction of unemployment.
- Negative economic growth (recession) could mean the government prioritises achievement of economic growth over greater equality of income and wealth.

TERMS

Economic growth: an increase in a country's productive potential measured by an increase in real GDP.

Recession: a period of six months or more of declining real GDP.

9.2 Economic growth and the business cycle – impact on business strategy

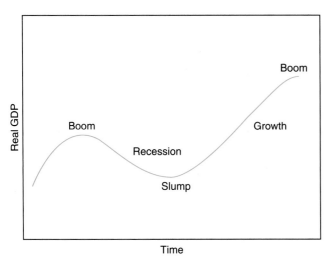

Figure 9.2 The stages of a typical business cycle

Gross Domestic Product (GDP): the total value of goods and services produced in a country in one year – real GDP has been adjusted for the effects of inflation.

Business (or economic) cycle: regular swings in economic activity, measured by real GDP, that occur in economies varying from boom conditions to recession.

Income elasticity of demand: measures the responsiveness of demand for a product after a change in consumer incomes.

Progress check A

1 What does 'an increase in real GDP' mean?
2 What is likely to happen to average incomes – or living standards – during a period of economic growth?
3 Why might you expect the demand for an inferior product to increase during a recession?
4 Explain an important feature of the 'boom' stage of the business cycle.
5 What would you expect to happen to the level of unemployment during a recession and why?

Stage of business cycle	Possible business strategies
Economic growth Average consumer incomes should be increasing	• Increase prices to take advantage of higher consumer demand – **but** will demand fall? • Develop new products that appeal to consumers with higher incomes – income elastic products **but** this could be an expensive strategy.
Recession Average consumer incomes likely to fall	• Lower prices as consumers have less to spend – **but** will perceived quality be lower? • Develop new products (perhaps 'inferior' goods) that appeal to consumers with lower incomes – **but** will this damage the brand image and existing consumer loyalty?

Table 9.1 How can businesses respond to swings in the business cycle?

9.3 Inflation and unemployment – impact on business activity

Causes of inflation

Inflation has two major causes:

1 Demand pull inflation: caused by too much demand for available supply of products. Businesses may be able to increase prices without demand falling – but this will depend on price elasticity.
2 Cost push inflation: caused by increased costs of production. Businesses may be forced to increase selling prices to avoid making a loss – but the impact on sales and revenue will depend on price elasticity.

Inflation: an increase in the average price level.

Causes of unemployment

Unemployment has several causes, such as cyclical, structural and frictional unemployment.

TERMS

Unemployment: exists when members of the working population are willing and able to work but are unable to find a job.

Cyclical unemployment: caused by low demand for products during recession stage of the business cycle.

Structural unemployment: caused by decline in important industries.

Frictional unemployment: caused by workers losing/leaving jobs and taking a long time to find others – perhaps because they have the 'wrong' skills.

Impact of unemployment on business

Unemployment can impact on businesses both negatively and positively.

Negative impact

- Reduces incomes of those unemployed – less to spend on products.
- May lead to increased taxes to pay welfare benefits – reducing retained profits (if corporation tax increased) or reducing consumer demand (if income tax increased).
- Unemployed workers lose skills and work incentives – reduces the quality of the labour force.

Positive impact

- May encourage work incentive of those in employment to reduce chances of losing jobs.
- Increased supply of available labour may allow firms to offer reduced wages – or not to increase wages.
- Unemployed workers may be prepared to move to regions of country where there is labour shortage.

Progress check B

1 Explain one reason why some unemployed workers might find it difficult to find a job during a period of economic growth.

2 Will all businesses be able to increase prices, with little impact on demand, during a period of inflation? Explain your answer.

3 Give **two** possible causes of cost push inflation.

4 Why might a business be able to reduce the average labour cost of production during a period of high unemployment?

5 Why might a business find it easier to retain (keep) staff during a period of high unemployment?

9.4 Government economic policies – how business strategy can adapt

Fiscal policy can be used to:

- raise revenue for government spending
- vary government spending levels, for example, on health and education
- boost spending on goods and services in the economy by using expansionary fiscal policy, for example, during a recession
- reduce demand for goods and services if inflation is a major problem
- cut the government's budget deficit if this is becoming too large.

TERMS

Fiscal policy: decisions about government spending, taxes and government borrowing.

Monetary policy: decisions about the rate of interest and supply of money in the economy.

Expansionary fiscal policy operates in the following way:

Figure 9.3 The impact of expansionary fiscal policy

Expansionary fiscal policy will encourage businesses to expand to meet the growing demand for goods and services from both government and households (consumers).

Monetary policy and interest rates are controlled in most countries by the Central Bank. This bank will have the objective of keeping inflation low. If inflation is too high the Central Bank may increase interest rates:

Figure 9.4 The impact of higher interest rates

Higher interest rates will lead businesses to borrow less and reduce investment in new projects – output may have to be cut back as demand from householders (consumers) is likely to fall.

TIP

You are unlikely to be asked technical questions about fiscal and monetary policy – but you will need to know how government policy decisions are likely to affect different businesses.

Progress check C

1   What decisions might a government take if it planned to introduce an 'expansionary fiscal policy'?

2   Why might the demand for some businesses' products be little affected by a reduction in income tax?

3   How might an increase in a country's rate of corporation tax (on profits) affect a multinational company's plans to invest in the country?

4   Which business is likely to be more affected by an increase in interest rates: a petrol retailing business or house construction business? Explain your answer.

5   Under what economic circumstances is a central bank likely to increase interest rates?

9.5 Exchange rates – how business activity can be affected

Impact of exchange rate appreciation

- Costs of imports fall – business may decide to import more materials/components from foreign suppliers; consumers may buy cheaper imported goods rather than those made domestically.
- Prices increase – this makes exports less competitive and foreign demand may fall.
- It would now be cheaper – than before the appreciation – for a domestically based business to locate in a foreign country.

Impact of exchange rate depreciation

- Costs of imports rise – domestically produced goods appear better value and demand for them might increase.
- Export prices fall – demand for exports might increase. Businesses may now be more likely to expand into foreign markets.
- It would now be cheaper – than before the depreciation – for foreign businesses to locate in the domestic country, creating more competition for local businesses.

TERMS

Exchange rate: price of a currency in terms of another.

Exchange rate appreciation: rise in the value of a currency relative to other currencies.

Exchange rate depreciation: fall in the value of a currency relative to other currencies.

TIP

Many students get the effects of currency appreciation or depreciation the wrong way round. Avoid this!

Progress check D

1 Give a numerical example of an exchange rate appreciation of your own country's currency.

2 Give a numerical example of an exchange rate depreciation of your own country's currency.

3 Explain why a business importing components and exporting completed products would **lose** and **gain** from a currency appreciation.

4 Why might a business be encouraged to begin exporting following a depreciation of the currency?

9.6 Further economic issues

Governments limit or constrain business activity, e.g. by legal controls or placing a tax on the products that business makes.

Governments can subsidise and support business activity, e.g. subsidies to businesses that are at risk of failing or grants to new business start-ups.

Governments often intervene in markets to limit market failure, e.g. controlling the activities of monopolies; taxing businesses that produce external costs; and giving grants to encourage training of employees.

Progress check E

1 Give an example of a product in your country that the government either bans completely or tries to limit the sale of.

2 Give one possible disadvantage of the government subsidising a business that is at risk of failing.

3 Give one reason why a government might provide financial support to businesses that train employees.

Exam-style question

Paper 3 (using an abbreviated case study)

TeePrint

Ahmed set up TeePrint with some friends. They each invested $5000. The business, located in Country A, produces printed T-shirts for teenagers called 'TeenTees'. These are printed on plain cotton T-shirts that are imported. These are cheaper than T-shirts produced in Country A. The T-shirts sold so well in the first few months that expanded production facilities were opened using old but cheap material printing machines. Production levels increased but print quality was often poor.

One year ago, the owners of TeePrint were approached by a venture capital business called Novak. It suggested that TeePrint should convert to a private limited company in which Novak would have a 50 per cent stake for an investment of $40 000. Ahmed and the other owners agreed to this. They realised that the capital injected could be used to purchase new computer-controlled material printing machines and pay website development costs for an online ordering system that would allow consumers to download the image they wanted printed on a T-shirt.

These developments have been successful. Many sales are now made to consumers in many different countries. Production quality is now much improved and online ordering is very popular. TeePrint is now planning to enter a new market segment. The market for dresses and shirts printed with flower and other patterns is dominated by middle income consumers, often between 20 and 40 years old, who want more than a basic printed T-shirt. Consumers could use the TeePrint website to order the dress or shirt style they wanted and the design of pattern to be printed on it. TeePrint would then print the material and outsource the making of the shirt or dress to a foreign clothing manufacturer. Ahmed estimates that the demand for these new products would be more income elastic than the demand for the T-shirts. Ahmed thought that the economic forecasts shown in Table 9.2 would be useful when making the decision about whether to enter this market segment.

	2017	2018	2019
Real GDP growth rate (%)	4	2	1
Inflation rate (%)	6	7	9
Interest rate (%)	5	7	8
Exchange rate index (2012 = 100)	100	90	85
Unemployment rate (%)	6	8	9

Table 9.2 Economic forecasts for Country A

1 Analyse the likely impact on TeePrint of a depreciation in Country A's currency. [10]

Student's answer

A depreciation of a currency means that one unit of it buys less of other currencies. If Country A's currency depreciates this will make imports coming into the country more expensive in Country A's currency. This could affect TeePrint negatively as the business buys in its unprinted T-shirts from other countries. Higher prices for its basic component could mean lower profit margins for TeePrint if they do not increase prices of the printed T-shirts. If the business wants to maintain profit margins then it will be forced to increase prices of the finished products. If the demand for the printed T-shirts is price elastic then a price rise will reduce demand by a high proportion, and total revenue will fall. This problem will be made worse if TeePrint buys in the material for the proposed dresses and shirts products from other countries. It could make the decision to enter this market an unwise one.

TeePrint also sells products abroad since the creation of its own website. The prices of these exports could now be reduced if Country A's currency depreciates as a lower price in foreign currency will still earn TeePrint the same amount in Country A's currency. These price reductions should increase the company's revenue and profit. Alternatively, Ahmed might keep the foreign prices the same and earn more of Country A's currency on each T-shirt sold. This will also have the effect of increasing the company's profit – but would have to be compared with the higher costs of imported unprinted T-shirts before a final decision is taken.

Authors' comments

The student has shown that depreciation is clearly understood as is the impact on both import and export prices. The latter is put into the context of TeePrint.

The student has also explained the link between depreciation, prices, sales and profits well – in terms of both import and export prices.

Additional exam-style question

Paper 3 (based on abbreviated case study above)

1   Evaluate the usefulness of the economic forecasts in Table 9.2 to Ahmed when making the decision whether to enter the market for printed dresses and shirts.   [14]

Unit 2
PEOPLE IN ORGANISATIONS

Management and leadership

10.1 Functions of management

Managers of a business perform many important functions:

Figure 10.1 Functions of managers

> **TERM**
>
> Management: the process of dealing with or controlling things or people.

Progress check A

1 Give **three** examples of how businesses could be badly managed.

2 Why are objectives important for managers?

3 Give examples of how a manager of a supermarket could undertake each of the five functions of management.

Mintzberg's management roles

To carry out these functions, managers have to undertake many different roles.

Interpersonal	Figurehead	Symbolic leader, for example, meeting important visitors to the business.
	Leader	Motivator, selector, for example, explaining his/her vision for the business.
	Liaison	Internal, external, for example, leading or 'chairing' meetings.
Informational	Monitor	Collector, for example, attending conferences and gaining information about the industry.
	Disseminator	Making information available, for example, communicating with key staff.
	Spokesperson	Communicating externally, for example, appearing on TV news programmes.
Decisional	Entrepreneur	New ideas/opportunities, for example, encouraging workers and managers to develop new ideas.
	Disturbance handler	Responding to change, for example, developing strategies to deal with competitive threats.
	Resource allocator	Deciding on spending, for example, approving budgets for the business and its departments.
	Negotiator	Representing the organisation, for example, meeting government ministers to influence policy.

Table 10.1 Mintzberg's managerial roles

10.2 Important leadership roles

TERMS

Director: senior manager elected into office by shareholders in an incorporated business.

Manager: person appointed to be responsible for setting objectives, organising resources and motivating staff so that the organisation's aims are met. This includes supervisors.

Worker representative: person elected by workforce to represent the workforce.

Progress check B

1. In a public limited company, which **two** types of leaders could be elected?

2. Give examples of activities corresponding to Mintzberg's leadership role of 'disturbance handler'.

3. What factors could influence the leadership style of a supermarket manager?

10.3 Qualities of leaders

Not everyone can show an effective leadership. Successful leaders often have all or most of the following personal qualities:

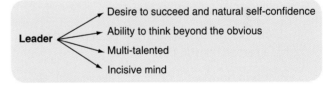

- Desire to succeed and natural self-confidence
- Ability to think beyond the obvious
- Multi-talented
- Incisive mind

Figure 10.2 Qualities of leaders

TERM

Leadership: the art of motivating a group of people towards achieving a common objective.

Progress check C

1. Give **two** features of a poor leader.

2. Give **four** features of a good leader and explain why each one is important.

3. Explain **two** problems a business might experience from poor leadership.

10.4 Styles of leadership

Leadership styles vary greatly. It is important to remember that there is never just one leadership style that is the best one to use in all business situations. The difference between leadership styles is shown clearly in Table 10.2 in the coursebook.

Progress check D

1 List **three** situations in which autocratic leadership might be appropriate.

2 Which leadership style might be appropriate in a research institution?

3 List **two** drawbacks of democratic leadership.

4 Which leadership style encourages staff involvement?

5 Why might the most suitable leadership style change in different situations?

10.5 McGregor's Theory X and Y

McGregor's famous Theory X and Theory Y did not claim that there are two different types of workers – but that there were two extreme management views about workers.

Progress check E

1 Is it true that McGregor claimed there are two types of employee?

2 Which theory, X or Y, attributes employees with accepting responsibility?

3 What style of leadership might a Theory X manager adopt?

10.6 Choice of leadership style

There is no one 'right' leadership style. The most effective leadership style depends on the following factors:

Figure 10.3 Choice of leadership style

Progress check F

1 Why is there no one right choice of leadership style?

2 If a decision is needed quickly, which leadership style might be adopted?

3 How might employees' attitudes to change be influenced by leadership style?

Informal leadership

So far we have only considered 'formal leaders' appointed by the business. They have formal authority over subordinates.

In many situations, such as a business, there are often informal leaders who also have influence over others.

TERM

Informal leader: a person who has no formal authority but has the respect of colleagues and some power over them.

Progress check G

1 Do informal leaders have formal authority? Explain your answer.

2 List **three** abilities that an informal leader might have.

10.7 Emotional intelligence (EI)

Goleman has suggested that effective leadership depends not just on the personal qualities we identified in 10.3 but also on whether people have emotional intelligence. Attempts to measure emotional intelligence lead to use of personality tests which produce an emotional quotient (EQ).

TERM

Emotional intelligence (EI): the ability of managers to understand their own emotions, and those of the people they work with, to achieve better business performance.

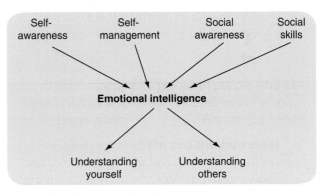

Figure 10.4 Emotional intelligence

Progress check H

1 Give three possible weaknesses of a manager who lacks high EI.

2 Explain **three** benefits of a leader having high EI.

Exam-style question

Paper 1 Section B

1 Analyse the differences between laissez faire and democratic leadership. [8]

Student's answer

Leadership requires giving people a vision and encouraging them to work together towards achieving it. Laissez-faire leadership gives substantial delegation to the workforce to make decisions and to organise their working lives. This may act as an incentive but depends on the nature of the employees and the work being performed. In a creative business, such as an advertising agency or a high technology business seeking new product ideas, laissez-faire leadership can encourage people to work originally to solve new problems. The leader hands over the authority to make decisions, which can be unwise if workers are not trained and experienced at handling issues for themselves. Some workers need clear leadership and guidance and they may struggle to work this way. Some tasks need clear guidance, such as health and safety issues. Laissez faire often involves little feedback and this may be demotivating for some workers who need a lot of reassurance.

Democratic leadership involves participation of the workers in business decisions. It provides more framework and guidance than laissez faire but workers are encouraged to become involved in solving business problems. This also means a wider range of ideas and opinions which could improve decisions.

However democratic leadership can be time-consuming and it is often more difficult to reach decisions than with, say, laissez-faire leadership. It is likely to be unsuited to situations that involve the need for immediate decisions, e.g. in emergency situations, and it would certainly not work well in the army. It is suited to situations involving highly trained and committed employees and in working situations where problems are best solved by the participation of all employees – workers and managers.

Authors' comments

This answer contains good knowledge about these leadership styles and there is some attempt to apply them to business situations. There is clear understanding of both laissez-faire and democratic leadership styles and an attempt to compare and contrast them. The student has demonstrated analytical skills as well as application of the concepts to realistic situations, for example by identifying and analysing situations in which laissez-faire leadership might be appropriate and why, and then analysing where democratic leadership might be better.

Additional exam-style questions

Paper 1 Section A

1 Explain the term 'emotional intelligence'. [3]

2 State Mintzberg's leadership roles. [3]

Paper 1 Section B

3 Discuss the view that an autocratic style of leadership is the most effective leadership style for a business in today's competitive business environment. [12]

Paper 2

The Kite Company (KC)

KC manufacture specialised kites. KC's employees are well motivated. Because the kites are made using job production the employees have high levels of skills. KC is thinking of growing the business to export worldwide. They will have to use flow production and are likely to use automation in the production line. There will inevitably be redundancies and the employees are concerned about their future. A new general manager has been appointed.

4 Analyse the factors that the new general manager should consider when deciding on a leadership style. [8]

Motivation

Chapter 11

Learning summary

After you have studied this chapter, you should be able to:

- [ ] explain the need to motivate employees
- [ ] analyse human needs in relation to work
- [ ] compare and evaluate the main motivational content theories (Taylor, Mayo, Maslow, Herzberg)
- [ ] compare and evaluate the main process theories (McClelland, Vroom)
- [ ] assess the main financial methods of motivation
- [ ] assess the main non-financial methods of motivation
- [ ] examine the ways in which employees can participate in the management and control of business activity.

11.1 The need for motivation

TERM

Motivation: the internal and external factors that stimulate people to take actions that lead to achieving a goal.

Why is motivation important?

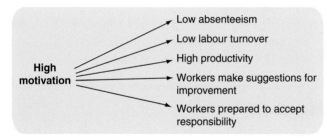

Figure 11.1 Benefits of high motivation

Progress check A

1. Give **three** examples of poor motivation in a business.
2. Why is a motivated workforce important for managers?
3. How might a supermarket benefit from a well-motivated workforce?

11.2 Motivation in relation to work

Human work needs often include:

- the ability for people to feed and clothe themselves
- the ability to provide shelter
- the respect of others
- improvement in lifestyle
- ability to make a positive contribution
- opportunity to satisfy ambition.

11.3 Content theories

Taylor's scientific approach

The Theory of Economic Man is based on the assumption that man is driven by money alone. Taylor's work has influenced the following areas:

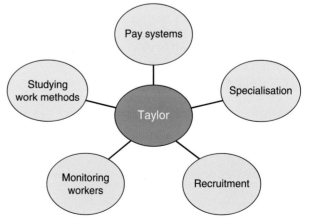

Figure 11.2 The impact of Taylor's scientific approach

Select ⟩ Observe ⟩ Record ⟩ Identify quickest method ⟩ Train ⟩ Supervise ⟩ Pay by results

Figure 11.3 Taylor's scientific approach to management

Progress check B

1 Why did workers mistrust Taylor?

2 How did Taylor have an impact on recruitment methods?

3 Why is the Economic Man principle considered simplistic?

Mayo

As shown by Mayo's observations which led to the 'Hawthorne effect':

Motivation improved by:

- consulting workers
- working in teams
- employees making decisions that affect themselves
- establishing targets.

Motivation was less affected by:

- working conditions.

Progress check C

1 How might a manager of a factory use the ideas of Mayo to improve productivity?

2 How does Mayo differ from Taylor in his views on money as a motivator?

3 How does employees' welfare fit into Mayo's ideas?

Maslow

Maslow's triangle is shown here:

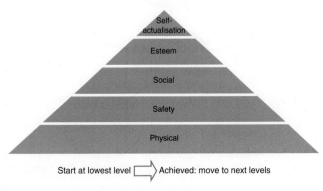

Figure 11.4 Maslow's hierarchy

- Self-actualisation is not reached by many people.
- Once a need is met it ceases motivating.
- It is possible to go down as well as up (reversion).

But

- Not everyone has same needs.
- When is a need met?
- Money may be needed to meet several needs.
- Self-actualisation is never permanently achieved.

Progress check D

1 Why is it difficult to achieve self-actualisation?

2 What might cause a reversion down the hierarchy?

3 Why do some managers think it is important to try to satisfy employees' needs?

4 Give examples of business conditions which allow for each type of Maslow's needs to be met.

TERM

Self-actualisation: a sense of self-fulfilment reached by feeling enriched and developed by what one has learned and achieved.

Herzberg

Herzberg's motivation theory is based on two factors:

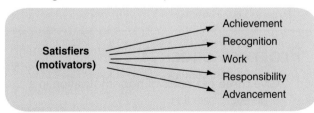

Motivators give workers positive feelings about their jobs and hence motivate.

Figure 11.5 Herzberg's two factors

Hygiene factors can give employees negative feelings about jobs when they are absent, so can demotivate. Improving them could prevent dissatisfaction but may not motivate.

For example, improving pay and working conditions removes dissatisfaction and may encourage work but not motivation whereas job enrichment is a motivating factor (motivator) and improves motivation.

Progress check E

1 List **three** of Herzberg's motivators.

2 How might pay demotivate workers?

3 Why might leadership style be a hygiene factor?

TERMS

Job enrichment: aims to use the full capabilities of workers by giving them the opportunity to do more challenging and fulfilling work.

Motivating factors (motivators): aspects of an employee's job that can lead to positive job satisfaction, such as achievement, recognition, meaningful and interesting work and advancement at work.

Hygiene factors: aspects of an employee's job that have the potential to cause dissatisfaction, such as pay, working conditions, status and over-supervision by managers.

11.4 Process theories

McClelland

McClelland said that there are three types of motivational need, the mix should depend on the characteristics of the workers/managers.

Achievement	Authority/ power	Affiliation
A strong motivational need to achieve. Need for feedback and sense of accomplishment.	A person with dominant need. Desire to control and make an impact.	Need for friendly relationships and interaction with others. Need to be liked.
Attitude of successful business people and entrepreneurs.	Strong leadership instinct.	Good team members.

Table 11.1 McClelland's motivational needs

Progress check F

1 Do leaders need a strong sense of affiliation?

2 Why do successful entrepreneurs need achievement motivators?

3 Explain the main difference between Maslow and McClelland.

Vroom

Vroom's process involves valence, expectancy and instrumentality as shown here:

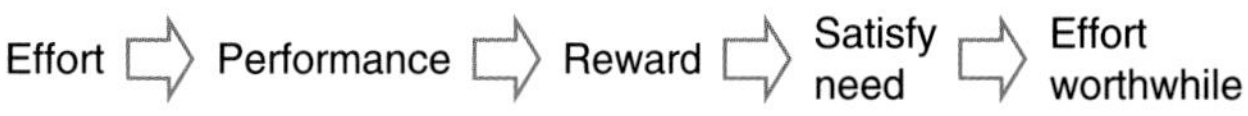

Effort ⇨ Performance ⇨ Reward ⇨ Satisfy need ⇨ Effort worthwhile

Figure 11.6 Vroom's process

TERMS

Valence: depth of want of employee.

Expectancy: degree to which people believe reward leads to performance.

Instrumentality: confidence that employees will get what they require.

11.5 Motivation in practice – financial methods

Piece rate and commission	• Encourages effort. • Unit costs known, helps in setting prices.	• Needs measurable output/sales. • May lead to falling quality/'bad' sales. • employees may only want to achieve target pay. • Provides little security. • employees discouraged from change.
Salary	• Should depend on experience, progress. • Security of income. • Linked to status. • Helps costing. • Suitable for where output is not measurable. • Suitable for management (unpredictable hours).	• Income not directly related to effort/ productivity. • May lead to complacency. • Regular appraisal essential, time-consuming.
Performance-related pay	• Staff motivated to improve performance. • Target setting important. • Appraisal may be of benefit.	• Will not motivate if staff not driven by financial rewards. • Team spirit can be damaged. • Could be subject to claims of manager favouritism. • May push conformity rather than innovation.
Profit sharing	• Potential conflicts between owners and employees. • Should lead to greater effort/cost reduction. • Attract better recruits. • Does not add to costs. • Could lead to increased profitability.	• Reward may not be related to individual effort. • Can be costly to operate. • Small profits may de-motivate. • Reduced shareholder dividends initially. • Reduced retained profits may reduce investments. • Could dilute value of existing shares.
Fringe benefits (perks)	• Provides benefits that employees might not otherwise have. • May be low-cost method.	• Unlikely to be as important as other methods of financial reward. • May have tax implications.

Table 11.2 Motivation - financial methods

TERMS

Hourly wage rate: payment to a worker for each hour worked.

Piece rate: payment to a worker for each unit produced.

Commission: a payment to a sales person for each sale made.

Salary: annual income that is usually paid on a monthly basis.

Performance-related pay: a bonus scheme to reward staff for above average work performance.

Profit sharing: a bonus for staff based on the profits of the business – usually paid as a proportion of basic salary.

11.6 Motivation in practice – non-financial methods

Job rotation	• Gives workers new skills.	• Increased workload. • Organisational problems.
Job enrichment	• Less supervision. • Workers have complete jobs. • Workers have more responsibility. • Challenging.	• Not easy to apply in practice. • Workers may not respond well. • May be seen as threatening jobs. • More work for same pay?
Job redesign	• Linked to job enrichment. • Can lead to improved recognition. • Allows introduction of team working. • More skills, better promotion chances.	• Difficult to implement. • May be seen as a threat.
Quality circles	• Good for finding solutions. • Involves participation.	• Time consuming. • Costly. • Needs support of management and employees.
Worker participation	• Participation in decisions. • Job enrichment. • More responsibility.	• Time-consuming. • Not suited to some styles of management.
Team-working	• Better motivation. • Makes better use of talents. • Can reduce costs. • Complete tasks can be allocated.	• Time consuming. • Not everyone good in teams. • Training costs. • Time costs.
Target setting	• Related to Management by Objectives. • Motivating.	• Bureaucratic.
Delegation and empowerment	See Chapter 14.	See Chapter 14.

TERMS

Job rotation: increasing the flexibility of the workforce and the variety of work they do by switching from one job to another.

Job enrichment: involves the principle of organising work so that employees are encouraged and allowed to use their full abilities - not just physical effort.

TERMS

Job enlargement: attempting to increase the scope of a job by broadening or deepening the tasks undertaken.

Job redesign: involves the restructuring of a job – usually with employees' involvement and agreement – to make work more interesting, satisfying and challenging.

Quality circles: voluntary groups of employees who meet regularly to discuss work-related problems and issues.

Worker participation: employees are actively encouraged to become involved in decision making within the organisation.

Teamworking: production is organised so that groups of employees undertake complete units of work.

Progress check H

1   Give **three** examples of non-financial motivators.

2   Explain the difference between piece rate and performance-related pay.

TIP

You should be able to do more than just describe/explain different methods of motivation.

You should be able to recommend which might be most suitable in particular situations and why.

11.7 Employees' participation in the management and control of business activity

Examples include:

- Team meetings
- Worker representatives
- Thorough training

- Quality circles, TQM
- Delegation
- Empowerment.

Exam-style question

Paper 1 Section B

1   Discuss whether a school should use non-financial methods to motivate its workers.   [12]

Student's answer

Non-financial incentives or rewards are methods of motivating employees that do not involve a monetary gain. These include training, quality circles, participation and more enriching work. Highly motivated workers can be a big advantage for schools who are often trying to encourage more students – and better qualified students – to study there.

If only money was used to motivate teachers and other workers at a school then this could be very expensive – schools often have limited budgets – and motivation might not be very high as money is soon taken for granted. Team or departmental meetings could be used to work out daily and weekly targets, e.g. for organising a given number of revision classes. Discussion and two-way communication will help to give teachers a sense of importance and involvement and targets they help set are more likely to be reached.

Although teachers are highly qualified, additional training could be offered in, for example, using IT in the classroom. By learning new skills teachers will have greater status and self-assurance and the new skills could be useful for the school too as teachers might be able to offer to teach more than one subject. A more flexible workforce is useful for the school when students' subject choices change.

Enriching the work done by teachers and other school workers could also be motivating. IT maintenance staff could be given some opportunities to investigate the best new computers for the school to buy. Teachers of each student could be encouraged to work closely together to help resolve problems that he/she might have or to push the student on to achieve an excellent university place. This will also reflect well on the teachers and give them a sense of achievement – one of Maslow's higher order needs.

Both the employees and the school will benefit from the use of non-financial methods. Herzberg

claimed that money is only a 'hygiene' factor and that real motivators involved changing the nature of the job itself. As schools often have little money to offer big new salary increases it only makes sense to use other methods – perhaps more effective ones – to motivate the people who work in them. However, the pay and salary levels of all school workers needs to be adequate to allow hygiene needs to be met first.

Authors' comments

The student avoids the risk of quoting all of the motivational theorists. The answer is very well applied to schools and teachers. A clear and well supported case is made for using non-financial methods. This is a very good answer.

Additional exam-style questions

Paper 1 Section A

1 Explain the term 'hygiene factor'. [3]

2 State **two** examples of financial motivators. [2]

3 Define the term 'empowerment'. [2]

Paper 2

Best Quality Supermarkets (BQS)

BQS is a national chain of supermarkets. Competition has increased and there is a threat to BQS's future. BQS is considering some methods to reduce cost in the hope that it will regain competitiveness.

BQS is considering:

- delaying a pay increase which means that pay will be less than that for competitors
- introducing flexible working contracts so that employees will not get paid if they are not needed
- greater staff discounts on goods purchased by staff
- payment of a bonus in the form of shares if the business does well
- longer working hours with no extra pay.

4 Discuss the impact that the proposals are likely to have on employees at BQS. [11]

Human resource management

12.1 Purpose and role of human resource management (HRM)

A business depends on the efficiency and motivation of some of its most important assets – the people who work for it. HRM is the tool to achieve the best from the workforce.

Figure 12.1 HRM roles

TIP

Small/medium firms may not have or need an HRM department. The functions are often carried out within other functional departments.

TERM

Human resource management (HRM): the strategic approach to the effective management of an organisation's employees so that they help the business gain a competitive advantage.

Progress check A

1 Why would a supermarket want an effective HRM department?

2 How can a small business survive without an HRM department?

12.2 Workforce planning

Having the wrong number of workers or workers with the wrong skills could be disastrous for a business. Workforce planning avoids such problems.

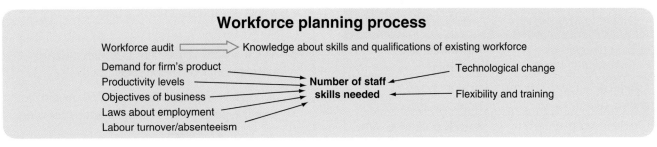

Workforce planning process

Workforce audit ⟹ Knowledge about skills and qualifications of existing workforce

Demand for firm's product
Productivity levels
Objectives of business ⟶ **Number of staff** ← Technological change
Laws about employment ⟶ **skills needed** ← Flexibility and training
Labour turnover/absenteeism

Figure 12.2 The workforce planning process

TERMS

Workforce planning: analysing and forecasting the numbers of workers and the skills of those workers that will be required by an organisation to achieve its objectives.

Workforce audit: a check on the skills and qualifications of all existing employees/managers.

TIP

Workforce planning should be closely linked with a firm's long-term objectives and with external factors influencing the firm.

Progress check B

1 Why should a business undertake a workforce plan if a global downturn is predicted?

2 Why would a car manufacturer about to open a new factory need a workforce plan?

3 Explain the possible consequences of not having a workforce plan.

12.3 Process of recruiting and selecting

Businesses use recruitment to get the best workforce possible within the constraints on them.

Establish nature of the job	What sort of person?	Attract applicants	Shortlist	Select
• Job description	• Person specification	• Job advertisement	• Chosen from applications/ CV/references	• Selection criteria • Achievements, intelligence, skills, interests, personal manner, physical appearance, personal circumstances
• Job title • Tasks to be performed/ responsibilities • Place in hierarchy • Working conditions • Assessment/ measurement	• Person profile in terms of qualifications, qualities and skills needed	• In business premises • Newspapers • Agencies • Job centres • Online	• A small number to interview selected	• Interviews • Aptitude tests • Psychometric tests • Tasks • Problem solving

Table 12.1 Recruitment and selection

A workforce with the wrong people would reduce the chances of meeting objectives. Most businesses will want to reduce the impact of labour turnover.

Internal advantages (external disadvantages)	External advantages (internal disadvantages)
Known to business	New ideas and practices
Candidate knows business and its culture	Wider choice of potential applicants
Quicker and cheaper	Avoids problems with staff not promoted
Workers have career structure, promotion chances	Candidates could be better qualified
Known style of management if recruiting for senior post	No further internal positions to fill

Table 12.2 Internal versus external recruitment

TERMS

Recruitment: the process of identifying the need for a new employee, defining the job to be filled and the type of person needed to fill it, attracting suitable candidates for the job and selecting the best one.

Job description: a detailed list of the key points about the job to be filled – stating all its key tasks and responsibilities.

Person specification: a detailed list of the qualities, skills and qualifications that a successful applicant will need to have.

Labour turnover: measures the rate at which employees are leaving a business. Calculated by:

$$\frac{\text{number of employees leaving in a given period}}{\text{average number of employees for that period}} \times 100.$$

TIP

Do not confuse job description and person specification.

Progress check C

1 Why might a software business seek to recruit product developers externally?

2 What are the benefits of a bank recruiting for senior positions internally?

3 What are the differences between a job description and person specification?

4 A business employs an average of 50 people. Last year five people left. What is the labour turnover?

12.4 Contracts of employment

In many countries it is a legal requirement to give an employee a contract of employment. Typically employment contracts will specify:

- Employee's responsibilities and duties
- Nature of contract (e.g. length if appropriate)
- Working hours, place of work, payment method
- Holiday entitlement
- Process for ending the contract (by employee or employer).

TERMS

Contract of employment: a legal document that sets out the terms and conditions governing an employee's job.

Dismissal: being sacked from a job due to incompetence or breach of discipline.

Unfair dismissal: ending an employee's employment contract for a reason that the law regards as unfair.

Redundancy: when a job is no longer required, so the employee doing this job loses the job through no fault of his or her own.

TIP

The precise legal requirements of employment contracts are likely to vary slightly between different countries. It would be useful to research what these legal requirements are in your own country.

12.5 Maintaining staff morale and welfare

Many businesses, especially those that believe in corporate social responsibility (CSR), will ensure that they care about the well-being of employees. In some countries, some of these ideas are incorporated into employment law. These functions are often undertaken by an HRM department:

- Ensuring effective health and safety in the workplace
- Support for resolving personal and family problems
- Providing medical facilities
- Providing equality and diversity guidelines
- Helping employees achieve a work-life balance.

12.6 Employee training

The costs of *not* developing/training employees are high as workers will be less productive and less motivated.

Development should be integrated into business activities with managers as well as the HRM department involved.

There are many forms of training:

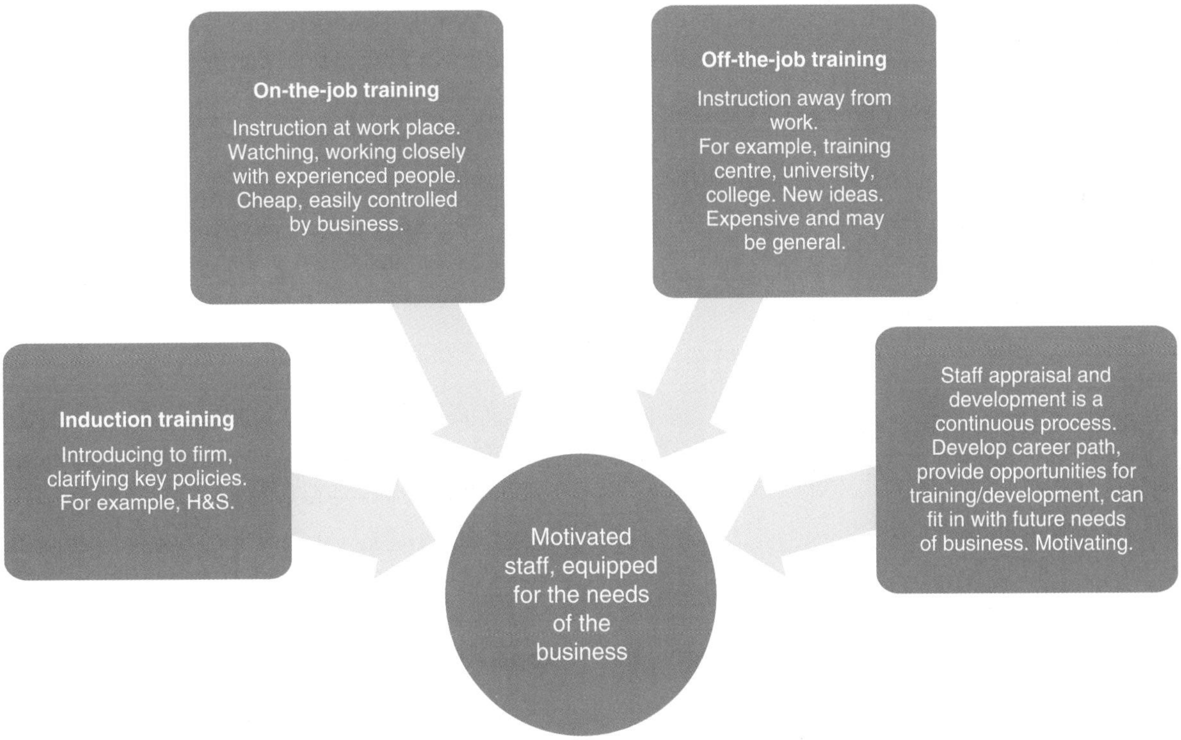

TERMS

Training: work related education to increase workforce skills and efficiency.

On-the-job training: instruction at the place of work on how a job should be carried out.

Off-the-job training: all training undertaken away from the business, for example, work related college courses.

Induction training: introductory training programme to familiarise new recruits with the systems used in the business and the layout of the business site.

Staff appraisal: the process of assessing the effectiveness of an employee judged against pre-set criteria.

On-the-job training

Instruction at work place. Watching, working closely with experienced people. Cheap, easily controlled by business.

Off-the-job training

Instruction away from work.
For example, training centre, university, college. New ideas. Expensive and may be general.

Induction training

Introducing to firm, clarifying key policies. For example, H&S.

Staff appraisal and development is a continuous process. Develop career path, provide opportunities for training/development, can fit in with future needs of business. Motivating.

Motivated staff, equipped for the needs of the business

Figure 12.3 Types of training

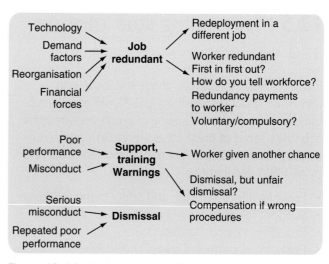

Figure 12.4 Redundancy and dismissal

Progress check D

1. Why might training help a car manufacturer introduce flexible working?

2. How does staff development fit in with the ideas of Herzberg?

3. What are the main differences between induction training and off-the-job training?

4. Why is it important to involve managers in employee development?

5. What sort of training would be best if a business is going to upgrade all of its computers?

12.7 Reducing the workforce

Circumstances may require a business to reduce the number of workers or individual workers may need to be sacked. Businesses have to go about solving these problems the right way.

Progress check E

1. Why might a global downturn lead to redundancies at a fashion shop?

2. What are the main differences between making someone redundant and dismissing them?

3. Why is it important to follow the correct procedures when making an employee redundant?

4. Give **three** reasons why redeployment is better than redundancy.

5. Give **two** reasons why a worker might legally be dismissed.

Exam-style question

Paper 2

Northwich College (NC)

NC is planning to gain extra revenue by hiring out its rooms and sport hall during school holidays. The Principal would like to appoint an Office Manager to manage these facilities and the letting of them during the school holidays. The manager would also be responsible for marketing the facilities. The job will be part time in term time and full time in holidays. Because it is a state owned college the salary is likely to be quite low.

1. Discuss the factors that NC needs to consider when recruiting and selecting an Office Manager.

[11]

Student's answer

The college has already started the recruitment process by identifying the need for a new manager and the roles to be undertaken. The job description should include the exact nature of the job to be done. The college should now focus on attracting applications from suitably qualified and experienced people. The job advert should stress the flexibility of the job with part-time work in term time helping to balance out the relatively low salary. A decision might have to be made about whether preference is given to internal or external candidates. It might be best to advertise the vacancy both internally in the college and externally through online job vacancy sites and then use good selection techniques to choose the best person for the job. It does not seem to be essential that the new manager has important 'internal experience' of this college so an external candidate could do a good job too. Once candidates have applied then the selection process begins.

A shortlist should be drawn up based on those candidates who come closest to the person specification – the skills and qualities most needed. The manager will need to 'sell' the facilities of the college to outside organisations, so self-confidence and an ability to communicate well will both be essential. CVs will be important in selection as experience in either a college environment or in property management, such as writing letting contracts, might be important. The quality of language used on the CV is important as writing letters will

be an important part of this job. Interviews will be essential to assess how the person presents themselves and to find out how ambitious and focused they are. The ideas they have for 'selling and promoting' the facilities of the college should be discussed with them and really original ideas should help the college decide which candidate to appoint. If a candidate says 'I don't know, I haven't thought about it', then this suggests they would not be the right person for the job. Interviews may take a lot of the college Principal's time but they will be the best way to select the right person in this case.

Authors' comments

The student showed depth of knowledge about the recruitment and selection and provides several examples of good application to the job vacancy in the question. Reasons for the recruitment and selection methods proposed are well analysed and there are some sound examples of evaluation. A very good answer.

Although the student made evaluative comments (a recommendation for the best selection method, a statement about the most important factor and a suitable conclusion) the comments need to be supported by the earlier discussion/analysis. This discussion should enable the student to put the factors into proper perspective with regard to the recruitment process.

Additional exam-style questions

Paper 1 section A

1   Briefly explain **two** roles of a Human Resource Manager.   [3]

2   Define the term 'on-the-job' training.   [2]

3   Give **three** ways in which a business may benefit from workforce planning.   [3]

Paper 1 section B

4   Analyse the importance of human resource management to a school.   [8]

5   'Training workers is a waste of time because employees leave a business and other businesses benefit'. Discuss.   [12]

Further human resource management

13.1 Approaches to HRM

Hard HRM	Soft HRM
Cutting costs	Developing staff
Increasing flexibility	Motivating through fulfilment
People treated like materials, equipment	People related
Strategy related	Fits ideas of Maslow, Mayo, Herzberg

Table 13.1 Hard versus soft HRM

13.2 HRM and flexibility in the workforce

There are several ways a business can manage its workforce, with different degrees of flexibility. Consider a business wanting to expand:

TERMS

Hard HRM: an approach to managing staff that focuses on cutting costs. For example temporary and part-time employment contracts, offering maximum flexibility but with minimum training costs.

Soft HRM: an approach to managing staff that focuses on developing staff so that they reach self-fulfilment and are motivated to work hard and stay with the business.

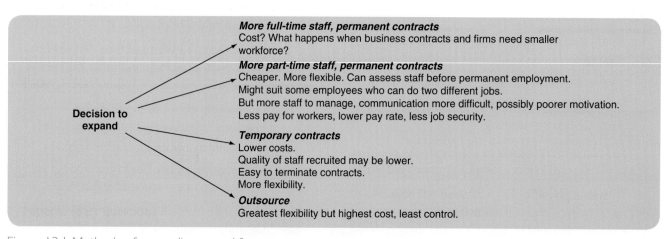

Figure 13.1 Methods of expanding a workforce

Two recent developments that increase flexibility are implementing zero hours contracts and using Handy's Shamrock organisation to identify key areas of the business as shown in Fig 13.2:

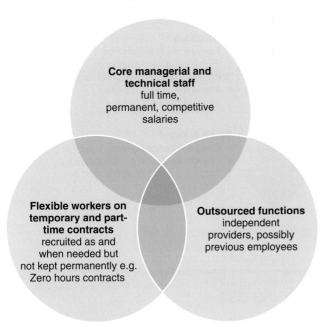

Figure 13.2 Handy's Shamrock Organisation

TERMS

Temporary employment contract: employment contract that lasts for a fixed period, for example, six months.

Part-time contract: employment contract that is for less than the normal full working week (of, say, 40 hours) for example, eight hours per week.

Flexi-time contract: employment contract that allows staff to be called in at times most convenient to employers and employees, for example, at busy times of day.

Outsourcing: not employing staff directly, but using an outside agency or organisation to carry out some business functions.

Zero hours contract: a contract in which there is no obligation on the employer to offer work, nor on the employee to accept work although 'employees' have some rights.

13.3 Measuring employee performance

The consequences of poor workforce performance can be damaging to a business. It is important to be able to measure workforce performance and take measures to improve it.

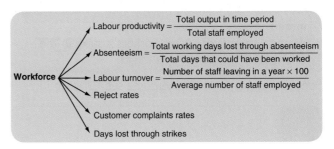

Figure 13.3 Measures of employee performance

TIP

There are other measures of employee performance. However, you should be prepared to use and refer to these results too e.g. reject rates; customer complaint rates, days lost through strikes.

Progress check A

1 Why is improving employee performance important to a business?

2 Give one way labour productivity could be measured in a fashion clothing shop.

3 Give **three** ways in which labour productivity may be reduced in a fashion clothing shop.

4 Why would high labour turnover be a problem at your school?

5 A business employs ten people. Last year each person was absent on average ten days. If the total number of days worked per person is 200 days, what is the rate of absenteeism?

13.4 Improving employee performance

Methods include:

- Performance appraisal – targets set and monitored.
- Training – stretch and challenge workers.
- Quality circles – identify and solve problems.
- Cell production/autonomous groups – multi-skilling and teamwork.
- Financial incentives – give workers a stake in the business.

For more detail on these measures see Chapter 11.

TIP
Low productivity may not be due to poor workforce performance. It could be due to poor machinery or supply disruptions such as strikes. High labour turnover may not be an indication of poor motivation. For example, businesses that employ students (for example, supermarkets) will always have high labour turnover.

Progress check B

1 Explain how training could improve employee performance in a hotel.

2 How could teamwork reduce absenteeism?

3 Why might giving workers a stake in an airline business improve labour productivity?

13.5 Management by objectives (MBO)

Management by objectives is a process for improving employee performance through the use of agreed objectives and a system of appraising performance against those objectives.

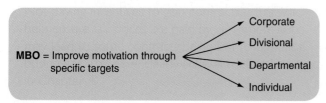

Figure 13.4 The role of targets in management by objectives

The advantages and disadvantages of management by objectives are shown here:

MBO has largely been succeeded by management imposed targets – the target culture.

Advantages
1. Feature of job enrichment
2. Everyone knows what to do
3. All working to same overall targets
4. Managers able to monitor success/failure

Disadvantages
1. Can be time-consuming
2. Objectives can be outdated quickly
3. Targets do not guarantee success

Figure 13.5 Management by Objectives

Progress check C

1 A school plans to introduce MBO. Give **two** possible objectives that a business studies teacher might agree with the management of the school.

2 Identify one possible problem with each of these objectives.

3 Why might targets not guarantee success?

13.6 The need for labour legislation

Laws may cover:

- Health and safety
- Gender and other equality issues including discrimination
- Trade unions
- Employment contract issues such as working hours, minimum wages, working ages, unfair dismissal.

TIP
You do not need to know the precise details of labour laws in any country – but you are advised to research the industrial relations laws in your own country.

Industrial relations legislation

In addition to laws governing labour, for example, Health and Safety, Equal Opportunities (see Chapter 8) the government influences relationships between it and trade unions.

Figure 13.6 The role of government in HRM

Progress check D

1 Why would the government in your country make laws regarding industrial relations?

2 Why might the requirement for 'secret ballots' in union votes be necessary?

13.7 Cooperation between the workforce and management

Employees, managers and owners may not share the same objectives so there is scope for **conflict**.

Industrial relations' tensions brought about by change could be:

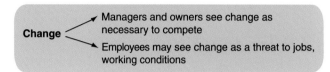

Figure 13.7 Management and change

Progress check E

1 Explain why good labour relations are important to employers.

2 State **two** benefits to an employee of collective bargaining with employers.

3 A fast-food business has 200 restaurants. Why would cooperation and negotiations between employees and management at a local level be difficult?

Management style	Advantages	Disadvantages
Autocratic management style – 'take it or leave it' attitude to employees.	• Low labour costs. • Quick, easy to make decisions.	• No security, poor motivation. • Often no training. • No common objectives. • No job enrichment, participation.
Collective bargaining at industry level (powerful unions negotiate with major employees/associations).	• Reduces needs for individual negotiations. • National agreements.	• Not suitable for small businesses. • Strikes likely – loss of output/sales. • Unions tend to resists essential changes. • May affect national competitiveness.
Co-operation at local level (e.g. works councils, quality circles).	• Fewer strikes. • Involves participation, so better motivation. • Working towards common goals. • Local decisions.	• More complex, time-consuming decisions.

Table 13.2 Approaches to labour-management relations

13.8 Workforce planning

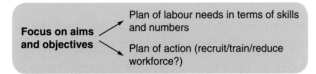

Focus on aims and objectives → Plan of labour needs in terms of skills and numbers

Focus on aims and objectives → Plan of action (recruit/train/reduce workforce?)

Figure 13.8 Role of a workforce plan

13.9 Trade unions

Trade unions **achieve:**

For employees

- Power through solidarity.
- Greater likelihood of success in relation to wages, working conditions through collective bargaining rather than individual bargaining.
- Protection for members (legal support).
- Pressure on employers to meet legal standards (for example, health and safety, equality).

For employers

- Negotiating with one body rather than many people.
- Useful channel of communication.
- Unions impose discipline on members.
- Responsible partnerships between unions and employers can bring benefits to a business.

TERM

Trade union: an organisation of working people with the objective of improving pay and working conditions of their members and providing them with support such as legal services.

Employers' attitude to unions

In many countries it is not a legal requirement to recognise trade unions. Employers can:

- Trade union recognition – may have benefits to employers

- have single-union agreements – makes negotiating easier, reduces inter-union disputes but union might be stronger, may not represent everyone.
- require no-strike agreements – can lead to better relationship with employer and the general public.

TERMS

Trade union recognition: when an employer formally agrees to conduct negotiations on pay and working conditions with a trade union(s) rather than bargain individually with each worker.

Single union agreement: an employer recognises just one union for the purpose of collective bargaining.

No-strike agreement: unions agree to sort problems out without resorting to strikes.

Industrial action: measures taken by the workforce or trade union to put pressure on management to settle an industrial dispute in favour of employees.

Possible union activities	Increased likelihood of conflict	Possible employer activities
Negotiations		Negotiations/ arbitration
Arbitration		Public relations
Go slow		Threat of redundancies
Work to rule		Changes of contract
Overtime ban		Closure
Strike action		Lockouts

Table 13.3 Likely success of union/business interaction

Progress check F

1 How could a teacher benefit from joining a teaching union?

2 Why would a 'no-strike' deal be important for the police service?

3 In your country there is a dispute over working conditions between the major airline and its cabin crew. Discuss the factors that will influence the outcome of the dispute.

4 A car manufacturer wants a single union deal. Why would the unions object to this idea to begin with?

Balance of negotiating power

Figure 13.9 Balance of negotiating power

Exam-style question

Paper 3

SS Engineering (SSE)

SSE manufactures specialist diggers and drills for use in the construction industry. It is a profitable business mainly because SSE's existing four factories are located in low-cost emerging market countries. Sales of SSE products are difficult to forecast as the construction industry is affected greatly by the economic situation especially interest rates. In addition, a major new competitor has started selling advanced digging equipment which can be programmed to perform tasks without the need for continuous worker control. This product was very popular last year in Country Y, where it was launched, and SSE sales fell in this country as a result.

Problems

Apart from varying sales and competition, the main problems experienced by SSE are all related to its existing factory employees and the quality of the output produced. Customer expectations are increasing in the construction industry and SSE's products, although very price competitive, are reported to be less reliable than those of competitors. Labour turnover is high in all four factories but SSE does not know why. Many junior managers also leave each year and the HR department is thinking of giving all those who leave a questionnaire to find out the reasons for them leaving.

New factory planned

SSE is planning to build a factory in a European Union country – its first outside of low-cost emerging market countries. The EU factory will give its products import tariff-free market opportunities in the huge EU market as well as access to a highly trained workforce. The proposal is to employ trained and experienced technicians who will programme and operate the computer controlled robotic equipment to be used in the new factory. SSE management would prefer to offer temporary, flexible employment contracts to these workers as it does to all of its existing factory employees in other countries. SSE

→

directors are prepared to allow its new EU workers to join trade unions, something that is illegal in the countries SSE currently operates in. Employment rights for workers are very extensive in the EU.

A new team in the marketing department will be set up with clear targets to enter the EU market successfully. It will report directly to Head Office as SSE still operates a largely centralised system.

Communication with stakeholders

SSE managers are not satisfied with the current communication methods used by the company. Factory managers are sent monthly budgets by email and they received the monthly SSE internal magazine. Suppliers and customers complain about difficulties in contacting SSE by telephone and shareholders complain about the huge cost of the large printed Company Report and Accounts posted to them each year. An IT consultant has advised the company to make much greater use of 'paperless' methods. The directors accept the need for change and the HR director in particular is keen to use electronic means to communicate with individual workers rather than the noticeboards used at present.

New product developments

SSE's basic product designs are now over ten years old. Directors understand the pace of change and have set up a small research and development department to develop new, technically advanced prototypes of digging and drilling machines. New employees are also being recruited to be responsible for planning the manufacture and marketing of the new products that R and D will be developing. Directors were reluctant to add yet another layer of management in SSE's tall hierarchical structure, divided on functional lines, and are considering other structures more suited to future expansion of the business.

1 Analyse the benefits to both employees and SSE's management from workers in the new factory joining a trade union. [10]

Student's answer

Trade unions are organisations of working people who combine together to protect their interests and work and to push for higher wages. Workers at SSE's new factory could benefit from joining a union to protect themselves from an employer which seems to have little experience of labour laws or negotiating/communicating with workers. The union would advise about their legal rights in the EU and help them to ensure that these rights are protected by SSE. For example, SSE plans to offer only temporary and flexible work contracts and this might be illegal in the EU. By forcing SSE to offer better employment contracts the workers will gain more job security and be paid at least the minimum wage. This is likely to improve the motivation of the employees which will help SSE achieve high productivity in the new factory.

SSE will also benefit from improved communication with workers which seems to be very poor in its existing factories. The trade union can act as a channel of communication between workers and SSE. Any problems that workers might be experiencing will be passed on to SSE managers and these could be solved by negotiation. This will make workers less likely to leave – labour turnover is high in other SSE factories. This will make workers less likely to leave – labour turnover is high in other SSE factories, which can be a big problem when technically trained workers are needed. This will make workforce planning much easier for SSE.

Authors' comments

Two relevant benefits are analysed in this answer – and the student recognises the fact that both SSE and the employees can benefit from trade union membership. The answer uses the context of the case study well and this is very important. This is a very good answer even though it is quite brief.

Additional exam-style question

Paper 3 (based on case study above)

1 Assess the importance of effective workforce planning to the success of the proposed new factory. [14]

Organisational structure

14.1 The purpose of organisational structures

Organisational structures:

- show responsibilities and line management
- show formal relationships between areas of a business and levels of management
- indicate accountability, management responsibilities and chain of command
- show formal channels of communication
- indicate links between departments/functions.

14.2 Key features of organisational structures

TERMS

Level of hierarchy: a position within an organisational structure at which the personnel have equal status and authority.

Chain of command: the route through which authority is passed down an organisation – from the chief executive and the board of directors.

Span of control: the number of subordinates reporting directly to a manager.

Formal structure: the levels of authority and channels of communication identified by an organisation chart.

Informal structure: a network of communication and, possibly, authority that develops independently of a formal structure.

14.3 Factors influencing organisational structure

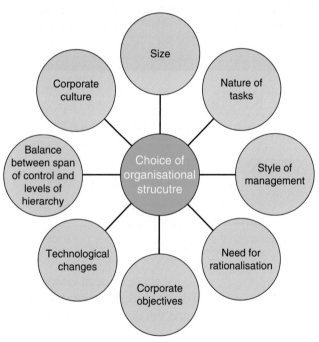

Figure 14.1 Factors influencing choice of organisational structure

14.4 Different types of organisational structures

Functional structures

These are businesses that are structured by functions (e.g. sales, marketing, finance, production, human resources) and these tend to be inflexible with little interaction between different functions. However, roles are clearly defined and it is easy to see where to go for information/help.

Hierarchical structures

Different layers, with authority/responsibility increasing the higher up the organisation, define these structures. A hierarchy can be flat (few levels of hierarchy with a wide span of control) or narrow (many levels of hierarchy but narrow span of control).

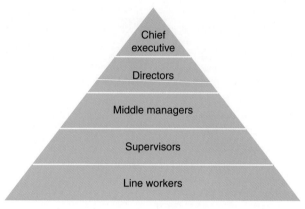

Figure 14.2 A hierarchical structure

The advantages and disadvantages of a hierarchical structure are shown in Fig 14.3:

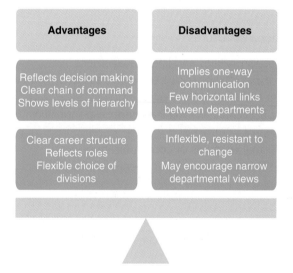

Advantages	Disadvantages
Reflects decision making Clear chain of command Shows levels of hierarchy	Implies one-way communication Few horizontal links between departments
Clear career structure Reflects roles Flexible choice of divisions	Inflexible, resistant to change May encourage narrow departmental views

Figure 14.3 Features of hierarchical structures

Matrix structure

The advantages and disadvantages of a matrix structure are shown in Fig 14.4:

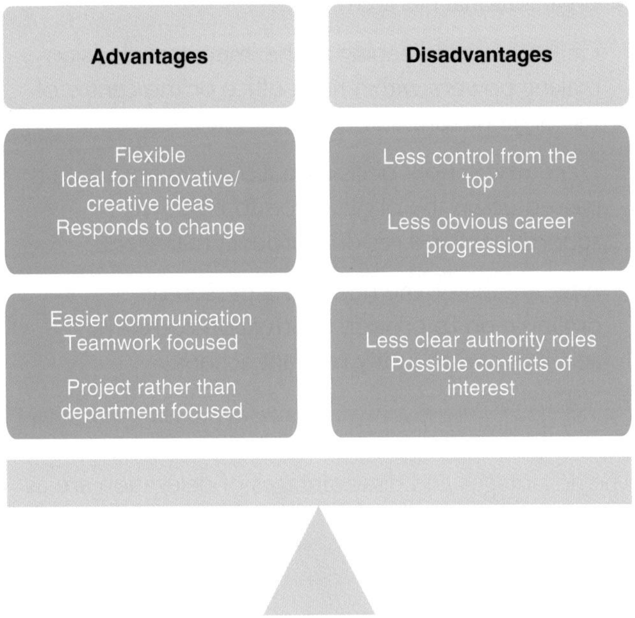

Advantages	Disadvantages
Flexible Ideal for innovative/ creative ideas Responds to change	Less control from the 'top' Less obvious career progression
Easier communication Teamwork focused Project rather than department focused	Less clear authority roles Possible conflicts of interest

Figure 14.4 Features of a matrix structure

TERM

Matrix structure: an organisational structure that creates project teams with team members from different functional areas.

The matrix structure (see Fig 14.5) is ideal for situations in which the business is task or project focused.

Progress check C

1 Explain **two** benefits of a matrix structure.

2 How could a matrix structure be used at your school/college?

3 Outline possible problems with a matrix structure for a multinational pharmaceutical company.

14.5 Reasons why structures change

Structures can change due to growth, a change in management approach, takeovers/diversification or globalisation.

Progress check D

1 Why might the introduction of email-based information flows have an impact on organisational structure?

2 Why is delegation more likely in a school than in a bank?

3 Explain why delegation is more likely in an organisation with a wide span of control.

4 Why would large businesses pay more attention to designing an organisational structure?

	Finance department	Production department	Marketing department	Human resources	Research & development
Project team 1					
Project team 2					

Figure 14.5 A matrix structure

14.6 Delegation and accountability

In decentralised organisations much of the work is delegated.

This contrasts with centralised organisations where head offices retain considerable control.

Delegation transfers the authority and accountability to undertake particular tasks but the final responsibility remains with the delegator.

Progress check E

1 Outline the importance of delegation in a school/college.
2 Explain why increased delegation might involve increased risk.
3 Distinguish between authority and responsibility.
4 Distinguish between authority and accountability.

TERMS

Delegation: passing authority down the organisational hierarchy.

Centralisation: keeping all the important decision-making powers within head office or the centre of the organisation.

Decentralisation: decision-making powers are passed down the organisation to empower subordinates and regional/product managers.

Accountability: the need for a person or organisation to provide information on relevant activities and to justify relevant actions.

The advantages and disadvantages of delegation are as follows:

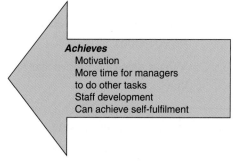

Achieves
Motivation
More time for managers
to do other tasks
Staff development
Can achieve self-fulfilment

But
Manager retains responsibility
Need for monitoring and control
Can be time-consuming
Depends on trust
Clear definition of task needed

Figure 14.6 Features of delegation

Advantages of centralisation	Advantages of decentralisation
• A fixed set of rules and procedures in all areas of the business should lead to rapid decision making – there is little scope for discussion.	• More local decisions can be made that reflect different conditions – the managers who take the decisions will have local knowledge and are likely to have closer contact with customers.
• The business has consistent policies throughout the organisation. This prevents any conflicts between the divisions and avoids confusion in the minds of customers.	• More junior managers can develop and this prepares them for more challenging roles.
• Senior managers take decisions in the interest of the whole business – not just one division of it.	• Delegation and empowerment are made easier and these will have positive effects on motivation.
• Central buying should allow for greater economies of scale.	• Decision making in response to changes, for example in local market conditions, should be quicker and more flexible as head office will not have to be involved every time.
• Senior managers at central office will be experienced decision makers.	

Table 14.1 Advantages of centralisation and decentralisation

TERMS

Line managers: managers who have direct authority over people, decisions and resources within the hierarchy of an organisation.

Staff managers: managers who, as specialists, provide support, information and assistance to employees without any authority or responsibility for them.

Progress check F

1   Explain why delayering has become increasingly more important for businesses that operate in global markets.

2   Why is it likely that businesses with tall organisational structures find it difficult to change?

3   Give examples of roles likely to be fulfilled by staff managers.

4   Would you advise a multinational food manufacturer to adopt a decentralised management structure?

    Explain your answer.

Exam-style question

Paper 3

Re-read the case study at the end of Chapter 13.

1   Discuss how SSE might change its organisational structure to become a more creative business with greater delegation for employees.   [14]

Student's answer

SSE currently operates with a 'tall and hierarchical' structure. This means that there are several layers of management with each layer having similar authority. This can make formal communication within the organisation slow and ineffective. There are also narrow spans of control so each manager has authority over a relatively small number of employees. This reduces the opportunity for delegation. A tall hierarchical structure appears not to be appropriate for SSE as there are suggestions that communication is poor and labour turnover high – both signs of a structure that does not allow for delegation and participation.

SSE's planned expansion also suggests that a new type of structure might be desirable. R and D and product development employees often work best in a structure that allows teamwork and a cross-over of ideas between departments. This will not be achieved in a hierarchical structure split into strict functional departments. A matrix structure is much more likely to achieve the kind of innovative new product and marketing ideas that SSE needs. The matrix structure would allow project teams – perhaps one team for each new type of digger – to be created by drawing people in from all departments to work on a particular project. This would require a substantial change of culture by SSE's managers who seem to like to control everything from the centre. It is not possible to tell whether SSE directors are prepared to make the changes required.

Marketing in new countries such as members of the EU will probably require different marketing strategies to those currently used. It is doubtful that the centralised and tall structure will give the kind of flexibility and rapid decision making needed for this. SSE directors could consider a structure in the marketing department that allows for divisions for each country/region so that specific and localised marketing budgets, targets and strategies can be adopted. Widening spans of control will also encourage subordinate managers to accept more authority and this will enrich the work that they do. This should help to motivate workers at all levels of the structure and reduce labour turnover. Fewer workers and managers leaving will make SSE's workforce planning easier and more accurate as well as reducing recruitment and selection costs.

So significant changes to the organisation's structure are needed to allow SSE to grow in the ways it plans. A combination of matrix teams and country divisions will allow for the creativity and flexibility that SSE will need to cope with new markets and new technology. Perhaps the outdated products and fear of new advanced technology and competition are results of SSE's tall and hierarchical structure and centralised decision making.

Author's comments

The student shows good knowledge of organisational structure. Many key concepts are introduced and understood. The answers are applied to the growth that SSE is planning. The points made are developed and analysed – the consequences of them are explained. Judgement is shown in the answer and in the conclusion. An excellent answer.

Additional exam-style question

Paper 3 (based on case study at the end of Chapter 13)

1   Discuss whether the directors should aim for SSE to remain a centralised business as it expands.   [14]

Business communication

15.1 Effective communication

Situations in which effective communication is essential:

- To pass instructions to employees
- To aid coordination of business activities

- To communicate with past, current and future customers
- To allow employees to participate in a business
- To share ideas, targets etc.

Effective communication is two-way. Barriers must be reduced or eliminated, and the appropriate communication media chosen.

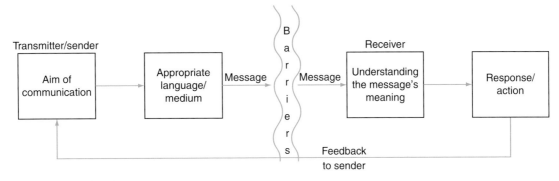

Figure 15.1 The communication process

The benefits of effective communication are shown in Fig 15.2:

Figure 15.2 Features of effective communication

TERMS

Effective communication: the successful exchange of information between people or groups, preferably with feedback.

Communication media: the methods used to communicate a message.

Feedback: the receiver of information sends back further information to the sender to indicate that the message has been received and understood.

15.2 Standard methods of communication

The choice of communication medium is dependent on the following factors:

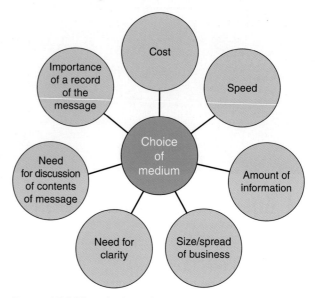

Figure 15.3 The choice of communication medium

Method	Strengths	Weaknesses
Oral	• Direct. • Can be varied to suit needs of receiver. • Easy to understand. • Can be questioned quickly.	• Need to listen carefully. • Affected by noise. • Passive. • No permanent accurate record. • Can be quickly forgotten.
Written	• Recorded – permanent record. • More structured. • Easy to distribute. • Cannot be distorted. • Can be referred to again.	• Often difficult to read. • Message identical to each receiver. • No body language. • Feedback lower. • No immediate response. • May be misinterpreted. • Costly and time consuming.
Visual	• More interactive. • Demands attention. • Often easier to remember. • Creates greater interest.	• Needs close attention. • Sometimes too fast. • Not always clear. • Interpretations by receivers can vary.
Electronic	• Great speed. • Interactive. • Creates interest. • Encourages response. • Ignores boundaries. • Good image for external communication.	• Cannot always be received. • Relies on receiver. • Is expensive in hardware. • Risk of communication overload. • Can be intercepted. • Diminishes personal contact.

Table 15.1 Strengths and weaknesses of communication methods

15.3 Channels of communication

TERMS

Channel of communication: the routes within an organisational structure through which information passes.

One-way communication: information that passes in only one direction in a hierarchy, usually top down. Often associated with autocratic leadership.

Two-way communication: information that passes in two directions in a hierarchy, often downwards and upwards. Often associated with democratic leadership.

Vertical communication: communication that flows from one level of a hierarchy to another.

Horizontal communication: communication that flows within a hierarchical level.

15.4 Barriers to effective communication

TERM

Communication barriers: influences that prevent effective communication.

Failure in one of the stages of communication

Failure can be due to:

- Wrong medium
- Channel of communication is too long
- Misleading or incomplete message
- Too much technical language or jargon
- Too much information
- Language/culture.

Poor attitude of sender/receiver

This is where:

- Sender not trusted by receiver
- Unmotivated receiver/sender
- Poor intermediaries.

Physical barriers

These can be:

- Too much noise
- Too much distance between sender/receiver
- Poor equipment/internet services.

Removing barriers to effective communication

Managers should ensure:

- Clear, concise and precise messages
- As short communication channels as possible
- Channels clear to all involved
- Built in feedback mechanisms
- Trust
- Appropriate physical conditions.

15.5 Informal/formal communications

Informal: unofficial, casual discussions between employees at any level – can be both a positive and negative force within a business. Known as the 'grapevine'.

Formal: can be chain, vertical, wheel, circle, integrated.

> **TIP**
> When discussing suitable communication methods, try to assess which type of communication network would be most appropriate in the given situation.

> **TIP**
> Try to link communication effectiveness with organisational structure. Traditional structures will tend to use vertical communication; matrix structures will use horizontal communication.

15.6 Achieving improvements in communications

Improvements come from: improving clarity of messages, reducing the communication chain, improving feedback, building trust.

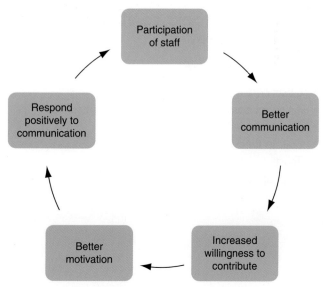

Figure 15.4 The virtuous circle of communication

Exam-style question

Paper 3

Re-read the case study at the end of Chapter 13.

1 Analyse the likely impact on employee motivation of improved worker-manager communications within SSE. [10]

Student's answer

Internal communication with employees is ineffective at SSE. Managers do not know why workers or junior managers leave. There is a tall hierarchical structure with messages suffering from passing through too many people. Temporary/flexible contracts do not encourage effective two-way communication. Improved methods could include team briefings and meetings, feedback briefings or interviews – such as appraisals and 'leaving' interviews – and email communications.

If employees and junior managers are made to feel more involved and important because of two-way communication methods, then this will increase their status and sense of importance. This will help to satisfy their needs for recognition, according to Maslow's hierarchy. This seems to be a particular problem for the junior managers at SSE who are given little delegated authority. Feedback from managers is an important aspect of Herzberg's job enrichment concept. Being made aware of how the work each employee or junior manager is contributing to the overall performance of the business can be satisfying and rewarding. Email communications from HR at Head Office to employees – as long as they are not just orders or criticism – can also lead to two-way communication, although these might be less effective than face-to-face meetings. Team briefings can help to build team spirit and if employees become involved in a group at work this can help satisfy social needs, as identified by Maslow.

Some or all of these changes should help to reduce labour turnover in all parts of SSE. This can also improve motivation as no one likes to work in an organisation where everyone else seems to be leaving.

Authors' comments

This is a good answer as it demonstrates an awareness of the original communication problems, some appropriate benefits from improved communication and an analysis of how these could benefit motivation, all within the context of SSE.

Additional exam-style question

Paper 3 (based on case study at the end of Chapter 13)

1 Recommend changes to SSE's communication methods to ensure more effective communication with external stakeholders and factory managers. Justify your answer. [14]

Unit 3
MARKETING

Chapter 16

What is marketing?

Learning summary

After you have studied this chapter you should be able to:

- ☐ understand what marketing is and the role of marketing
- ☐ understand the difference between consumer markets and industrial markets
- ☐ know how marketing objectives link with corporate objectives
- ☐ distinguish between market orientation, product orientation and societal marketing and apply these concepts to different businesses
- ☐ understand how supply and demand determine price in a free market

- ☐ calculate market size, market growth and market share from given data
- ☐ understand how marketing can be used to add value to a product in different business situations
- ☐ distinguish between niche marketing and mass marketing
- ☐ understand the importance of market segmentation.

16.1 The role and importance of marketing

Marketing is one of the important functional departments of all businesses. Marketing is more than just 'selling'. The role of marketing in a business is to:

- find out what customers are prepared to buy
- communicate this to other departments, e.g. operations/production
- sell the product (i.e. either a physical good or a service) to customers at a profit.

Marketing varies for different types of products. Cars are still usually sold through a physical location such as a car dealer but books are increasingly bought online and not through high street book shops.

16.2 Consumer and industrial markets

Businesses can sell products in either consumer markets – to the final users of the products – or to industrial markets where businesses buy the product to be used in further production. This distinction is important because products will be sold in different ways in these markets. For example, trade fairs and industry exhibitions might be used to sell industrial

products but most consumer products are sold through retailers or the internet.

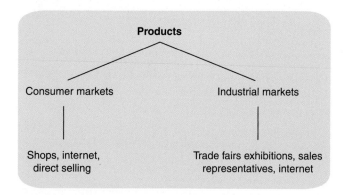

Figure 16.1 Consumer and industrial markets

16.3 Marketing objectives

Effective marketing departments have clear objectives. These should be aimed at achieving the objectives of the corporation. They should be coordinated with the objectives of other departments to try to ensure that resources are available for meeting the marketing objectives.

TERM

Marketing objectives: the goals set for the marketing department to help the business achieve its overall objectives.

Figure 16.2 Marketing objectives

16.4 Distinguish between market orientation and product orientation

A market or customer oriented business (often called 'market led') will put the customer first and use market research to identify needs and potential demand. This information is then used to develop products that will meet this demand.

Product oriented (or product led) firms focus on the production process and 'getting the product right' before attempting to sell it to customers.

So, market oriented firms put much more focus on market research but product oriented firms put the focus on selling a product that has already been developed or produced.

Two other approaches to marketing are:

1 Asset led marketing – basing new products on a firms' existing products and strengths, such as Apple focusing on consumer electronics – not electric heating!

2 Societal marketing – making marketing decisions based not just on consumer wants but 'what is good for society' such as wooden furniture made from sustainably sourced materials.

Market or customer oriented (market led)	Product oriented (product led)
Customer first.	Product design first and then get 'the product right'.
Use market research to find what customers want.	Then find market.

Table 16.1 Market orientation and product orientation

TERMS

Market (consumer) orientation: bases product decisions on consumer demand as established by market research.

Product orientation: focuses on products that can be made or have been made for a long time and then trying to sell them.

Asset led marketing: bases marketing strategies on the firm's strengths and assets instead of purely on what the customer wants.

Societal marketing: marketing strategies consider not just the demands of consumers but also the effects on society.

TIP

You should be able to evaluate these different approaches to marketing. For example, whether market orientation reduces risks or the extent to which societal marketing will increase in importance in countries where consumers are becoming increasingly worried about the environment.

16.5 Demand, supply and price

In free markets – with no government controls and where many firms operate – prices are determined by the 'forces of demand and supply'. The prices of oil and other basic raw materials fell in 2015/16 due to falling demand and supplier's unwillingness to cut back on output.

TERMS

Demand: the quantity of a product that consumers are willing and able to buy at a given price in a time period.

Supply: the quantity of a product that firms are prepared to supply at a given price in a time period.

Equilibrium price: the market price that equates supply and demand.

TIP

Make sure you draw the demand and supply curves correctly!

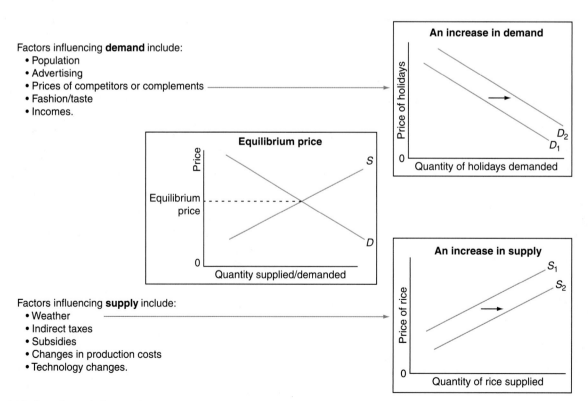

Factors influencing **demand** include:
- Population
- Advertising
- Prices of competitors or complements
- Fashion/taste
- Incomes.

Factors influencing **supply** include:
- Weather
- Indirect taxes
- Subsidies
- Changes in production costs
- Technology changes.

Figure 16.3 Supply and demand

16.6 Market size, market growth and market share

Marketing objectives are often expressed in terms of 'increasing annual sales by five per cent' or 'increasing market share by ten per cent'. A high market share gives a business more influence and power over retailers and suppliers. If a product becomes a brand leader it can use this in its advertising.

$$\text{Market share (\%) in a time period} = \frac{\text{Sales of business} \times 100}{\text{Total market sales}}$$

It is therefore very important for a marketing manager to know:

- How big is the market in which we sell our products?
- Is it getting bigger or smaller?
- Are our sales a greater or smaller share of the total market than last year?

It is often easier for a business to increase the sales of a product if the total market is growing but increasing product sales does not necessarily mean that the market share of the business has increased. Competitors might have increased sales at an even faster rate!

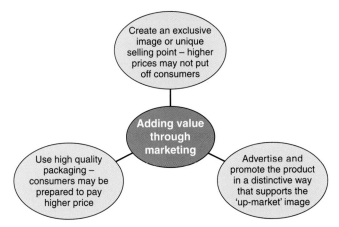

Figure 16.4 Ways marketing can increase value added

TERMS

Market size: the total level (or value) of sales of all producers within a market.

Market growth: the percentage change in total market size over a period of time.

Market share: the percentage of total market sales in a market sold by one business in a given time period.

Progress check B

1 Draw a graph showing a 'typical' demand curve for one brand of television. If consumer incomes increased by five per cent, draw a new demand curve on the graph.

2 Draw a graph showing a 'typical' supply curve for crude oil. If there is a major disaster at a large oil field, draw a new supply curve on the graph.

3 In both Q1 and 2, explain what is likely to happen to the equilibrium price of each product after these changes.

4 Calculate the percentage annual growth in market size if the total value of the mobile (cell) phone market in one Country Z was $90m in Year 1 and $110m in Year 2.

5 Refer to Q4. Company A sells mobile phones in Country Z. In Year 1, its sales value was $30m. In Year 2, its sales increased to $35m. Calculate Company A's market share in both years.

6 If Company B has 15 per cent market share for a product and total market size is $230m, calculate the value of Company B's sales.

7 Explain why it is important to a producer of breakfast cereals to have a high market share.

16.7 Adding or creating value

This links with Chapter 1. Marketing managers have an important role to play in increasing the value added to a product.

TERM

Unique selling point (USP): the special feature of a product that differentiates it from competitors' products.

TIP

If a question asks you to explain how a business can add value to its products, make sure your suggestions are based around the products the firm is selling – apply your answer!

16.8 Niche marketing and mass marketing

TERMS

Niche marketing: identifying and exploiting a small segment of a larger market by developing products to suit it.

Mass marketing: selling the same products to the whole market with no attempt to target groups within it.

TIP

Niche marketing is increasingly common because modern production techniques allow much more product flexibility of design and built-in features – once you have studied Operations management, you should be able to make these links in your answers.

	Advantages	Disadvantages
Niche marketing	• Small firms are often able to survive by exploiting niche markets. • Allows big business to create separate and exclusive images for products. For example, Lexus owned by Toyota. • Unexploited niche markets may allow higher prices to be charged to the business that enters them first.	• No economies of scale in terms of production and marketing. • Quite a risky strategy if the tastes of niche market consumers change. • Total sales – and possibly profits – will be lower than mass marketing. • Cost of developing products to suit different niche markets.
Mass marketing	• Potential for economies of scale. • High sales likely – could be more profitable than niche marketing.	• Profit margins could be lower than niche marketing if the mass market is very competitive. • Business may have a low image or status if it does not develop any niche market products.

Table 16.2 Advantages and disadvantages of niche and mass marketing

16.9 Market segmentation

This marketing concept is becoming much more important for many consumer products. As consumer incomes rise in most of the world, so expectations change. Many consumers would prefer to buy products that are specifically designed for their needs supported by a marketing strategy that focuses on them and their needs.

TERMS

Market segmentation: identifying different segments within a market and targeting different products or services to them.

Market segment: a sub-group of a whole market in which consumers have similar characteristics (similar consumer profile).

Consumer profile: a quantified picture of consumers of a firm's products showing age groups, income levels, gender and social class.

Progress check C

1 Explain **two** ways in which a supermarket could add value to the fresh produce (for example, meat and vegetables) that it sells.

2 In the global market for computers there are many 'market niches'. Identify **four** of these.

3 Explain the benefits to a computer manufacturer of only focusing on niche marketing.

4 Explain **three** ways in which a large car manufacturer could segment its market.

5 Explain **two** benefits to the car manufacturer of segmenting the market in one of these ways.

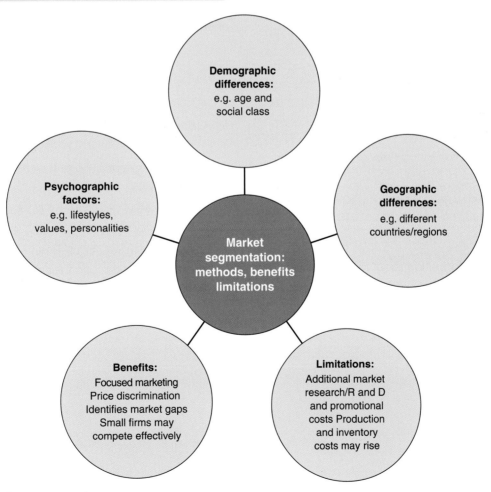

Figure 16.5 Market segmentation

Exam-style question

Paper 2

HiQ Fashion

HiQ Fashion sells children's clothing through two out-of-town retail stores. The business buys in school uniforms, jeans, sport clothes and other children's clothing from some of the lowest-cost suppliers. HiQ Fashion stores contain a huge range of items but they are poorly displayed and most of the employees just operate the tills or fill the shelves. There is very little consumer service provided. The Marketing Director has just reported to the other directors these key points about the company's recent sales:

- 'Our sales increased by 15 per cent this year from last year's total of $4m.
- The total market size of the children's clothing market was $32m last year and $35m this year.
- Our average prices are ten per cent lower than competitors'.

The Managing Director was pleased with these results but wanted the company to expand further. She said, 'I suggest we do some market research into the consumer needs for adult sports clothing. I think this is a fast growing market which we could move into. Consumer incomes are rising. People are playing more sport and demanding very high quality sports clothing. With our market research results we could then decide which sports to focus on'.

1 Briefly explain the term market oriented.   [2]

Student's answer

A market oriented business uses market research. It collects information about what consumers want to buy and uses this to decide what to produce. This makes the business less risky as only those things that consumers want are being made. As HiQ has not sold adult sports clothing before, market research will help the business decide what items to sell.

Authors' comments

This is a very good answer. Brief and accurate, the definition of market orientation shows full understanding. There is also a useful reference to the data – and the reason why HiQ might use market orientation is well applied.

Additional exam-style questions

Paper 1 Section 1

1 Explain what is meant by 'market segmentation'.   [3]

2 Explain two ways in which a camera manufacturer could segment markets.   [5]

Paper 2

Use the above information about HiQ to answer the following:

3 Briefly explain what is meant by 'market size'.   [3]

4 Calculate the change in HiQ Fashion's market share between the two years.   [3]

5 Explain the importance of the trend in HiQ's market share.   [3]

6 Analyse two ways in which HiQ could segment the sports clothing market.   [8]

7 Would you advise HiQ Fashion to sell adult sports clothing through their existing two stores? Justify your answer.   [11]

Market research

Chapter 17

Learning summary

After you have studied this chapter you should be able to:

- know the importance and scope of market research
- distinguish between primary research and secondary research and assess the relative advantages
- understand methods of information gathering
- know how to use sampling methods and present market research results
- evaluate usefulness and cost-effectiveness of market research undertaken in different business situations.

17.1 Need for market research

Market orientation is explained in Chapter 16. This concept, adopted by most businesses these days, requires market research to be undertaken before product and other key decisions are taken. Market research is often a continuous process. It is helpful not just to decide what to produce and sell but also to keep the business as aware as possible of changing consumer needs or market trends.

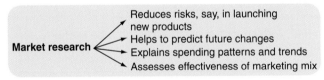

Figure 17.1 Benefits of market research

TERM

Market research: the process of collecting, recording and analysing data about customers, competitors and the market.

17.2 Market research process

Market research can be an expensive process. It is important to make sure that the time and money spent on it is geared towards solving clear marketing problems. This can be done by the market research process shown in Table 17.1.

Progress check A

1. How can market research improve the effectiveness of business decisions?
2. Why is it important for a business to know about its customers?
3. How does market research support new product development?

Problem	Objectives	Sources	Advantages
Market size? Falling sales? New market? New competitors?	Set SMART objectives to achieve a solution to the problem through market research. **Example 1** How many people are likely to buy our product in Country X? (quantitative data needed)	START with secondary research. (desk research) • Government • Libraries • Trade organisations • Market intelligence reports • Newspapers • Company records • The internet.	Widely and quickly available. Some reports may be expensive to buy – but often cheaper than primary research. May not be recent.
Which customers to target? Which new products to develop?	**Example 2** Why do consumers prefer Company Y's products to ours? (qualitative data needed)	Primary research (field research) • Qualitative • Quantitative • Focus groups • Observations • Test markets • Surveys.	Not available to competitors. Up-to-date. Designed to meet specific information needs of the business.

Table 17.1 The market research process

17.3 Primary and secondary research; quantitative and qualitative research

It is important to remember these distinctions.

TERMS

Primary research: the collection of first-hand data that is directly related to a firm's needs (field research).

Secondary research: collection of data from second-hand sources (desk research).

Qualitative research: non-numerical research into the in-depth motivation behind consumer buying behaviour or opinions.

Quantitative research: research that leads to numerical results that can be statistically analysed.

Focus group: a group of people who are asked about their attitude towards a product, service, advertisement or new style of packaging.

Progress check B

1. List **three** advantages of primary data over secondary data.

2. Why should secondary data usually be collected first?

3. Under what circumstances will secondary data collection be impossible?

4. Why might qualitative research be useful? Give a business example.

17.4 Sampling methods

In most market research situations it is impossible to address questions to the whole 'population' or target market. This is because of the cost involved or the distances that would have to be covered by researchers or, perhaps, because the identity of all consumers is not known. In these cases a sample must be selected. Different sampling methods are outlined in Fig 17.2.

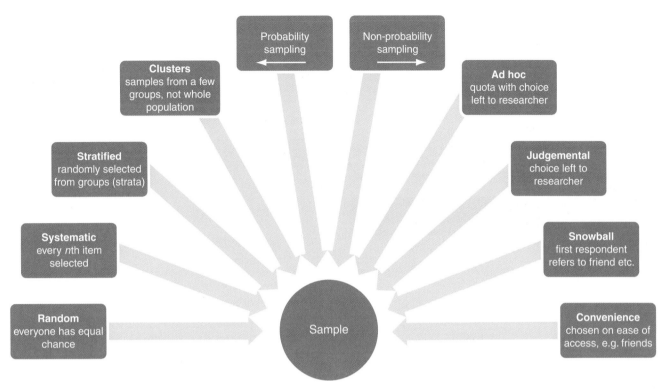

Figure 17.2 Methods of sampling

TERMS

Sample: the group of people taking part in a market research selected to be representative of the overall target market.

Random sample: every member of the target population has an equal chance of being selected.

Systematic sample: every nth item in the target population is selected.

Stratified sampling: this draws a sample from a specified sub-group or segment of the population and uses random sampling to select from each stratum.

Quota sampling: when the population has been stratified and the interviewer selects an appropriate number of respondents from each stratum.

Cluster sampling: using one or a number of specific groups to draw samples from and not selecting from the whole population, for example, using one town or region.

Progress check C

1   Give **four** types of non-probability sampling.

2   For **two** methods listed in Q1, outline a business situation in which it might be the best method of sampling.

3   Why use samples during primary data collection?

17.5 Questionnaires and interviews

Much primary data collection is gathered by means of questionnaires. These can either be self-completed or the questions can be read out during an interview.

Questionnaire design should:

- be based on clear objectives
- be unambiguous
- have a logical sequence
- avoid leading questions
- use easy to understand language
- give results that allow analysis.

Open questions: those that invite a wide-ranging or imaginative response – the results will be difficult to collate and present numerically.

Closed questions: questions to which a limited number of pre-set answers is offered.

Self-completed questionnaire	Direct face-to-face or telephone interview
Response rate often poor with postal questionnaire – better if online or mobile used.	Skill of interviewer important to success.
Questions easily misunderstood.	Follow up questions can be asked.
Cheap – but does this make it cost-effective if the data is less reliable?	Expensive but may give more accurate data.

Table 17.2 Questionnaires and interviews

17.6 Is primary data always reliable?

The short answer to this is no! Fig 17.3 explains why:

17.7 Presentation of information

This is an important part of the market research process. Effective presentation of results can improve managers' understanding of them.

Progress check D

1　Give one disadvantage to open questions.

2　Give **three** types of bias.

3　Give one advantage of self-completed questionnaires.

4　An entrepreneur researched the potential market for a new gardening service by surveying ten members of her family. Explain why the results are likely to be unreliable.

TERMS

Range: the difference between the highest and lowest value.

Interquartile range: the range of the middle fifty per cent of the data.

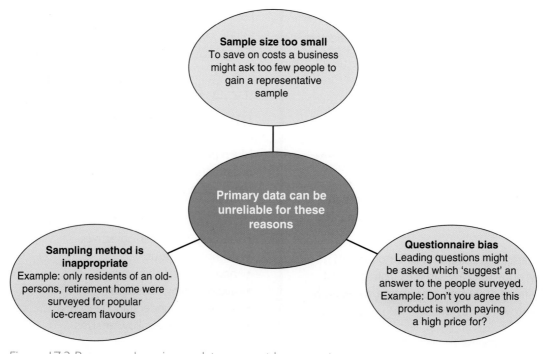

Figure 17.3 Reasons why primary data may not be accurate

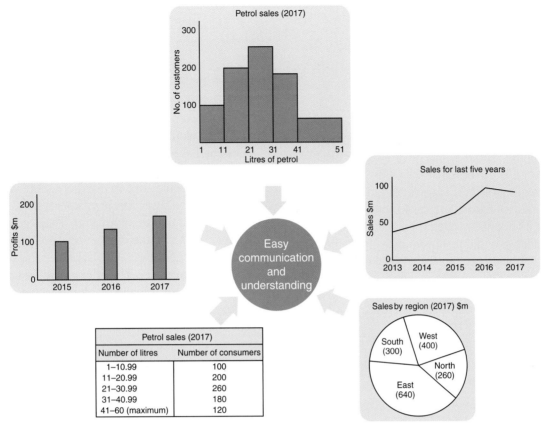

Figure 17.4 Ways of presenting statistical data

17.8 Statistical analysis

Here are some ways in which statistical data can be analysed:

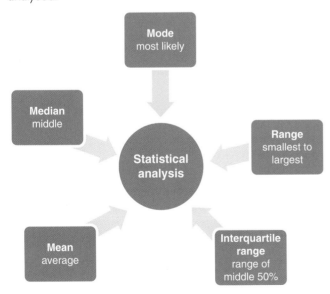

Figure 17.5 Ways of analysing statistical data

Exam-style question

Paper 2 (part question)

New City Hospital (NCH)

NCH is a public sector hospital. The managers are planning to spend money providing extra facilities. To raise finance for the hospital, these facilities would then be rented out to private sector health organisations. They sell their services to fee-paying private patients. NCH managers plan to undertake market research before spending money on providing additional facilities. They want to collect both qualitative and quantitative data about the market for private health care. One of the managers knows a doctor who works in a private sector hospital. He has offered to ask six other doctors what extra facilities they think NCH should provide.

1 a i   Define the term 'qualitative data'.   [2]

    ii   Briefly explain what is meant by the term 'quantitative data'.   [3]

  b   Analyse **two** benefits to NCH of undertaking market research before spending money on providing additional facilities.   [8]

  c   Discuss the most suitable methods of market research that NCH could use to help managers decide which facilities to improve.   [11]

Student's answer to 1(c)

NCH is a hospital in the public sector. As it obtains its finance from the state, it might have limited funds so cost-effective market research will be important.

The managers should undertake secondary research first. This is data that has already been collected. They could find other hospitals that provide similar facilities and try to get information on how busy these are and how much they charge to private companies. However, the other hospitals may be reluctant to give this information. It might be possible to get information about the market for private health care and its overall size and growth from market research agencies. However, these reports can be expensive and are often out of date. The demand for health services might change quickly over time, for example,

as a population ages it will need more care facilities for the elderly.

The NCH managers should then do primary research. NCH managers could visit private sector hospitals and interview doctors about the facilities they most want. They could ask the doctors how much they would pay for the additional facilities at NCH. The NCH could send a questionnaire out to a sample of the private health providers in the country. This could contain questions such as how much they would pay for new facilities at NCH – this would be quantitative information. They could also ask what would be the most important factor that would make them use NCH facilities – this would be qualitative information. This data would be up-to-date and specific to NCH's needs. However, the response rate to questionnaires might be low and this could make the primary research inaccurate.

NCH managers should use both secondary research and primary research as they have different advantages. The secondary information – which should be gathered first – might tell them that the market for private health care is not growing. This might make NCH managers think again before spending government money on expensive primary research and health facilities which they planned to rent out to the private sector.

Authors' comments

The student clearly has a good grasp of the situation described in the case study. They also understand the difference between primary and secondary research as well as the need to undertake secondary research first. The need for cost-effective research is well explained and in context.

There are analytical points made. For example, the student recognises that information gained from secondary research might make the managers think again, so avoiding spending money on expensive primary research. Evaluation is effective throughout the answer – suggesting that secondary data should be undertaken first; comparing the advantages of the two methods; justifying the need for cost-effective research; recommending that both secondary and primary research should be undertaken. This is an excellent answer.

Additional exam-style questions

Paper 2

1   Answer parts. (a) and (b) from the New City Hospital case study above.

Paper 1 Section A

2   Distinguish between random sampling and stratified sampling.   [3]

Paper 1 Section B

3   Discuss the most appropriate forms of market research an entrepreneur might use before setting up a new food retailing business.   [20]

Chapter 18

Marketing mix: product and price

Learning summary

After you have studied this chapter you should be able to:

- understand what the marketing mix is (4Ps)

- analyse the role of the customer and importance of customer relationship marketing (4Cs)

- assess the importance of product decisions in different business situations

- understand the product life cycle and its significance

- calculate price elasticity of demand and understand the results

- assess different pricing methods and apply them to business situations

- evaluate the importance of pricing as one element of the marketing mix.

18.1 The marketing mix

The traditional marketing mix comprises the '4Ps' but others can also be added to this list, such as People and Processes.

> ### TERM
>
> Marketing mix: the four key decisions that must be taken in the effective marketing of a product.

Product
The good or service being offered for sale to the customers including the packaging of it

Price
The amount the customers pay to purchase the product

Marketing mix
These 4Ps need to be linked or integrated

Promotion
Ways in which the product, its features and brand image are communicated to customers

Place
The ways in which products are made available for sale to customers

Figure 18.1 The marketing mix

18.2 Customer relationship marketing (CRM) and the 4Cs

This recent development moves away from the 4Ps to focus on how a business can establish a long-term relationship with customers. The aim of CRM is to keep existing customers – the focus of the 4Ps is to gain new customers.

> ### TERM
>
> Customer relationship marketing (CRM): using marketing activities to establish successful customer relationships so that existing customer loyalty can be maintained.

This emphasis on customer loyalty has been encouraged by estimates that suggest it often costs five times more to win a new customer (for example, through promotional costs) than to keep an existing one (for example, by offering excellent after-sales service). Recent research suggests that by keeping just five per cent more of their existing customers, some companies could increase profits by nearly 100 per cent!

Customer solution	What the business needs to provide to meet the customers' needs and wants.	The product and the service provided with it must meet customers' requirements – these requirements have to be monitored by market research and this information may allow for more effective market segmentation.
Cost to customer	The total cost of the product including actual price plus guarantee cost, delivery, finance costs.	This needs to be maintained at a competitive level.
Communication with customer	Promoting the product to customers – but also gaining information back from them.	Two-way communication will help to improve relationships with customers.
Convenience to customer	Providing easy access to both the product (the place where it is sold) and information about it.	This may be becoming easier for many customers with increased access to the internet – but this is not always the most 'convenient' channel for all products.

Table 18.1 The 4Cs

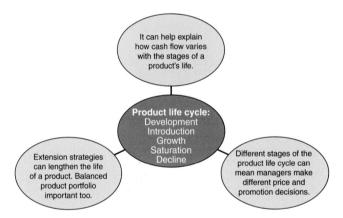

Figure 18.2 The product life cycle

Progress check A

1 Using any relevant example of a product that you are familiar with, outline the meaning of the '4Ps'.

2 Explain how a restaurant could attempt to retain a higher proportion of its customers than it currently does.

3 Explain why customer relationship marketing is important for:

  a a bank b a mobile (cell) phone network provider.

18.3 Product decisions and the product life cycle

A product – any good or service – needs to meet customer expectations if customer loyalty is to be retained. A market map helps to identify the most suitable 'position of new products'. The product life cycle concept can help marketing managers analyse the product portfolio and take decisions about products and other parts of the marketing mix.

TERMS

Product life cycle: the pattern of sales recorded by a product from launch to withdrawal from the market.

Product portfolio analysis: assessing the performance of the products of a business.

Extension strategies: marketing plans to extend the maturity stage of the product life cycle.

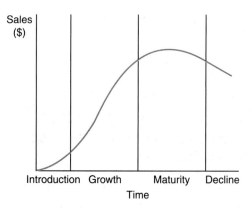

Figure 18.3 Typical stages of a product life cycle

This life cycle can often be lengthened by the use of extension strategies. Analysing the product portfolio with this technique and by ensuring not all products are in the 'decline stage' increases the chances of a business achieving its marketing objectives.

TIP

The product life cycle is difficult to predict for any new product – and for an existing product it may be difficult to determine which stage it is currently at. These are possible limitations of this model.

Progress check B

1   Do you think that 'more advertising' could lead to long-term success of any product? Explain your answer.

2   Draw and label a typical product life cycle diagram.

3   Give examples of 'extension strategies' for a well-known product of your choice and explain the likely impact of them.

4   Explain how the type and level of promotion spending on a product might change as it passes through its life cycle.

5   Explain **two** limitations of using the product life cycle in decision making.

18.4 Product differentiation and USP

TERMS

Product differentiation: making a product distinctive so that it stands out from competitors' products in consumers' perception.

USP: Unique Selling Point (or Proposition) the special feature of a product that differentiates it from competitors' products.

An effective USP helps a business:

*   Differentiate itself from rivals in competitive markets.
*   Achieve customer loyalty.
*   Establish low price elasticity of demand which gives potential for higher revenue (see Section 18.5).

18.5 Price elasticity of demand

This is an important concept as it measures the responsiveness of customers' demand for a product as the price of it is changed.

$$\text{Price elasticity of demand (PED)} = \frac{\text{\% Change in quantity demanded}}{\text{\% Change in price}}$$

To calculate a percentage change, use this formula:

$$\frac{\text{Change (in demand or price)}}{\text{Original (demand or price)}} \times 100$$

The PED formula can also be used to answer questions such as these:

If demand increased by ten per cent and PED is estimated to be −2, what was the change in price?

$$PED = \frac{\text{\% Change in quantity demanded}}{\text{\% Change in price}}$$

$$-2 = \frac{10}{x}$$

$$\text{so, } x = \frac{10}{-2} = -5\%$$

The price was reduced by five per cent in order to achieve an increase in sales of ten per cent.

Progress check C

1 Copy and complete this table (based on demand per week in units sold).

Original price	New price	Original demand	New demand	PED	Comment
$5	$6	1500	1050		Demand is elastic and revenue should fall if the price is increased.
$1000	$1050	300	270		
$1	$0.95	5000	6000		
$10000	$11000	200	195		

2 Explain what you understand by the statement: The demand for Product X is more price elastic than the demand for product Y.

3 A marketing manager estimates that the PED for Product C is −0.5 and the PED for Product D is −2.3. Explain, with the aid of demand curve diagrams, what would happen to total revenue if the manager increased the prices of both products.

4 State **two** factors that could influence the PED of a product.

> **TIP**
> PED is nearly always a negative result because for most products, when the price is increased the quantity demanded falls – and vice versa with a price reduction.

18.6 Pricing decisions

Setting the price for a product is one of the most important of all marketing decisions. Some of the factors that influence this decision are shown in Figure 18.4.

18.7 Pricing methods

There are several different pricing methods or techniques that business can use to determine the actual price to be charged.

> **TIP**
> It is important, if you are asked to recommend or justify a particular pricing method, to consider the level of competition that exists in the market and the extent to which the product is very different from that of competitors' products.

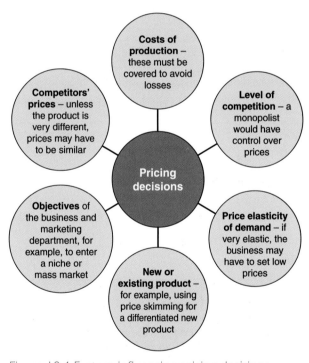

Figure 18.4 Factors influencing pricing decisions

18.8 Why pricing is important

- Has major influence on sales and profits of a product.
- Psychological impact on consumers.
- Needs to be constantly reviewed especially in fast-changing or competitive markets.
- Essential that the price charged matches and integrates with the rest of the marketing mix.

Method	Key term definition	Potential benefits	Potential limitations
Full-cost pricing	Calculating unit cost and adding a fixed profit margin.	Profit will be made if all output sold. Easy to calculate for single product firms.	Difficult to calculate for multi-product firms, for example, may lead to inaccurate allocation of fixed costs. Does not take market conditions into account.
Contribution pricing	Basing prices on covering variable costs and making a contribution to fixed costs and profit.	Flexible as the price charged can vary considerably with market/competitive conditions. Variable costs should be covered.	Fixed costs may not be covered (and a loss recorded) if total contribution does not exceed fixed costs.
Competitive pricing	Basing price on prices charged by competitors.	Allows the business to remain competitive. Small firms with little market power may have to use this method.	Costs may not be covered – for example, if larger competitors have lower unit costs of production. Price may vary frequently as competition changes.
Psychological pricing	Basing price on customers' perceived value of the product.	Customers do not feel they are being charged 'too much' for the product's value. Customers do not feel that a product appears 'too cheap'.	Market research will be necessary to discover customers' perception of value. The psychological price may not cover unit costs.
Penetration pricing	Setting a relatively low price in order to achieve high sales volume/market share.	Customers should be attracted to the new (or existing) product as it has a price lower than most competitors.	This price may not cover unit costs. It may be difficult to raise prices later due to customer resistance.
Market skimming	Setting a high price for a unique or highly differentiated product.	Should gain high revenue if PED is low. High profit margins.	High prices may attract competitors into the market, reducing sales. Customers may be resistant if prices are lowered later if they consider quality is being reduced too.

Table 18.2 Pricing methods/strategies

Progress check D

1 Use a simple numerical example to explain full cost pricing.

2 Explain how a hotel might use contribution or marginal cost pricing.

3 Under what market conditions would a business be most likely to use competition based pricing.

4 Explain, using a simple example, what 'price discrimination' means.

5 Distinguish between market skimming and market penetration pricing methods.

6 Give one example each of a business situation when

a market skimming and

b market penetration pricing might be used.

7 Give an example of psychological pricing and explain why this method might be used.

Exam-style question

Paper 2

Redgate Bakers (RB)

RB produces specialist cakes for festivals and birthdays. It has a shop that also sells a large variety of bread loaves, sandwiches and snack foods of bread of different types. These are all bought in from another bakery. RB spends $100 per week on advertising and promotion.

The costs of producing each specialist cake are:

Materials and labour (variable costs) $15

Weekly fixed costs of cake department $200

Ten cakes are produced and sold each week.

The business does not offer free delivery for its cakes and does not use IT to keep customer records or to sell its products. However, RB has an excellent reputation for its cakes and many customers think they are the best available in town.

The market for bread is very competitive and RB has a small market share. Several large supermarkets also offer a wide range of bread. Some of them sell it as a 'loss leader' and the manager of RB is worried about the effect on his business.

1 a i   Define the term 'market share'.   [2]

      ii Briefly explain the term 'loss leader'?   [3]

   b i   Calculate the selling price for each specialist cake if RB uses full cost pricing and expects to make a profit of 20 per cent of total cost per cake.   [3]

      ii Calculate the selling price if RB buys in cheaper materials and variable costs are reduced to $12 per cake.   [3]

   c Analyse two pricing methods that the manager of RB could use for the bread sold by the business.   [8]

   d Discuss whether RB should use some of its resources to undertake customer relationship marketing.   [11]

Student's answer to 1(c)

There are many pricing methods that RB could use. They could use market skimming which means charging a very high price for bread and then, later reducing prices when competitors offered low prices. This would not work well in this case as competitors already exist. A skimming pricing strategy would lead to very low sales of bread for RB. This pricing strategy would work best with a newly developed product with few competitors – and this is not the case with bread which is difficult to make different from the products made by competitors.

Contribution pricing could be used. This means the price would at least cover the variable costs of buying in the bread and anything extra would be profit. This would allow RB to vary the price, and the contribution made, depending on what competitors charge their customers. If a basic loaf is sold very cheaply by other bakeries, then RB would have to accept a low contribution on this type of product. If RB are buying in some specialist breads – perhaps made from organic flour – then it might be able to earn a high contribution on these products by charging a price much above the buy-in variable costs. This would particularly be the case if competitors did not sell specialist bread like this.

Authors' comments

This is a good answer which is well applied to RB and bread! It is almost evaluative – it shows judgement in suggesting when price skimming might best be used – **but** the evaluation is wasted in this case (the clue is the command word 'analyse').

Two pricing methods are explained and analysed and this makes it a good answer.

Additional exam-style questions

Paper 2

1 Answer parts (a), (b) and (d) from the RB case study above.

Paper 1 Section B

2 a Explain why a shoe retailer might use customer relationship marketing. [8]

b Discuss the usefulness of the product life cycle model to a soft drinks manufacturer. [12]

Chapter 19

Marketing mix: promotion and place

Learning summary

After you have studied this chapter you should be able to:

- understand the different forms of promotion

- know why setting objectives for a promotion campaign is important

- analyse factors that influence promotion decisions and apply these to different business situations

- understand why 'place' is an important element of the marketing mix

- discuss the suitability of distribution channels in different business situations

- analyse the reasons for and impact of internet marketing such as online advertising, dynamic pricing, social media, viral marketing, e-commerce

- evaluate the importance of a consistent and integrated marketing mix.

19.1 Different forms of promotion

Promotion is about communicating with customers or potential customers – to tell them about a product, to offer special deals on that product and to convince customers that they should buy it.

Figure 19.1 Types of promotion

TERMS

Promotion: the use of advertising, sales promotion, personal selling, direct mail, trade fairs, sponsorship, public relations and viral marketing to inform customers and persuade them to buy.

Above the line promotion: promotion (such as advertising) paid for directly by the business, e.g. use of mass media advertising.

Below the line promotion: promotion that is not a directly paid for means of communication but based on short-term incentives to buy.

Promotion mix: the combination of promotional techniques that a firm uses to sell a product.

Advertising: paid for communication with consumers to inform and persuade, for example, TV and cinema advertising.

Sales promotion: incentives such as special offers or special deals directed at consumers or retailers to achieve short-term sales increases and repeat purchases.

Promotional budget: the amount of money made available by a business for spending on promotion during a certain time period.

19.2 Promotional objectives

Effective decisions about promotion, such as how much to spend and which methods to use, require a business to establish clear promotional objectives. These could include:

- Establishing or reinforcing a distinctive brand image - this differentiates products from competitors and encourages customers to 'ask for the product by brand name'
- Increase sales by a target per cent
- Increase market share to a target per cent
- Increase repeat sales to existing customers
- Attract a target number of new customers.

These promotional objectives should be closely linked in with the overall objectives of the marketing department (which should themselves be linked to the corporate objectives of the business).

How can a business check if these objectives have been achieved?

- Consumer feedback, for example, focus groups.
- Sales before and after the promotion campaign.
- Response rates to advertisements and sales promotions.
- Website 'hit' rates.

TIP

When discussing promotion and how much a business might spend on promotion it is important to refer to promotional objectives, how to assess whether these have been met, finance resources available and the nature of the market.

Progress check A

1 Why is promotion important when launching a new product?

2 If a product is already well established in the market, why might a business still spend money on promoting it?

3 State **three** methods of 'below the line' promotion and outline one possible advantage of each one.

4 What is meant by a 'promotional budget'?

5 Should a computer manufacturer that is launching a new model spend as much on advertising as its competitors? Explain your answer.

6 Why is it important for a business to measure the success of a promotion campaign?

Key factor	Why important
Product	• Consumer product or industrial product – only one of these is likely to be advertised on television. Which one? • New product or existing product – which one of these is likely to need 'informative' advertising? • Product life cycle – different approaches to promotion are likely to be used at different stages.
Target market	• If the product is targeted at the elderly (for example, walking aids) then magazines or newspapers with a high proportion of elderly readers might be an effective medium to use. • If the product, such as a computer game, is targeted at young consumers, then viral marketing through social networking sites might be more effective.
Cost	• The cost of different promotions needs to be weighed against the potential revenue/profit gains. Would it be worthwhile for a local home cleaning service business to advertise in national newspapers?
Finance available	• Related to cost. The finance available – promotional/marketing budget – will often limit what forms of promotion can be used.
Competitors	• Is it a good idea to copy how competitors advertise and promote their products? Will consumers be attracted to alternative methods?
Packaging	• Needed to protect physical products but also a means of promoting the brand image of the product, e.g. boxes for expensive perfumes.

Table 19.1 Factors influencing promotion decisions

19.3 Promotion decisions – the key factors

When marketing managers make decisions about how to promote a product there are a number of key factors that should be considered, as outlined in Table 19.1.

Progress check B

1 State one product/service for which TV advertising might be ineffective – and explain your choice.

2 State one product for which TV advertising might be effective – and explain your choice.

3 State one product for which 'point of sale' displays could be an effective form of promotion – and explain your choice.

4 Explain with examples how the promotion of a product might change as it passes through its life cycle.

5 Suggest one suitable promotion objective for a petrol company about to undertake a new promotion campaign.

19.4 Why 'place' is important – channels of distribution

When studying the 4Cs, 'convenience to customer' is an important consideration. The place element of the marketing mix is closely related to this. By place, we do not necessarily mean a physical location where a product can be bought – although the position of a shop may well be an important aspect of customer convenience in buying a product. The place element

refers to the method or channel of distribution used by the business and how and where the product is to be sold to the customer.

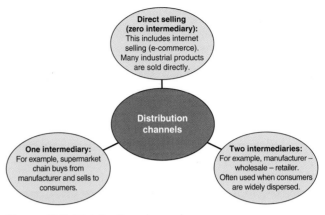

Figure 19.2 Distribution channels

19.5 Deciding which distribution channels should be used

Important factors to consider include:

- Need to keep costs low to maintain competitiveness – intermediaries may add to 'channel cost'
- Importance of product freshness
- How widely dispersed the market is
- Cost of holding inventories
- Level of service expected by consumers
- Technical complexity of product.

19.6 The impact of the internet on marketing

The rapid growth of internet marketing has had an impact on most elements of the marketing mix – for consumer products but also for products sold between businesses (B2B) (see Table 19.2).

Advantages	Disadvantages
Customers can compare prices easily – the business might be the cheapest.	Customers can compare prices easily – the business might not be the cheapest!
Global promotion is possible though the website – much cheaper than global TV advertising!	Millions of websites are available – how will customers access yours?
Global online selling is possible through a suitably designed website – cutting out intermediaries.	Some customers prefer face-to-face contact and personal selling – and the ability to 'see and try before they buy'. Transport costs of individual items to customers (and return costs if products not suitable).
Dynamic pricing is possible – charging different prices to different consumers based on information about them.	Customers may object to not always being offered the lowest possible price.
Easy to record web 'hits' and success of online promotions. Easy to respond to customer questions and feedback.	Negative qualitative feedback from customers about products or services can 'go viral' very quickly.

Table 19.2 Internet marketing – advantages and disadvantages

19.7 Integrating the marketing mix

The four elements of the marketing mix must be consistent and integrated with each other. This means that the '4P' decisions cannot be taken in isolation to each other. Consumers need to be given the same 'message' about a product through its design, price level, method of promotion and 'place' of sale.

TERM

Integrated marketing mix: the key marketing decisions complement each other and work together to give consumers a consistent message about a product.

TIP

Explaining the importance of an integrated mix to the success of a marketing campaign is a very good conclusion.

Progress check C

1 Explain why expensive jewellery is usually sold through shops with high quality fittings and décor, using well-trained staff.

2 Why would a computer controlled manufacturing machine usually be sold through 'direct selling'?

3 Why might a furniture manufacturer sell most of its products to retailers rather than directly from its factory?

4 Why might a sweet manufacturer use a two-intermediary channel of distribution?

5 Explain the importance of e-commerce for a type of product of your choice.

6 Explain how social media can be used to promote a product.

Exam-style question

Paper 1

1 a Analyse the advantages and disadvantages to a clothing retail business of starting to sell products online via the internet. [8]

b Discuss the factors that might influence the marketing mix for a newly launched soft drink. [12]

Student's answer to 1(b)

The marketing mix is the combination of factors that businesses can decide on which influence the sales of a product – the 4Ps are product, price, promotion and place. It would be important for the manufacturer to set a clear marketing objective for the new product – this could be five per cent market share within 12 months. The main benefit of having an objective like this is that it will help to integrate the 4Ps to make sure that they all aim to achieve this target. There is no point in setting a really high price for a mass market soft drink – it will not send a consistent message to consumers and it will not allow the business to gain five per cent market share.

If the product is aimed at the mass market – perhaps this decision was taken after a product positioning analysis – then it must have flavours which appeal to a large number of consumers. These might have already been tested by market research. Getting the product right will be essential as there are so many soft drinks on the market, the new product will need to offer something 'special' to stand out from the competition.

The price must reflect the mass market the product it is aimed at and not be too high. It could be priced using penetration pricing – a very competitive low price – as this will make it more likely that the market share objective is achieved. The potential risk of this strategy is that potential consumers might think the drink lacks quality ingredients.

Promotion will be the factor that most determines whether a successful brand image is created. Coca-Cola and Pepsi have such well-known brand names that the products now almost 'sell themselves' as customer loyalty is so high for them. Internet, web-based and social media advertising would appeal to young consumers. As they might be the group that buys the most soft drinks, these methods of promotion would be best. In contrast, selling over the internet is not a good idea as soft drink is cheap and often an impulse buy. Customers will not order a can of drink online for delivery tomorrow if they are thirsty now.

The most important feature of the marketing mix will be its integrated nature. A tested product with unusual flavours, perhaps aimed at the youth mass market, sold at reasonable prices with teen focused internet promotion should lead to success. Making the product widely available through a range of retailers, vending machines, gyms and night clubs will be the final part of a consistent marketing mix.

Authors' comments

This answer is quite brief but it has real strengths. It is well applied to soft drinks throughout. The importance of a consistent and integrated mix is stressed several times. The importance of marketing objectives is well understood. There are several, well supported, recommendations and these represent good evaluation and judgement. This is an excellent answer.

Additional exam-style questions

Paper 1

1   Answer part (a) above.

Paper 2

HiTech Cameras (HTC)

HTC manufactures cameras. Sales of low priced cameras have been hit by the growing use of mobile phones with cameras. Five years ago HTC decided to focus only on expensive cameras with advanced features. The lowest priced camera the business sells has a retail price of $300. HTC has developed a revolutionary new camera made with very light materials. It is called 'Lightpix'. It is planned to be launched at the end of 2017. The Marketing Director plans not to use traditional methods of advertising but to use only online and mobile phone communication methods. She is convinced that viral marketing through social media will have as big an impact on sales as a huge and expensive advertising campaign. As a result, she has only allocated a promotion budget of ten per cent of expected first year's sales of Lightpix. The camera is expected to capture two per cent of the national market for cameras, forecast to be worth $120m in 2018, in its first 12 months after the launch.

The directors of HTC are confident of the new camera's success as it has a clear USP. However, competitors are working hard to catch up and mobile phone cameras are improving with each new model launch. HTC is also taking a major decision to close all 50 of its camera shops and will, in future, only sell online.

2   a   i   Define the term 'advertising'.   [2]

ii   Briefly explain the term 'viral marketing'.   [3]

b   i   Calculate the 2018 promotion budget for HTC.   [3]

ii   Explain one way in which HTC could assess the success of its promotion campaign for Lightpix.   [3]

c   Analyse **two** potential benefits to HTC of only selling cameras online.   [8]

d   Evaluate the extent to which an integrated marketing mix will ensure success of the new model of camera.   [11]

Marketing planning

20.1 Marketing plan

Marketing decisions in large businesses can lead to significant expenditure and can have a huge impact on the future success of the business. These decisions need to be planned for – not taken on the spur of the moment.

TERM

Marketing plan: a detailed fully researched report on marketing objectives and the marketing strategies to be used to achieve them.

The key contents of a marketing plan are:

- Purpose of the plan, for example, prepare for launch of new product.
- Background to the business including mission statement (useful for external stakeholders such as potential investors).
- Situational analysis – SWOT and PEST analysis will help to establish the current strengths of the business and its products, actual and potential competitors, market trends and external problems and opportunities.
- Marketing objectives – to give clear focus and direction to the marketing plan.
- Marketing strategies proposed – the ways in which the business intends to achieve its objectives, for example, developing new markets for existing products or promoting in existing markets to

increase market share. The strategy used will need an integrated marketing mix to be effective.
- Marketing budget – having a plan but no resources will lead to disaster!
- Executive summary and time frame for putting the plan into effect.

Potential benefits	Potential limitations
An important part of a business plan, for example, for a new business or a significant development by an existing business.	Detailed plans can be time-consuming and costly, for example, external market research may have to be 'bought-in'. Are they justified for small businesses? Are they justified if similar marketing decisions have been taken before?
Encourages integration and close working with other functional departments.	Fast-changing markets require a flexible approach to planning – a marketing plan that is not adjusted to changing external conditions, for example, would lead to incorrect decisions being taken.
Improves the quality of marketing decision making and reduces risks of these decisions failing.	Planning cannot guarantee success – effective management of the strategic decision will still be essential.

Table 20.1 Evaluation of market planning

20.2 Elasticity

Estimating the following measures of elasticity could be an important part of the situational analysis for a market plan. They are based on the same principle as price elasticity of demand: measuring the relative impact on demand for a product following a change in a variable.

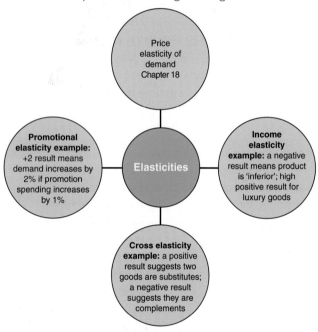

Figure 20.1 Different elasticity measures

Key formulae

$$\text{Promotional elasticity of demand} = \frac{\%\ \text{Change in demand}}{\%\ \text{Change in promotion spending}}$$

$$\text{Income elasticity of demand} = \frac{\%\ \text{Change in demand}}{\%\ \text{Change in consumer incomes}}$$

$$\text{Cross elasticity of demand} = \frac{\%\ \text{Change in demand of Good A}}{\%\ \text{Change in price of Good B}}$$

Using elasticity results – words of caution:

• Often based on estimates
• Assumes other factors did not affect sales
• May only apply to a certain time period – last year's elasticity estimates may not be accurate for today's market conditions.

TIP

Elasticity results are not necessarily accurate figures that can be relied upon by marketing managers for future decision making – the results can act as guidelines, no more.

20.3 New product development

TERM

New product development (NPD): the design, creation and marketing of new goods and services.

Stages in NPD

Generate new product ideas

For example, from R and D, employees, adapting existing products.

Idea screening

Is it technically feasible and will it benefit consumers whilst making a profit for the business?

Concept development and testing

What features should the product have? How will consumers react to it?

Business analysis

Assessing costs, likely sales and potential profits.

Develop a prototype product.

Product testing

Testing the product in terms of its durability and function; modifying it in response to consumer group feedback.

Test marketing

Small-scale market launch to test customer reaction. Is it worthwhile launching nationally?

Commercialisation

Full-scale launch of the product.

20.4 Research and development (R and D)

TIP

Don't forget that only a small proportion of 'new product ideas' ever reach the final stage of commercialisation — this is an evaluation of the NPD process.

TERM

Research and development (R and D): the scientific research and technical development of new products and processes.

TIP

Never confuse research and development with market research!

Potential benefits	Potential limitations
Creates new products.	It is expensive and may take years for new products to lead to higher profits.
Develops new production processes, for example, robots to reduce unit costs.	Rival firms may be spending more on R and D or using resources to develop even better products and processes.
Unique selling point may be created – higher prices may be charged, increasing profit margins.	If the new product or process is not differentiated enough to patent it, other companies will copy the development.
Can create a progressive and forward-looking image for a business.	R and D is not guaranteed to lead to successful new developments.

Table 20.2 Evaluation of R and D

Progress check C

1 State **three** possible sources of new product ideas.

2 Why is 'idea screening' a necessary stage of the NPD process?

3 Explain the benefits of using a test market for a new product.

4 Why are some industries more focused on R and D than others?

5 Explain how a change in government laws that restricted the use of powerful motor cars might:

   a lead some car manufacturers to increase R and D spending and

   b make some new car developments less successful.

6 Distinguish between 'offensive' and 'defensive' R and D strategies.

20.5 Sales forecasting

What are the potential benefits to sales forecasting?

- Preparing marketing plans, for example, are sales forecast to increase faster in some markets than others?
- Changing marketing strategies, for example, in response to forecasted sales decline.
- Reducing risk of decision making, for example, not launching a new luxury product when a recession is forecast to reduce sales in this market segment.
- Preparing resources in other departments, for example, if sales are forecast to increase.

20.6 Sales forecasting methods

Key stages in the moving average method:

- Calculate moving total.
- Divide by the number of time periods included to give the moving average (trend).
- Centre the moving average if necessary.
- Graph the trend results and extrapolate.
- Estimate future trend results.
- Adjust by the average seasonal variation.

Progress check D

1 Using an example, explain what the term 'positive correlation' means.

2 What does 'average seasonal variation' mean?

3 Under what circumstances might market research data be the only possible method of sales forecasting?

4 Calculate the seasonal variations from the following data:

Quarter	Sales $000	Trend (quarterly moving average) $000	Seasonal variation $000
1	56	63	
2	67	66	
3	80	70	

Table 20.3

5 Why might sales for a manufacturer of mobile phones be subject to cyclical variations?

6 Explain **two** business situations in which sales forecasts could turn out to be very inaccurate.

7 Explain the difference between cyclical variations and seasonal variations.

Figure 20.2 Sales forecasting methods

TIP

Be ready to evaluate any of the methods of sales forecasting – and remember that sales forecasts can never be fully relied on. The future is not certain!

20.7 Marketing strategies

Should be focused on the marketing objective(s)

If the key marketing objective is to 'increase consumer loyalty' a strategy of entering a new market in another country is inappropriate. If the objective is to increase sales by ten per cent each year, then a strategy just focusing on customer relationship marketing (to increase customer loyalty) will not achieve this. Marketing strategies will need to change if the marketing objective changes.

Should be integrated with other departments

This will help to ensure that the necessary finance, people and production capacity are available to put the marketing strategy into operation.

Should be coordinated with all elements of the marketing mix

The mix must be consistent (see Chapter 19) and must support the strategy in a coherent way.

Exam-style question

Paper 3

RCC

RCC is a limited company that manufactures cosmetics, shampoos and creams for women and men. 80 per cent of RCC's products are sold in its domestic market in Country P. The company has transformed its image, mainly through successful research and development. It used to only make products for sale by supermarkets under their 'own brand' label. Recent work by RCC's small research and development team has led to a new range of products sold under the 'Sunsafe' brand name. These were supported by a major advertising campaign that promoted the unique selling point of the products as: 'Sunsafe is an entirely natural product, not tested on animals and guaranteed to protect skin from sun damage'. Sales of Sunsafe products were 50 per cent above target in the last two years despite market skimming pricing.

The success of Sunsafe encouraged competitors to launch similar creams. RCC started to develop other new products. 'Sunsafe Junior' is almost ready for launch. It is to be targeted at young consumers. It is a cream that RCC claims offers complete sun protection for 12 hours and is suitable for young people's sensitive skin. This is much more effective than all products sold by competitors. It has cost $m to develop and test. The Marketing Director is planning the marketing strategy to be used by RCC to sell Sunsafe Junior in Country P. The marketing objective is to gain just five per cent market share in the first year as RCC do not plan for it to be a low-priced, mass market product. The Marketing Director is using the data in Table 20.4 to help plan the

→

marketing strategy. The marketing budget has been set at only $1m as expensive, traditional media such as TV and newspapers will not be used.

Total value of sun-cream market	$600m
Sales of 'young users' sun cream as percentage of total market	15
Estimated income elasticity of demand for young people's sun cream	2
Forecast increase in consumers' annual incomes in Country P	5%
Number of other sun creams targeted at young people	8
Proportion of sun creams sold through low price supermarkets	45%
Proportion of sun creams sold through exclusive beauty salons	6%

Table 20.4 Market data for sun creams for young people – Country P (2017)

1   a   Analyse **two** benefits to RCC of spending on research and development (R and D).   [10]

    b   Recommend a suitable marketing strategy for 'Sunsafe Junior'. Justify your recommendation.   [14]

Student's answer to 1(a)

Research and development (R and D) is when a business spends money on developing new products for sale and new ways of making products. It can be very expensive as RCC have spent $1m on developing 'Sunsafe Junior'. However, it seems to have given RCC a USP as it offers 12-hour protection, which is much better than competitors' products. This USP, if combined with effective promotion, can lead to RCC setting a high price for the product. Other products in the 'Sunsafe' range have sold well despite using price skimming. This high price should give high profit margins which will help to earn profits to repay the original investment and also increase retained profit.

R and D has also helped to transform RCC and its brand. It used to sell creams under supermarkets' 'own labels' and this is a mass market, low-priced strategy. By developing differentiated products through R and D, RCC has been able to develop its own brand and identity. New market segments are being entered. This approach is being supported with the social responsibility policy of not testing on animals and using natural materials. This has allowed RCC to create much more value than the previous strategy. RCC's shareholders will benefit from higher returns and will encourage them to support further investment by RCC in research and development.

Authors' comments

This student knows about R and D – and they have not confused it with market research! The analysis of the benefits of R and D is also impressive. The two points made about extending sales into new market segments and creating a USP are well explained and developed. They are both applied to RCC. Although rather briefly expressed this answer is well on the way to being an excellent one!

Additional exam-style question

Paper 3

1   Answer part (b) from the RCC case study above.

Chapter 21

Globalisation and international marketing

Learning summary

After studying this chapter you should be able to:

- [ ] understand what globalisation is
- [ ] assess the implications for marketing of increased globalisation and economic collaboration, e.g. BRICS
- [ ] analyse the relative benefits of different approaches to international marketing
- [ ] apply and evaluate international marketing strategies.

21.1 Globalisation of markets

The trend towards increased globalisation is being driven by:

- less protectionism and freer international trade
- expansion of multinational corporations
- fewer restrictions on movement of capital and workers
- internet and other technological developments.

TERMS

Globalisation: the growing trend towards world markets in products, capital and labour with less protectionism.

Multinational corporations (MNCs): businesses that have operations in more than one country.

The number and size of MNCs have increased greatly in recent years because of globalisation. Globalisation has both potential benefits and drawbacks for businesses. The benefits include not just increased opportunities for selling in foreign markets but also setting up production operations in other countries and integrating with foreign companies.

The main drawback is one of increased competition – from lower-cost producers in other countries and from MNCs setting up in a firm's domestic market.

Progress check A

Copy out the following factors in two lists – one with globalisation benefits to businesses and one with globalisation drawbacks to businesses:

a   New markets open up.

b   More foreign competitors in home market.

c   Costs may be lower in foreign markets.

d   Cultural differences exist in foreign markets.

e   Increased competition can force a business to increase efficiency.

f   Integration with foreign businesses more likely.

g   Takeovers by foreign businesses more likely.

21.2 Impact of globalisation on marketing

The growth of world trade is creating more opportunities for businesses to sell in foreign markets – international marketing. Many businesses have started selling to the BRICS countries or have plans to do so – or set up joint ventures with businesses already operating in these emerging economies.

International marketing: selling products in markets other than the home or domestic market.

Emerging market economies, e.g. BRICS: economies that have experienced fast (but variable) economic growth in recent years and which have potential to be very large economies such as: Brazil, Russia, India, China and South Africa.

Reasons why businesses market products in other countries are shown in Fig 21.1:

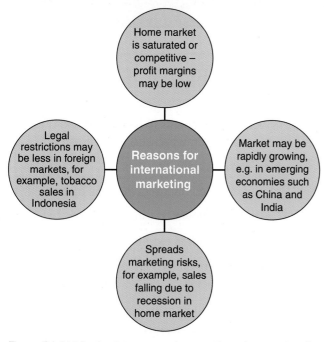

Figure 21.1 Why businesses market products internationally

21.3 Differences between selling in home markets and international marketing

- Legal differences – for example, laws controlling advertising to children or unethical business practices.
- Cultural differences – for example, language, religious beliefs relating to whether meat can be eaten and from which animals, role of women in society.

- Economic and social differences – for example, average income differences, ageing or youthful population.

- Political differences – for example, some countries are less politically stable than others.
- Business and market differences – for example, small shops are much more significant (in terms of percentage of total consumer spending) in India than in the UK.
- Different approaches to ethical issues such as child labour or bribery to gain business contracts.

Progress check B

1 Find out about the economy of Indonesia. Do you think it should be included in the BRICS group of countries?

2 Explain why a food processing business must find out about cultural differences before exporting products to a country for the first time.

3 What are likely to be the major reasons why European car makers have all set up sales operations in China?

21.4 How to enter foreign markets – factors that influence the method chosen

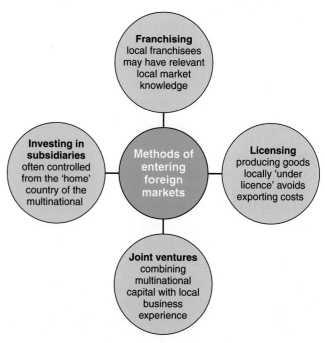

Figure 21.2 Different methods of entering foreign markets

Choosing between these methods will depend on:

- cost of different methods of entry.
- the risk involved.
- likely returns/profits to be made.
- the experience of the business in entering foreign markets.

21.5 International marketing strategies

The two main strategies for selling products in foreign markets are pan-global marketing or global localisation.

The key differences between these two strategies are that 'pan-global' attempts to reduce marketing costs and new product development costs but 'global localisation' attempts to satisfy local market conditions, perhaps by developing a product for a specific foreign market – even if this means marketing costs are higher.

TERMS

Pan-global marketing: selling the same products in the same way in all international markets.

Global localisation: adapting the marketing mix, including differentiated products, to meet national and regional tastes and cultures.

Progress check C

1 Aston Martin, a maker of expensive luxury cars, recently announced it was planning to sell in India for the first time.

   Explain **two** possible reasons why the company took this decision.

2 Apple Corp's latest high-tech products are sold in most countries in the world with few, if any, adaptations.

   Is this an example of pan global marketing or global localisation marketing?

   Explain your answer.

3 How might the fact that there are different laws in different countries affect a company's international marketing decisions?

4 The average (median) age of Brazil's population was 30.3 years in 2016.

   In Japan the median age was almost 50 years.

   Explain how these data might influence the marketing strategy of an international clothing retailer operating in both countries.

5 Explain why an international food retailing business might establish a joint venture with a local retailing business when selling in an emerging market country for the first time.

6 Explain **two** benefits to a soft drink manufacturing business of using pan global marketing rather than global localisation.

Exam-style question

Paper 3

Meaty Burgers (MB)

MB is one of the world's best known 'fast-food' restaurant chains. It has expanded internationally as trade barriers have been reduced over recent years. It uses suppliers from several different countries – always using the lowest-cost provider. It has a diverse workforce in nearly all of its restaurants. It offers competitively priced meals, quick service and a family friendly atmosphere to millions of consumers all over the world, every day of the year. Recent research suggests that the average age of its customers is 32 years. MB offers six core food products in all of the countries it sells in – all these products are based around, according to its advertising, 'the largest meat burgers in the world'. MB has many international rivals competing for a share of the global fast-food market.

→

Sales at MB restaurants are increasing in all countries except Country B. Country B has a youthful population of 500 million people – a huge potential market. Over half the population do not eat meat for religious and cultural reasons. Average incomes are much lower than in most of the countries MB operates in.

1 a Analyse the benefits to MB from globalisation. [10]

  b Recommend changes that MB should make to its marketing strategy to achieve success in Country B. Justify your answer. [16]

Student's answer to 1(b)

MB is using a 'pan-global' marketing strategy. This means it adopts the same marketing mix in all of the countries that it operates in. It could use 'global localisation'. This would mean adapting key parts of its marketing strategy to fit in with the consumer profile, tastes and national cultures of each country. I would recommend that MB uses the global localisation strategy as this will allow the company to adapt to the major differences between Country B and its other main markets.

MB needs to do some market research in Country B. It needs to find out consumer tastes in this country and the social and cultural factors that can influence demand for fast-food products. Without accurate market information MB will not be able to take the product decisions that will lead to sales success in the country. It could be that vegetarian or fish options will be necessary because in Country B there are social or religious reasons for not eating meat. The age structure of the population might be different from other countries that MB trades in. Knowing the age structure of the population can help with both product decisions but also promotion decisions. The 'large youthful' population might be more responsive to social media

promotions than more traditional media which is still read by older people, such as daily newspapers.

The colour scheme of the MB restaurants might not be suitable for people's tastes in Country B. The colour used might be associated with sadness or with religion and therefore inappropriate. The uniforms worn by serving staff in MB restaurants might cause offence to many people in Country B so these will need to be changed too.

Pricing is another factor that MB must investigate. 'Incomes are lower than other countries MB operates in' so prices might need to be lower than in other countries. Fast food is not an essential product and if MB food is priced too high in Country B very few people will be able to afford it. MB might still make a profit if it uses cheaper non-meat ingredients in its food. All of these changes are referred to as 'global localisation'.

MB needs to adapt both product and promotion to local needs but it can still benefit from its huge size by gaining marketing, purchasing and financial economies. These can still help to make it a low-cost fast-food provider in Country B but with a marketing mix much more likely to lead to high sales there. Perhaps the most important factor that MB must undertake is detailed market research within Country B. Without this it will be impossible for MB to adapt its marketing strategy effectively to meet the population's needs, taking into account cultural and religious differences with the other countries MB sells in.

Authors' comments

This is a clearly argued and well-balanced answer. There are very good application points, relating to MB and/or Country B. The analysis is clear and there is a definite recommendation to MB which is well supported. This has the structure required of an excellent answer.

Additional exam-style question

Paper 3

1 Answer part (a) from the Meaty Burgers case study above.

Unit 4
OPERATIONS AND PROJECT MANAGEMENT

Chapter 22

The nature of operations

Learning summary

After you have studied this chapter you should be able to:

■ understand inputs, outputs and the transformation process

■ explain resources used in production (land, labour and capital)

■ distinguish between effectiveness and efficiency

■ explain the links between value added, the production process, marketing and production decisions

■ discuss how to increase value added

■ discuss the difference between labour and capital intensity.

22.1 The transformation process

Operations management is concerned with the processes involved in converting *inputs* into *outputs* suitable for the customer. The transformation process is shown in Fig 22.1:

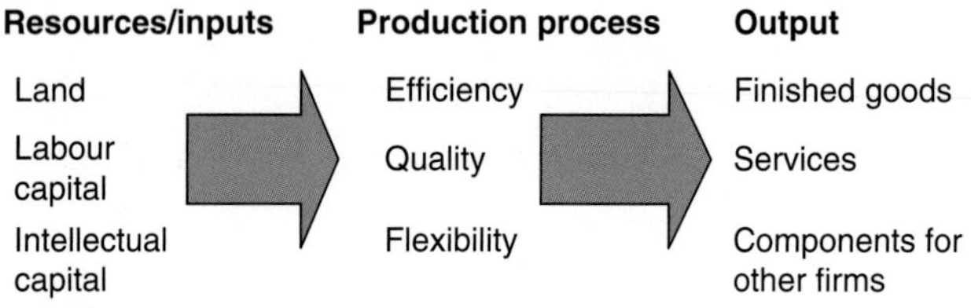

Resources/inputs
Land
Labour
capital
Intellectual
capital

Production process
Efficiency
Quality
Flexibility

Output
Finished goods
Services
Components for
other firms

Figure 22.1 The transformation process

TIP

Do not think that operations management is only for manufacturing businesses. Businesses such as banks, supermarkets, petrol stations also have to plan to use resources productively and effectively. The term 'production' can refer as much to a business providing a service as to a firm manufacturing a product.

TERMS

Land: natural resources such as land, minerals.

Labour: work done by people including managers/decision makers.

Capital: machinery, equipment, finance, buildings, raw materials.

Intellectual capital: ideas, patents, skills etc.

Progress check A

1 Explain the resources that would be needed for an oil refinery.

2 Who would buy the output from a cement manufacturer?

3 What are the resources used by a shoe shop?

4 Give examples of resources that can be categorised as 'land'.

22.2 The production process

Customer needs → Suitable product →
Quality method/ ← Production system ←
standards

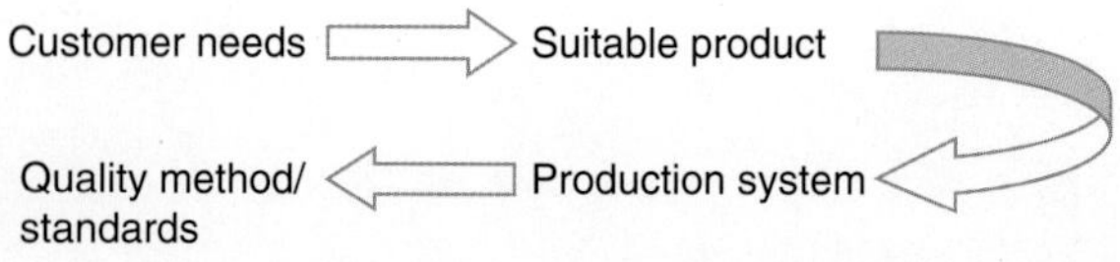

Figure 22.2 The production process

22.3 Effectiveness, efficiency and productivity

TERMS

Effectiveness: a measure of how well a product/ production system meets the designed purpose, e.g. target output.

Efficiency: producing output at the highest ratio of output to input: efficiency = inputs/outputs × 100 per cent.

Productivity: the ratio of outputs to inputs during production, for example, output per worker per time period.

Higher efficiency = lower unit costs.

TIP

'Efficiency' and 'effectiveness' have different meanings and need to be used correctly. Productivity – a common measure of efficiency – needs to refer to a specific time period.

Labour productivity	Capital productivity
Measured by: $\dfrac{\text{Output in period}}{\text{Workers employed}}$	Measured by: $\dfrac{\text{Total output in period}}{\text{Capital employed}}$

Improved by:
- training of employees
- increasing motivation
- better management including improvements to processes
- investing in better equipment including latest technology.

Table 22.1 Labour versus capital productivity

Labour intensive	Capital intensive
Production relies heavily on workforce, for example, hand-made furniture.	Production relies heavily on capital equipment (for example, machinery) such as car manufacturing.

Choice:
- Nature of product
- Traditions of business and desired image
- Relative price of inputs (for example, cheap labour favours labour intensive)
- Size of firm and available capital.

Table 22.2 Labour versus capital intensity

For example, if furniture maker A makes ten chairs each day and employs five people; and furniture maker B makes 100 chairs a day and employs 40 people, then which has the highest labour productivity?

Labour productivity of business A: 10/5 = two chairs per employee per day

Labour productivity of business B: 100/40 = two and a half chairs per employee per day

So business B has the higher labour productivity.

Possible consequences for the business of increased productivity:

- Can reduce unit costs
- Only useful if the product remains profitable and production levels remain consistent with consumer demand

But:

- Workers may want higher wages
- Workers may fear redundancies
- May give the business a competitive advantage.

TIP

The terms 'production' and 'productivity' can easily be confused. Make sure you use them correctly. Increasing productivity does not necessarily mean increasing production.

It is possible for a business to achieve an increase in labour productivity but to reduce total sales/output too.

If demand for a product is falling, it might be necessary to reduce the size of the workforce – but by a smaller proportion than the reduction in output.

22.4 Value added/creating value

The production process *adds value* – the customer wants the finished products not the raw materials.

For example, for furniture:

- Unsawn timber has little value.
- Sawn timber has greater value.
- Furniture made from sawn timber has even greater value.
- Furniture conveniently displayed in the shop for sale has even greater value.

At each stage the value added is the final value of that stage less the costs of the inputs.

For example, take a firm that sells chairs for $100. Materials (screws, glue etc.) cost $3, the wood costs $30 so the added value is $67.

Progress check C

1 How does a retail outlet add value?

2 If the leather for handbags costs $10 per handbag and other costs are $20 per handbag, what would customers value the handbag at if the value added is $30 per handbag?

22.5 Increasing value added

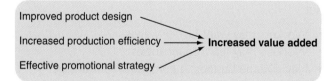

Figure 22.3 Increasing value added

Progress check D

1 Explain how promotion can increase the value added of a model of car.

2 How could new software add value to a laptop?

TERMS

Value added: the increase in value of a product/ service a business from one stage of production to another.

Production: converting inputs into outputs.

Level of production: the number of units produced during a time period.

Progress check E

1 Explain the difference between efficiency and effectiveness at a school.

2 Outline **two** ways a soft drinks manufacturer could increase its capital productivity.

3 Outline **two** ways a college could increase its labour productivity.

4 Explain why teachers might be concerned if they were asked to improve their productivity.

5 A clock manufacturer has decided to change from labour intensive methods of production to capital intensive methods.

What could be the effects of this decision on the employees?

22.6 Labour versus capital intensity

Labour intensive: involving a high level of labour input compared with capital equipment.

Benefits: suited for personal services, can produce unique items, low start-up costs.

Capital intensive: involving a high quantity of capital equipment compared with labour input.

Benefits: suitable for mass production, where labour is relatively expensive, less need for skilled employees.

Decision influenced by:

- size of business
- method of production
- relative costs of land and labour
- need to meet customers' specific needs.

Exam-style question

Paper 2 [part question]

Big Sofas (BS)

Sam, the Managing Director of BS, a furniture manufacturer, has been examining production data for the two factories owned by the company. The data is:

	Factory in Country A			Factory in Country B		
	2014	2015	2016	2014	2015	2016
Output (sofas)	1000	1200	1400	2000	1800	1600
Employees	20	22	24	50	50	50
Machines used	10	9	8	15	15	15

Table 22.3

The furniture made in Country B is of an old design whereas that made in Country A is more modern. Country B has very strict employment laws. The managers in Country A have gradually been replacing old machines but falling revenues in Country B have not allowed Country B's managers to do the same. Employees in Country B are paid a salary but Country A operates a piece rate pay system.

1 a Calculate for each year and each factory:

    i labour productivity [3]

    ii capital productivity. [3]

  b Briefly analyse the likely reasons for the trends in the productivities you have calculated. [6]

  c Recommend ways the managers in country B could improve productivity. [11]

Student's answer

1 a i Factory A: 50, 54.5, 58.3

      Factory B: 40, 36, 32

   ii Factory A: 100, 133, 175

      Factory B: 133, 120, 107

  b Factory A is benefiting from improving labour productivity and improving capital productivity. More efficient machines are contributing to these improvements. Total output is increasing. Growth in the market has been met by improved productivity, and the piece rate paid to employees has probably helped.

    Factory B is suffering falling production and productivity. However, there has been no investment in more efficient machines and no retrenchment of employees, probably because of the employment laws. Although a salary provides security of income it does not necessarily motivate employees to increase output.

    B is falling behind A with A having improving capital productivity (50 to 58.3) and significantly improving labour productivity (100 to 175). In contrast B has falling capital productivity (40 to 32) and falling labour productivity (133 to 107). For both types of productivity in B, not only is the trend down but also the absolute levels.

c The factory manager in B needs to motivate employees more effectively and to update machinery. The two might be linked. If workers are asked to work with old and unreliable machinery it can lead to demotivation. Possibilities for improving productivity include new machinery. However, the cost will be a major constraint as revenue is falling in this country. If B produces more and increases productivity it does not necessarily mean that BS will sell more unless lower unit costs allow a reduction in prices to consumers. If sales are inevitably going to fall then it is difficult to justify new machines and productivity is inevitably going to fall, but if they are falling because prices are too high then lower unit costs from higher productivity should help to solve this problem.

Possibilities for improving the efficiency of labor, apart from new machines, include changing the payment method to have an element of 'productivity bonus'. Non-financial means of motivation such as job enrichment or participation in decision making might make the employees more interested and committed at work. This would help to improve productivity but if no more units are sold, jobs could be lost through redundancy. B's strict labour laws might make this difficult.

The final recommendation depends on whether any additional output could be sold. If not, then redundancies would seem to be the only way to improve productivity and decrease costs. If additional product could be sold, perhaps through reduced prices arising from rising productivity, then either new machinery or incentives to employees (or both) could work, the choice depending on the relative costs.

Authors' comments

1 a The productivity calculations are correct. Good answer.

b The comments are succinct and to the point, and use all of the information provided.

c This is a good answer as it looks at more than one possible 'solution' and assesses them both. Answers clearly apply to this case study business. Clear and relevant final conclusion.

Additional exam-style questions

Paper 1 Section A

1 Define the term 'added value'. [2]

2 Explain what is meant by 'labour intensive'. [3]

Paper 1 Section B

3 a Analyse the importance to a manufacturer of specialist computers of improving efficiency. [8]

b Discuss the factors that the computer manufacturer should consider when deciding between a labour intensive or capital intensive production system. [12]

Operations planning

Learning summary

After you have studied this chapter you should be able to:

- ☐ explain the influence of marketing, availability of resources and technology (e.g. CAD and CAM) on operations decisions

- ☐ recognise the importance of flexibility and process innovation

- ☐ describe and evaluate different production methods

- ☐ discuss problems of changing from one method to another

- ☐ analyse the factors that determine location and relocation decisions

- ☐ recommend the best location

- ☐ identify the factors that influence the scale of a business

- ☐ use the concepts of economies and diseconomies of scale

- ☐ discuss the limitations of enterprise resource planning (ERP).

23.1 Influences on operations decisions

Operations planning is preparing input resources and managing resources and systems to meet expected demand.

Forecast demand is the critical factor in this process so it is important for Production and Marketing functions to work together effectively with operational flexibility.

It is also important to ensure that a business has the right resources available so that planned production can be achieved. This involves the areas of:

- Marketing: match output to demand levels, produce the right product.
- Resources: minimise wastage, choose right production method, plan purchases and inventories, workforce planning, choose right location.
- Technology: use automation, CAD, CAM where appropriate, plan necessary investments, appropriate capacity.

Progress check A

1. What is meant by 'operations planning'?

2. How might an increase in forecast sales have an impact on operations in a shipbuilding firm?

3. Give **three** reasons why flexibility in production is important.

TIP

Operations management provides a good example of how business functions need to be integrated.

TERMS

Operations planning: preparing input resources to supply products to meet expected demand.

Operational flexibility: the ability of a business to vary both the level of production and the range of products following changes in customer demand.

CAD: the use of computer programs to aid the design process by creating graphical representations of objects.

CAM: the use of computer software to manage and control the production process often linked in with CAD.

Capacity: the notional maximum output a business can achieve with existing resources. May be possible to exceed in urgent situations.

23.2 Flexibility and innovation

The business world is changing rapidly. It is difficult to predict future demand. So businesses need to adjust to changing demand. This requires flexibility in product design, production levels and delivery which can be achieved through flexible production systems, flexible and adaptable employees, and appropriate stock control systems. One possibility of achieving this is through subcontracting.

An important way of achieving flexibility is through process innovation using automation, robotics, and improved work flows.

When working together CAD and CAM offer accuracy, increased productivity, consistency of output and the ability for products to be accurately reproduced. They can be an important part of enterprise resource planning (ERP) see 23.7.

But: can be expensive, training is needed, may need different skills with possible redundancies of existing workers.

TERM

Process innovation: the redesign of production systems or service provision systems that incorporates innovation system improvements.

23.3 Production methods

TERMS

Job production: producing a one-off item specifically designed for the customer.

Batch production: producing a limited number of identical products – each item in the batch passes through one stage of production before passing to the next stage.

Flow production: producing items in a continually moving process.

Mass customisation: the use of flexible computer-aided production systems to produce items to meet individual customers' requirements at mass-production cost levels and using features of flow products.

TIP

Some products produced in batches, for example soft drinks, are actually produced on continuous production lines so are closer to flow production than batch production.

If a question asks you to recommend a method of production in a given situation it is important to weigh up the advantages and disadvantages of each production method in the context of that situation and then justify your decision.

Choice of production system

Choice of production system depends on:

- Nature of the product
- Size of business
- Volume of production
- Available technology
- Nature of the market
- Relative cost of labour and capital
- Skills of available workforce
- Time available
- Flexibility required.

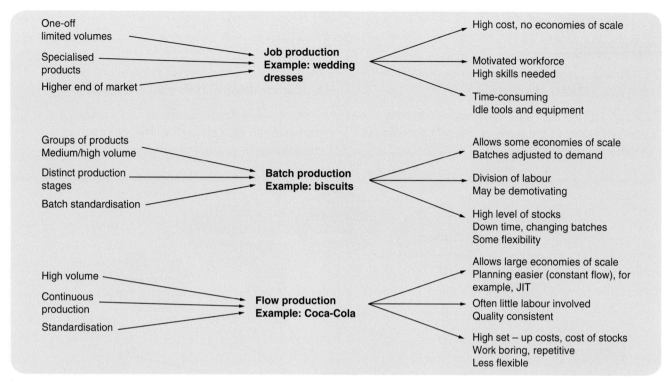

Figure 23.1 Features of production methods

Mass customisation

Computer aided design (CAD)
Computer aided manufacturing (CAM) ➡ Mass customisation
Process innovation

Figure 23.2 Mass customisation

Mass customisation uses the latest technology with multi-skilled workforce on production lines (usually flow) but with the ability to make a range of products to meet customer requirements. For example, Dell Computers allows for differentiated marketing.

Progress check B

1 Give **three** examples of products likely to be produced using job production.

2 Give **three** advantages batch production has over job production.

3 Explain why flow production is suited to the manufacture of high-volume cars.

4 Analyse how mass customisation can now be applied to the production of high-volume cars.

5 Why might mass customisation be chosen for personal computers?

23.4 Problems of changing production methods

Typical problems that result from changing production decisions:

• Takes time, planning, capital
• May be resisted by workforce
• Possible impact on motivation, training
• Lost production and disruption during changeover.

23.5 Location decisions

TERMS

Optimal location: a business location that gives the best combination of quantitative and qualitative factors.

Quantitative factors: these are measurable, in this instance in financial terms, and will have a direct impact on the costs of a site and/ or the revenue from it and hence its profitability.

TERMS

Qualitative factors: these are non-measurable factors that may influence decisions.

Offshoring: the relocation of a business process done in one country to the same or different company in another country.

Multinational: a business with operations or production bases in more than one country.

Trade barriers: taxes (tariffs) or other limitations (for example, quotas) on the free international movements of goods and services.

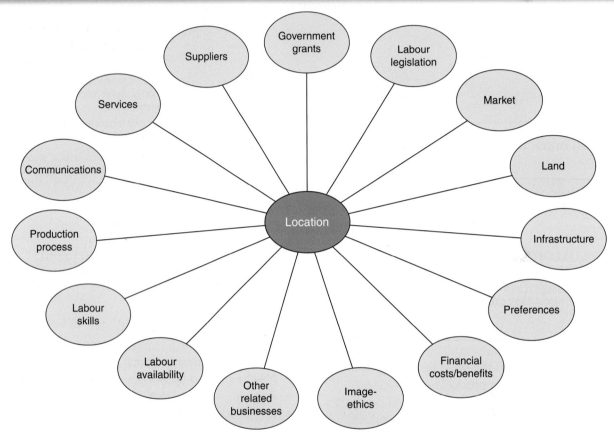

Figure 23.3 Factors involved in location decisions

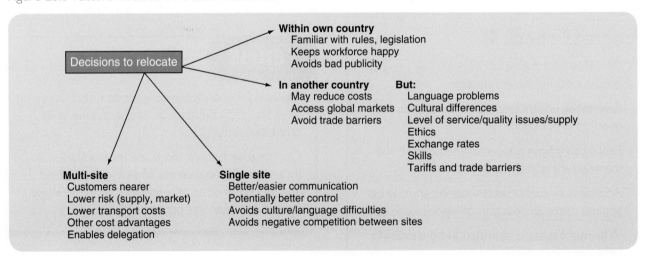

Figure 23.4 The types of relocation

Progress check C

1 What factors are important for the location of a supermarket?

2 Why might a UK bank relocate its call centre to India?

3 Analyse **two** ways that the location of a theatre might affect its competitiveness.

4 How might the increasing use of the internet affect the location decisions of a computer manufacturer?

5 Why have Japanese car manufacturers located in the USA?

6 Explain the difference between offshoring and outsourcing.

23.6 Scale of operation

The scale of operation (size) of a business could be determined by:

- the decision of the owners to stay small or expand the business,

- the nature and size of the market, the number and size of competitors,

- financial resources available, the age of the business.

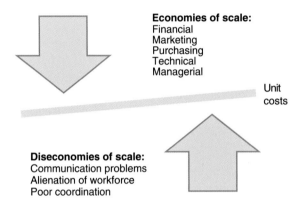

Economies of scale:
Financial
Marketing
Purchasing
Technical
Managerial

Unit costs

Diseconomies of scale:
Communication problems
Alienation of workforce
Poor coordination

Figure 23.5 Impact of scale on unit costs

Avoiding diseconomies of scale

- Improve coordination through reorganisation.
- Decentralisation – departments behave like smaller businesses.
- Reduce diversification – concentrate on 'core' activities.

Progress check D

1 How might a bank benefit from economies of scale?

2 Explain the meaning of 'managerial economies of scale'.

3 Explain how a bus company could benefit from economies of scale.

4 In many countries electricity is supplied by one company. Explain how it might suffer from diseconomies of scale.

23.7 Enterprise resource planning (ERP)

Enterprise resource planning can be used to improve the firm's efficiency of a business..

TERMS

Enterprise resource planning (ERP): the use of integrated software systems to plan and manage information from all areas of a business in order to simplify complex processes and make them more efficient.

Supply chain: all of the stages in the production process from obtaining raw materials to selling to the consumer – from point of origin to point of consumption.

Supply chain management (SCM): ERP software that focuses on the supply chain.

Figure 23.6 The impact of ERP

Limitations of ERP

- Costs.
- Single system for whole firm may mean change which could cause resentment.
- Takes a long time to implement.
- Difficult to identify all possible information links.

Progress check E

1 Amazon is an international, online bookshop. Explain why ERP is essential to its operations.

2 Explain how a firm manufacturing car engines will benefit from supply chain management.

3 Explain the difference between ERP and lean production.

4 Why is it easier to use JIT stock control when ERP is in operation?

Exam-style question

Paper 2 (part question)

HealthEquip (HE)

HE manufactures equipment for use in hospital operating theatres. It is important that equipment is manufactured to the highest quality and safety hygiene standards. The directors of the business are considering three possible locations for relocating production. The Managing Director has prepared the following information:

Location – comments from Managing Director

Our current factory in the centre of town is old and too small. Our products need to be manufactured in a clean, modern environment. The two locations being considered are:

Site	Situation	Rent	Type	Potential	Operating costs	Grants
Southwood	Close to present site	Low rent	Disused car factory needing conversion	No potential for expansion	Low operating costs	Government grants available
Westfield	New site outside of town	High rent	New building	Space for expansion	High operating costs	No grants available

Table 23.1

1 a Explain the term 'director'. [3]

  b Explain why quality is an important issue for HE. [6]

  c Recommend which location (Southwood or Westfield) would be best for the relocation of HE's factory. Justify your choice. [11]

Student's answer to 1(c)

An important feature of the Southwood location is that government grants are available. This will help to reduce the impact of the development costs. This is important because businesses involved in the health industry are short of finance because hospitals, the main customers, have to compete for government funding.

The site also has low operating costs and low rents helping to make it affordable for HE. Being an old building, all of the problems will have been sorted out compared with a new building. However, the building will not be purpose built which could be a disadvantage. The closeness to the present site means that transport costs remain about the same which presumably means the business remains close to the hospitals. In today's economic climate, survival is more likely to be important than growth so it is not important that there is little room for expansion.

On the other hand, Westfield is a new site, out of town. The main benefit of this is that the building could be purpose built to the highest hygiene standards, which is very important for the medical equipment. Unhygienic or faulty equipment could be disastrous for HE. This very important factor has to be balanced against the higher operating costs and lack of government grants, although an out-of-town site might be cheaper than converting the old building. The other major advantage is the scope for expansion but this would depend on whether growth is anticipated in the longer term once economic conditions improve.

Without knowing the actual costs involved, and the extent to which problems with equipment would damage HE, it is difficult to make a recommendation. However, it would be hard to argue against a medical equipment company seeking the highest hygiene conditions, so that so long as HE can afford the Westfield option they should choose that option.

Additional exam-style questions

Paper 1 Section A

1 a Explain the term 'CAM'. [3]

  b State **two** advantages of job production. [2]

  c Define the term 'mass customisation'. [2]

Paper 1 Section B

2 a Analyse the possible advantages and disadvantages to a computer manufacturer of using mass customisation. [8]

  b Evaluate the factors that would influence whether a car manufacturer would locate in your country. [12]

Paper 2

3 Answer parts (a) and (b) from the HE case study above.

Inventory management

24.1 The purposes of inventory

TIP

The ideas of inventory control apply just as much to retail outlets as they do to manufacturing businesses.

TIP

Remember to apply the ideas of inventory control to the business in the question. So, for example, a business that sells greetings cards is likely to hold high levels of inventory at festive times. A supermarket will aim to turn inventory over as quickly as possible, a furniture shop will hold high levels of inventory so that customers are able to look at a range of styles.

TERM

Inventory (stock): materials and goods required to allow for the production and supply of finished products to the customer as well as work-in-progress.

Progress check A

1 Explain why a shoe shop will hold inventories of shoes.

2 Why is a building firm likely to have more work in progress than a fast-food outlet?

3 What raw materials would a soup manufacturer require?

4 Give **three** examples of seasonal goods that may require high inventory levels.

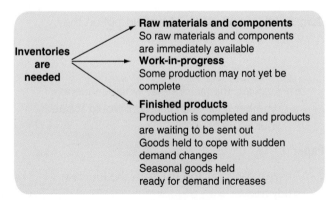

Figure 24.1 The need for inventories

24.2 The costs and benefits of holding inventories

Amount of **inventory** held is a trade-off between costs and benefits:

Costs of insufficient inventory

Lost sales
Idle resources if no raw materials
Difficult to meet new orders
Order quantites small, no economies of scale

Benefits of low inventory levels

Reduced opportunity cost
Reduced storage costs
Reduced risk of wastage/obsolescence

Figure 24.2 Forces on inventory levels

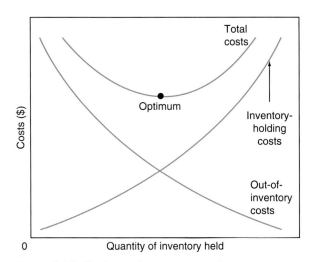

Figure 24.3 Optimum inventory levels

Fig 24.3 shows how a balance between the costs of holding stocks and the penalties arising from running out of stock can provide the best (optimum) level of stocks at which to operate.

24.3 Interpreting inventory control charts

Inventory levels in a firm will be **dynamic** as shown in Fig 24.4:

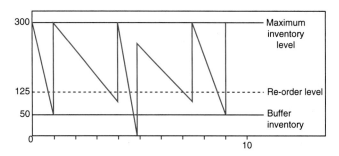

Figure 24.4 Typical inventory control chart

TERMS

Economic order quantity: the optimum or least-cost quantity of inventory to re-order taking account of delivery costs and inventory-holding costs.

Buffer inventory: safety inventory in case of sudden increases in demand or supply problems.

Re-order level: when inventories fall to this level, new supplies are ordered.

Lead time: the normal time taken between ordering new inventories and their delivery.

TIP

You will not be asked to calculate the optimum order size but it is advised that you remember the costs of holding inventory and the costs of being out of inventory – and apply these ideas to the business in question.

24.4 Just-in-time (JIT)

Just-in-time is an operating system based on lean production techniques (see Chapter 26) that includes minimising inventories as far as possible.

Raw materials:

Delivered only when needed.

Work-in-progress:

Kept to a minimum by efficient production process.

Finished products:

Dispatched to customers as soon as completed.

It can also be a system used by retail outlets, for example, supermarkets in terms of products arriving at a supermarket branch from suppliers.

It is difficult to get JIT to work effectively as a number of wide-ranging conditions have to be met:

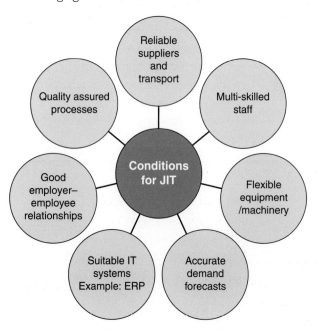

Figure 24.4 Conditions for successful JIT

Situations in which JIT will not work

- Some of the conditions are not easy to achieve, especially concerning staff and suppliers.
- Small firms may not be able to afford to implement it.
- Circumstances (for example, inflation) may make holding inventories attractive.
- The costs of stock-outs (having insufficient inventory) are prohibitively expensive so that buffer inventories are essential.

Exam-style question

Paper 2

HealthEquip (HE) manufactures high quality medical equipment for hospitals. Amongst the problems they have is inventory levels. The Operations Director of HE has made the following comments:

'Our present system of inventory control is not working effectively as we have shortages in some components and far too much inventory in others.'

This is illustrated in the following inventory data:

Component	Lead time of component from supplier (weeks)	Components held in inventory (weeks)	Supplier of component	Demand for component
A	2	4	Reliable	Rising
B	1	6	Reliable	Constant
C	3	9	Unreliable	Falling
D	4	5	Unreliable	Unpredictable

Table 24.1

1	a	Explain the term 'lead time'.	[3]
	b	Explain why it might be important for HE to hold inventories of components?	[4]
	c	Discuss the possible usefulness of JIT (just in time) to HE.	[11]

Student's answer to 1(a) and (b)

a   Lead time is the time it takes between ordering inventory from a supplier and when the delivery arrives at its destination.

b   If there is insufficient inventory of components HE may not be able to produce its equipment. This will mean that the production equipment and employees will be idle if deliveries from suppliers have not arrived on time. This is a waste of resources – and patients will be kept waiting. This not only risks losing customers such as hospitals and doctors' practices but could bring a bad reputation as medical equipment could be life saving.

Authors' comments

a   Excellent answer to both parts. Answer to (b) is clearly applied to this business. Although brief, it has adequate explanations.

Additional exam-style questions

Paper 1 Section A

1	a	Explain the term 'buffer inventory'.	[3]
	b	State **two** benefits of maintaining low levels of inventories.	[2]
	c	Define the term lead time.	[2]

Paper 1 Section B

2   Analyse the advantages and disadvantages to a book publisher of holding inventories of books. [8]

Paper 2

3   Answer part (c) from the HealthEquip case study above. [11]

Chapter 25

Capacity utilisation

Learning summary

After you have studied this chapter you should be able to:

- understand how to calculate and interpret capacity utilisation
- understand implications of operating under/over capacity
- recommend strategies for improving capacity utilisation
- evaluate benefits of outsourcing.

25.1 How to calculate capacity utilisation

Capacity utilisation measures one aspect of business efficiency. It measures what percentage of a business's potential output is actually being achieved.

$$\text{Capacity utilisation} = \frac{\text{Current output level}}{\text{Maximum possible output level}} \times 100$$

Capacity utilisation up = average fixed costs down leading to average unit costs down

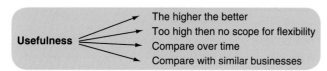

Figure 25.1 Usefulness of calculating capacity utilisation

TIP

Capacity utilisation relates to the output of a business. If a firm is working at less than maximum capacity, as output increases the business will gain from improved capacity utilisation. Even though unit costs fall, it does not gain from economies of scale.

TERMS

Capacity utilisation: the proportion of maximum output capacity currently being achieved.

Production capacity: total level of sustained output that can be produced in a given time period.

25.2 Implications of operating under or over maximum capacity

TERM

Full capacity: when a business produces at maximum output.

Working close to or above 100 per cent full capacity is a trade-off:

Benefits of high utilisation

- Average costs down
- Sign of success
- Employees get sense of security.

Disadvantages of high utilisation

- Staff under pressure
- No flexibility for new orders
- Insufficient time for machine maintenance
- Greater unreliability.

Progress check A

1 A hotel has 75 rooms. On average 50 rooms are filled each night. What is the average capacity utilisation?

2 The daily overhead cost for the hotel is $500. What is the average overhead cost per room if 50 rooms are occupied?

3 If the hotel could increase its utilisation to 80 per cent what would the average overhead cost become?

4 Why might a restaurant want to increase its capacity utilisation?

5 Explain **two** reasons why a cell-phone manufacturer might not want to work at full capacity for long periods of time.

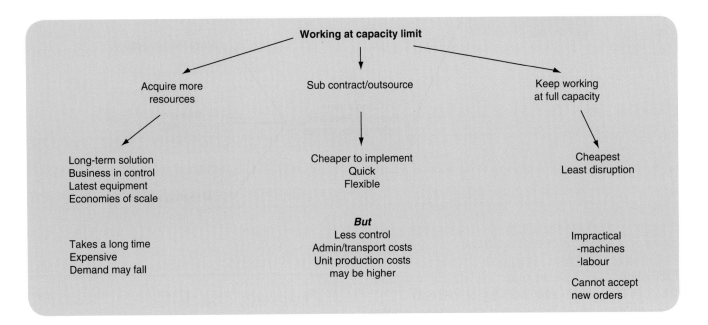

Figure 25.2 What to do if capacity utilisation is too high

Progress check B

1 Explain **two** disadvantages of working at 100 per cent capacity utilisation.

2 Explain **two** advantages and **two** disadvantages of sub-contracting as a way of solving a capacity shortage for an oil refining company.

3 Why might capacity shortages be dealt with differently if the problem is short term rather than long term?

Working below maximum capacity

Reasons for excess capacity

- Product might be seasonal.
- Demand might have fallen.
- Efficiency might have increased.
- Improved technology.

TERM

Excess capacity: exists when the current levels of demand are less than the full capacity output of a business – also known as spare capacity.

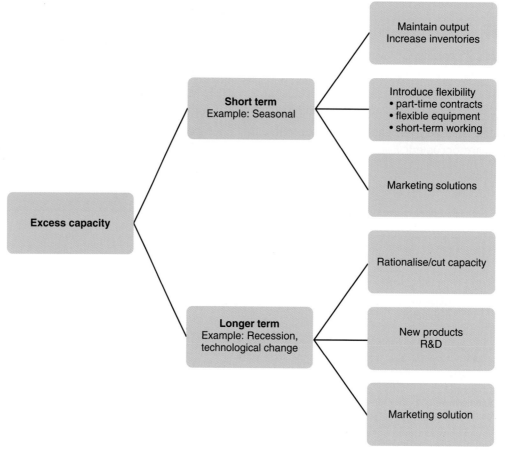

Figure 25.3 Solutions to excess capacity

Each method will have an impact on workforce directly (through lost jobs, shorter working) or indirectly (through motivation). The method also depends on the nature of the product. For example, it is not suitable to maintain production for a perishable product.

TIP

When making decisions about how to deal with excess capacity it is important to consider both the timescale and cause of the problem.

TERMS

Rationalisation: reducing capacity by cutting overheads to increase efficiency of operations, such as closing a factory or office department, often involving redundancies.

Capacity shortage: when the demand for a business's products exceeds production capacity.

Progress check C

1 Give **two** reasons why a greetings card manufacturer might have excess capacity.

2 A car manufacturer has six assembly plants. What do you think the best way would be to solve overcapacity due to a recession?

3 How realistic is producing new products a way of dealing with excess capacity for a hairdressing business?

4 Explain how marketing might solve the problem of overcapacity in a chocolate factory.

25.3 Outsourcing

TERMS

Outsourcing: using another business (a 'third party') to undertake a part of the production process rather than doing it within the business using the firm's own employees.

Business process outsourcing (BPO): a form of outsourcing that uses a third party to take responsibility for certain business functions such as HR and Finance.

Core activity: activity or activities within a business which are central to the business's aims and objectives of the business.

High capacity utilisation is not the only reason for outsourcing. The advantages and disadvantages of outsourcing are shown in Fig 25.4:

TIP

You may be asked for your advice on outsourcing an activity.

Generally, the more important an activity is to the overall aims and reputation of the business, the less likely it is that outsourcing will be appropriate.

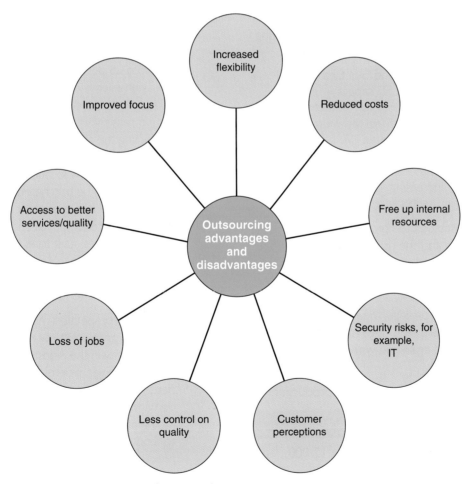

Figure 25.4 Advantages and disadvantages of outsourcing

Progress check D

1 Would you advise a school to outsource its HRM functions? Explain your answer.

2 Are there some functions that a newspaper business should not consider outsourcing? Explain your answer.

3 Explain **two** benefits to a bank of outsourcing its customer service call centre.

4 Why might a business outsource to another country?

Exam-style questions

Paper 3

TTC

TTC manufactures high quality safety equipment, such as automatic fire extinguishers, for the chemical and oil industries. Although it has an excellent reputation for quality and customer service it is experiencing falling capacity utilisation. The Operations Director of TTC has made the following comments:

'Because of falling demand our factories only worked at 75 per cent capacity utilisation last year. With a recession affecting the chemical and oil industries this year I don't see things getting any better. We have closed one production line but this will only delay a solution to the problem, not solve it. We are experiencing increasing competition in the market for high-tech safety equipment.'

The directors discussed the problem of falling capacity utilisation and the rising average costs resulting from it. One director suggested cutting the costs of the HR department by outsourcing nearly all of its functions to a business in a low cost country 3000 km away. Unsurprisingly, the HR Director argued that this would be a huge mistake, especially if demand increased again and with it the need for more employees.

The following figures give the trend in production:

	Last year	This year
Output	24 000	12 000
Capacity	32 000	24 000

Table 25.1

1 a Calculate the capacity utilisation for this year. [3]

b Analyse possible reasons for the trend in capacity utilisation. [10]

Student's answers

1 a Capacity utilisation (percentage) is
12 000/24 000 × 100 = 50%

b Capacity utilisation has fallen from 75 per cent to 50 per cent. Although the capacity of the business has been reduced from 32 000 to 24 000, a 25 per cent reduction, production has fallen even more, from 24 000 to 12 000, a 50 per cent reduction. This is probably because of two reasons. Firstly, the recession which is affecting the chemical and oil industries. As businesses in these industries will not be investing in new locations, less safety equipment will be purchased. However, the business produces important safety equipment. When the recession ends and the chemical and oil industries start to expand again, then they will definitely need more safety equipment. So the low capacity utilisation at TTC might be a temporary problem.

Increasing competition might be more of a long-term problem. New rivals will increase total capacity in the industry producing safety equipment. Even if demand for such equipment does not fall, TTC may experience a fall in demand with chemical and oil businesses having more choice of supplier. If TTC is able to fend off this competition with its quality products and reputation for customer service – very important for complicated safety equipment – then this fall in demand might also be temporary and the fall in capacity utilisation that is a consequence of it.

Authors' comments

1 a Correct.

b The analysis is as detailed as it can be given the limited information provided. The student not only comments on the trend, but also analyses clear reasons for it and commenting on what may happen in the future. It clearly uses the context. Good answer.

Additional exam-style questions

Paper 3

1 Discuss the factors that TTC should consider when deciding whether to outsource its HRM functions. [12]

2 Discuss whether TTC should close down some of its capacity permanently. [12]

Lean production and quality management

26.1 Lean production

Lean production involves a systematic approach to changing production/supply systems in order to minimise waste. Techniques may involve Kaizen, just-in-time (JIT) methods, TQM, flexible specialisms, simultaneous engineering, cell production, employee involvement such as quality circles. The 'mix' of techniques chosen will be dependent on the nature of each individual organisation to meet the specific needs of that business.

Progress check A

1 Explain how JIT can contribute to lean production.

2 Classrooms at school are empty during school holidays. How might the school use classrooms to reduce waste?

3 Why might car manufacturers use flexible specialism?

4 Describe the main features of cell production.

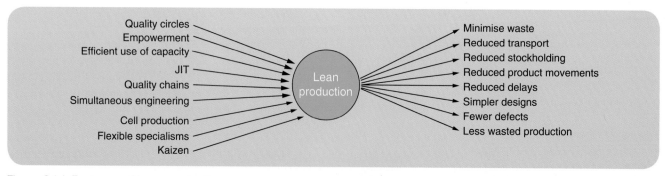

Figure 26.1 Features of lean production

26.2 Kaizen

A key element of lean production is Kaizen, a built-in process of continuous improvement within an organisation. The conditions for successful Kaizen (continuous improvement) are:

- Management culture
- Team working
- Empowerment
- Staff involvement.

But

- Some changes may need to be radical
- Resistance from managers and staff
- Additional costs, for example, training
- 'Diminishing returns' may lead to abandonment.

TIP

It would be good analysis to link the Kaizen principle to the work of Herzberg on job enrichment.

Progress check B

1 Why might Kaizen not be suitable in responding to a major change in technology?

2 Why might the impact of Kaizen diminish over time?

3 Explain why involving staff is essential to successful Kaizen.

4 Give **three** advantages of teamworking.

26.3 Just-in-time in the context of lean production

The ideas behind the just-in-time concept can be applied beyond just stock control so that it is relevant to flows and inventories throughout the whole production/supply processes. Systems can be designed to ensure that:

- supplies of raw materials arrive only when they are needed, avoiding raw material inventories
- production systems are scheduled so that work-in-progress is minimised at all stages of the process
- finished products are supplied to customers when they are needed.

This may mean higher set-up costs, high reliability in all stages including suppliers, and complex processes, but can lead to reduced costs (and other issues associated with high inventories) and reduced waste – a feature of lean production.

26.4 Quality

Associated with the ideas of lean production is the process of improving quality. Quality is defined in terms of what the customer wants. Some customers may want a perfect product which implies a very high price or other customers may be happy with an adequate product at a lower price.

- **Benchmarking:** a variation of quality assurance in which standards are set by reference to external developments such as competitors, recognised standards.
- **TQM:** an integrated approach to quality that involves every aspect of a business striving for zero defects.

TERMS

Quality control: systems for finding faulty products. Includes: inspection, testing, random sampling.

Quality product: a good or service that meets customers' expectations and is therefore 'fit for purpose'.

Quality standards: the expectations of customers expressed in terms of the minimum acceptable production or service standards.

Quality assurance: a system of agreeing and meeting quality standards at each stage of production to ensure customer satisfaction.

TIP

Quality is often viewed by students as an absolute concept and erroneously not a relative one. Quality must be explained with reference to the expectations of the target market customers. The level of quality selected by any business must be based on the resources available to it, the needs of the target market and the quality standards of competitors.

26.5 Quality methods

Improved quality has to be balanced against costs:

Costs	Benefits
Determining customer needs	Increased customer satisfaction/business
Training costs	Good publicity
Rejection costs (materials/products)	Improved reputation
Equipment costs	Easier to launch new products on existing reputation
Inspection costs	Brand building
Reworking faulty products	May allow premium pricing
Tracing problems costly, time-consuming	Improves customer loyalty

Table 26.1 Aiming for high quality - costs and benefits

Quality can be achieved by means of:

- **Quality control:** using inspection, testing, random sampling to check the quality of the finished product (prevention, inspection, correction).
- **Quality assurance:** improving processes such that at every stage agreed standards are achieved.

Progress check C

1 Explain the difference between quality assurance and quality control.

2 Explain why improving quality is important for an aircraft manufacturer.

3 Are consumer expectations on the quality of clothes the same for everyone? If not, why not?

4 Why does sampling not lead to zero defects?

5 Why is quality an issue for all businesses, not just manufacturing?

26.6 Benchmarking

The process of benchmarking is shown in Fig 26.2:

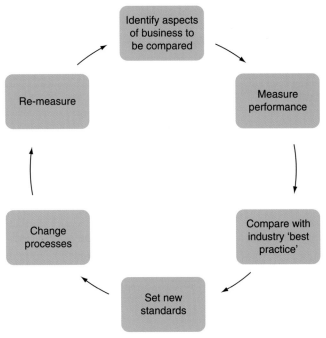

Figure 26.2 Comparing methods of achieving quality standards

TERM

Benchmarking: identifying the best firms in the industry and then comparing the performance standards – including quality – of these businesses with their own business.

Benchmarking can also includes achieving recognised standards such as ISO9000.

Progress check D

1 Why is ISO9000 not a guarantee of quality?

2 How could benchmarking discourage innovation?

3 How do quality circles fit in with the ideas of Herzberg?

4 Why could it be difficult to get sufficient information for benchmarking?

TIP

Quality is not just an issue for large businesses. Small and medium-sized firms also need to give consideration to this vital operations management concept. They must ensure that the quality level selected and the quality assurance methods used are within their resources. By reducing waste levels and staff checking quality levels, businesses can save money in the long run.

26.7 Total quality management

TQM is the integrative philosophy for ensuring continuous improvement in products, processes, services to achieve zero defects. Tools to achieve TQM include:

- Kaizen.
- Quality chains to ensure that quality is maintained from one stage to the next.
- Quality circles to identify problems, make improvements and empower employees.
- Internal customers to provide mechanisms for identifying problems at all stages.

TERMS

ISO9000: an internationally recognised certificate that acknowledges the existence of a quality procedure that meets certain criteria.

Quality circles: groups of employees who meet to discuss problems and identify improvements.

Quality chains: setting up business procedures that identify sequences of internal customers.

26.8 Choosing between methods of improving quality

Quality control	Quality assurance	TQM
Prevention.	Setting standards.	Culture of quality.
Inspection.	Checks processes.	Interdependencies.
Correction/improvement.	Changes systems.	Everyone involved.
Based on sampling of finished product.	Standards throughout processes: • product design • inputs • production • delivery • customer service.	Zero defects. Internal customers.
Negative culture.	Costly to set up.	Completely changes culture.
Inspection is tedious.	Time-consuming setting standards.	Whole business needs to be committed.
Sampling so failures get through system.	What are appropriate standards?	Are workers prepared to accept responsibility?

Table 26.2 Comparing quality methods

TERMS

TQM (total quality management): an approach to quality that aims to involve all employees in the quality improvement processes.

Internal customers: people within the organisation who depend on the quality of work being done by others in the organisation.

Zero defects: the aim of achieving perfection every time.

Exam-style question

Paper 3

Saucy Foods (SF)

SF manufactures food products using Indian-style spices. SF produces bottles of curry sauces for 'people in a hurry' so that customers simply add the sauces to their meat, vegetables or pasta. SF uses many suppliers for their spices and two suppliers of the bottles for the sauces. Quality often varies between the suppliers. SF uses batch production methods, with variations of the ingredients for

each batch. SF is receiving increasing numbers of complaints about the finished product with customers complaining that some sauces taste different each time they buy them.

Workers use old mixing and bottling machinery in the production process. The work is repetitive and the kitchen managers have been told by the managing director to 'keep an eye on employees who are not committed to the business'.

1 a Evaluate whether adopting TQM would be sufficient to solve the quality problems of SF. [14]

Student's answer

TQM aims at zero defects by introducing a series of quality assurance standards or targets throughout the operations of the business and with its suppliers. It requires the full cooperation and involvement of workers as everyone is responsible for quality – not just 'quality inspectors'. TQM would certainly help improve quality and ensure greater consistency of output. Suppliers would have to agree to a supply contract for materials and ingredients of a certain minimum standard. This would be easier to achieve if SF greatly reduced the number of suppliers. All materials and ingredients should be checked against quality standards as soon as they arrive at SF and free replacements must be offered by suppliers if these standards are not met. SF might decide to only buy supplies from firms that can show they have met international standards of quality.

Workers will need training in setting, agreeing and monitoring of quality standards. This requires a committed workforce that accepts that zero defects is a realistic objective. Managers should be there to advise and guide and not to 'watch over' workers as the assumption with TQM is that they want to achieve high quality output.

Quality circles could be used regularly to sort out any production of quality issues that arise as soon as they are seen – and not wait for customer complaints.

TQM can be very effective but there are some reasons why it might not work effectively at SF at present. Workers may be bored and unmotivated – just what is not needed for TQM to work. Managers and workers could meet to discuss how the tasks could be shared or possibly how autonomous work groups might be used to allow workers some control over the allocation of tasks. By enriching work in these ways, the issue of boredom and low motivation could be overcome. However, managers will have to change their leadership style completely – perhaps to a democratic style – so that workers are considered as key parts of the quality system – not just there to be watched and checked. Unless these two issues are resolved then TQM will not give SF the quality production it is seeking.

Authors' comments

This is a very well-focused answer. There is clear understanding of the distinction between TQM and quality control through inspection. The essential conditions for TQM to work are analysed. The context is well used – especially in the conclusion.

Additional exam-style questions

Paper 3

Lack of competitiveness threatens Top Toys (TT)

TT is a large manufacturer of traditional toys. It is struggling to survive due to increasing competition from Asia. Many of these new competitors have taken advantage of advanced technology such as CAD and CAM and have also introduced modern management techniques such as lean production including JIT, and TQM including Kaizen. The Board of TT are deciding whether to adopt the practices of their competitors and focus on the mass market for toys or aim for the higher income market segment of custom-made toys. This smaller market segment has demand that is less price elastic so cost competitiveness is not so important.

The Finance Director has reported that if TT decides to take on rivals 'at their own game' this will involve:

- Large investments which may mean cutting dividends and obtaining extra finance from loans
- New flexible working practices – however workers are concerned at the prospect of redundancies if nothing is done
- Introducing simultaneous engineering and flexible specialisms into an otherwise traditional business
- Production efficiencies which should reduce average costs
- A new approach to marketing.

1 Analyse the problems for TT resulting from the decision to change to lean production. [10]

2 Discuss whether JIT would be appropriate for a toy manufacturer such as TT. [14]

Project management

27.1 The need for projects and project management

A project consists of specific tasks that arise from the need for a business to change. Examples of projects could include opening a new shop, launching an advertising campaign, building a new factory, designing and launching a new product. Projects, large as well as small, need managing. The nature of a project is shown here:

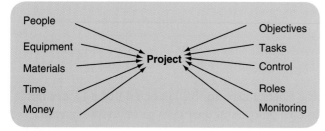

Figure 27.1 Features of a project

TERMS

Project: a specific and time limited activity with a starting and ending date, clear goals, defined responsibilities and a budget.

Project management: using modern management techniques to carry out and complete a project from start to finish in order to achieve pre-set targets of quality, time and cost.

Progress check A

1 Why do projects need planning?

2 Why do projects need monitoring?

27.2 Why do projects fail?

There have been spectacular failures in project management, mainly time overruns and cost overruns, for example: Millennium Dome, Wembley Stadium, the Tacoma Bridge in the US, Microsoft digital villages in Africa, Airbus 380. Can you think of examples in your country?

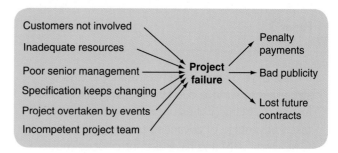

Figure 27.2 Reasons for project failure

Progress check B

1 Why is it important to involve customers in a project implementing a new IT system for a bank?

2 How could bad publicity concerning the building of a major sports complex affect a building business involved in the project?

3 Why is it important to complete a project on time?

4 Give an example of inadequate resources when building a new airport.

27.3 Elements of a network diagram (CPA)

A network diagram shows:

- Sequence of activities (usually denoted by letters)
- Logical dependencies
- Duration of each activity (shown adjacent to activity line)
- Earliest start time of each activity (EST)
- Latest finish time of each activity (LFT).

TERM

Critical path analysis: a planning technique that uses a network diagram to identify all tasks in a project, puts them in the correct sequence and allows for the identification of the critical path.

TERMS

Network diagram: the diagram used in critical path analysis that shows the logical sequence of activities and logical dependencies between them.

Critical path: the sequence of activities that must be completed on time for the whole project to be completed in the shortest time. **Node:** diagrammatic representation of the beginning/end of an activity.

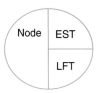

EST (earliest start time): Found by looking at earliest finishing times of preceding activities. EST for last activity is overall minimum duration of project.

LFT (latest finish time): found by working backwards in time from subsequent activities (only possible to calculate once all the ESTs have been calculated).

Dummy activity: an artificial activity used to ensure the logical representation of a project is not ambiguous – for example 'C and D follows A and B' needs to be shown differently to 'C follows A and B, D follows B'.

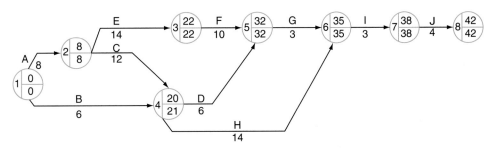

Figure 27.3 A typical network diagram showing activities, durations, EST, LFT

27.4 Floats

'Float' shows how much potential slack there is in the network. For any activity:

Total float = LFT – duration – EST

Free float = EST of next activity – duration – EST of activity under consideration.

Critical activities all have zero float.

TERMS

Total float: how much an activity can be delayed without delaying the overall project.

Free float: how much an activity can be delayed without delaying the next activity.

Progress check C

1 How is the earliest start time calculated?

2 Why is it useful to know the project duration?

3 Why is it more important to monitor critical activities than it is to monitor activities with large floats?

4 What is the free float on a critical activity?

5 Distinguish between free float and total float.

27.5 Using CPA in project management

CPA helps in estimating and negotiating delivery dates so that other operations can be planned.

- Helps knowing when activities start/end – helps allocation of resources and coordination including sub-contractors.
- Helps monitor progress especially through finishing times.
- Can see consequences of delays.
- Knowing critical path helps focus resources, and resources can be moved from non-critical activities if delays are likely.
- Main use is in 'what if' analysis.

27.6 Evaluating CPA

The advantages and disadvantages of CPA are shown in Fig 27.4:

Benefits
- Helps plan completion date
- Floats help ordering equipment, reorganinsing tasks, coping with delays
- Fits in well with ideas of ERP
- Creates a planning culture
- Effective easy analysis of changes in assumptions

Disadvantages
- Can be costly, time-consuming
- Relies on assumptions
- Cannot guarantee success, plan is only as good as the management
- No technique can guarantee success

Figure 27.4 Benefits and disadvantages of CPA

Progress check D

1 Outline **two** benefits of using CPA.

2 Outline **two** limitations of CPA.

3 What is meant by the 'critical path'?

4 Why does using CPA not guarantee successful completion of a project?

5 Suggest **three** real-life situations that would benefit from the use of CPA.

6 Explain when dummy activities are used.

7 Would you use CPA for planning your revision? If not, why not?

Exam-style question

Paper 3

Tulloch Farms (TF)

TF Farms is planning some new buildings. Contractors will be used for each stage of the project. It is important that the project is completed before the start of the rainy season in 17 weeks.

Activities for completing the building project:

Activity	Explanation	Preceded by	Duration (weeks)
A	Order materials and await delivery	–	3
B	Prepare land	–	2
C	Prepare a marketing strategy	–	8
D	Build foundations	A, B	3
E	Fit walls and windows	D	5
F	Fit electrical connections	E	2
G	Install bathrooms	E	4
H	Fit roofs	E	3
I	Paint buildings	F, G, H	1

Table 27.1

1 a Using the data above construct a network diagram (CPA) for the project, showing all earliest start times and latest finish times. [10]

b If activity B is delayed by two weeks, briefly advise TF on what steps he could take to avoid the project taking longer than 16 weeks. [4]

c Discuss the extent to which this CPA will ensure the successful completion of the project on time. [12]

Student's answers to 1(a) and (b)

a The critical path is A, D, E, G, I and takes 16 weeks.

b If B is delayed by two weeks it makes B critical rather than A and this would delay D and subsequent activities and the whole project by two weeks unless something is done. Since C remains non-critical and has a float of eight weeks it may be possible to move resources from C to any of the critical activities for up to eight weeks to try and get two weeks saving on these critical resources.

Authors' comments

The network diagram should be completely right and neatly drawn.

The answer to 1b is correct.

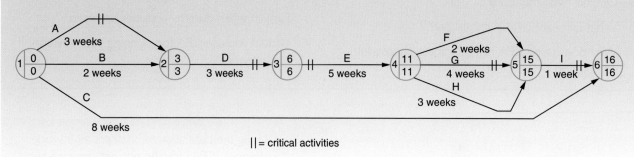

|| = critical activities

Additional exam-style question

1   Answer part (c) for the Tulloch Farms case study above.

Unit 5
FINANCE AND ACCOUNTING

Chapter 28

Business finance and its sources

Learning summary

After you have studied this chapter you should be able to:

- ■ explain why businesses need finance

- ■ explain why different needs might mean different sources are appropriate

- ■ explain the meaning and significance of working capital

- ■ explain the significance of and distinction between revenue expenditure and capital expenditure

- ■ analyse the relationship between legal structure of a business and its sources of finance

- ■ distinguish between short and long term sources of finance

- ■ evaluate internal and external sources of finance

- ■ analyse the factors influencing the choice of sources of finance

- ■ evaluate the appropriateness of each possible source in a given situation.

28.1 The need for finance

Start-up
- Buildings
- Inventory
- Other start-up costs

Working capital
- Day-to-day spending
- Inventory
- Expenses
- Bills
- Operating costs

Capital expenditure
- New machinery
- Takeovers
- Research and developments

Contingencies
- Changed economic circumstances
- Unexpected developments
- Cash shortages

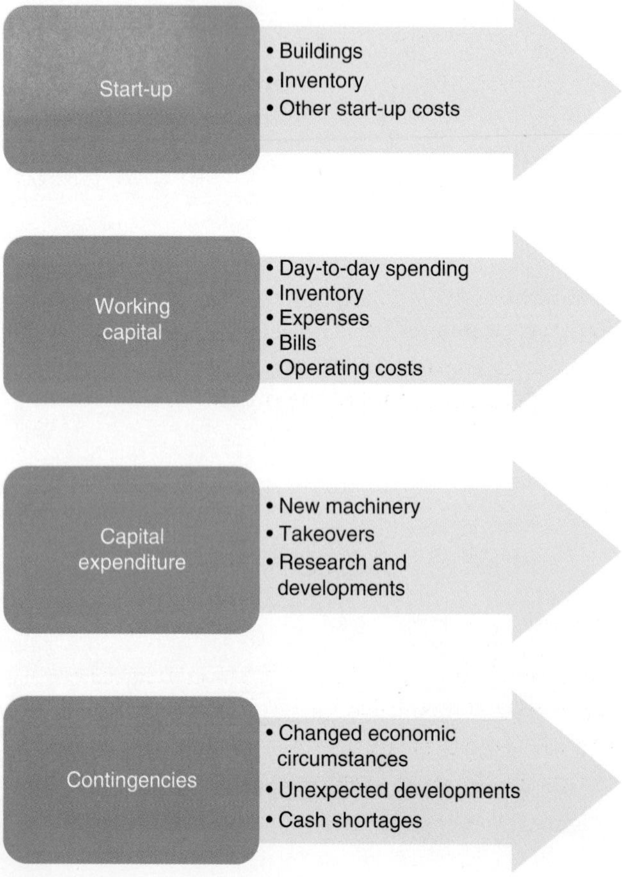

Figure 28.1 The need for finance

TERMS

Start-up capital: capital needed by an entrepreneur to set up a business.

Capital expenditure: involves the purchase of assets that are expected to last for more than one year, such as buildings and machinery.

Revenue expenditure: spending on all costs and assets other than fixed assets. It includes wages and salaries and materials bought for inventory.

28.2 Needs and sources

Some needs will require long-term sources, e.g. mortgages for buildings.

Other needs will require short-term sources, e.g. overdrafts for temporary cash shortages.

28.3 The meaning and significance of working capital

The finance needed for day-to-day operations:

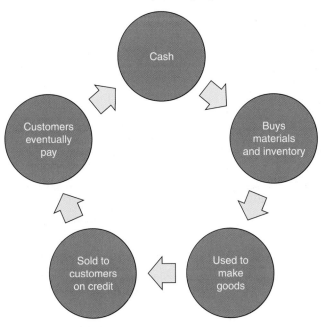

Figure 28.2 The working capital cycle

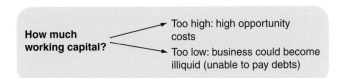

Figure 28.3 Levels of working capital

Without working capital, a business cannot function or survive.

28.4 Significance of and distinction between revenue expenditure and capital expenditure

Revenue expenditure: essential for everyday running costs. Usually paid for from income and appears in income statement (P&L account).

Capital expenditure: essential to pay for fixed assets and usually paid for from long-term sources. Usually appears in the statement of financial position.

Progress check A

1 State **two** needs for finance for a new business.

2 Distinguish between capital expenditure and working capital.

3 Explain why a business may need finance to meet contingencies.

4 Give **two** examples of capital expenditure.

28.5 Relationship between legal structure and sources of finance

Unincorporated businesses have restricted sources since they are unable to raise finance through share issues. It is unlikely that a public limited company would rely on personal savings of the owners as a source.

28.6 Sources of finance (internal/external; short term/ long term)

The various sources of finance are discussed here. These are not all suitable for unincorporated businesses who are more likely to borrow from friends, relatives, and sources of micro finance.

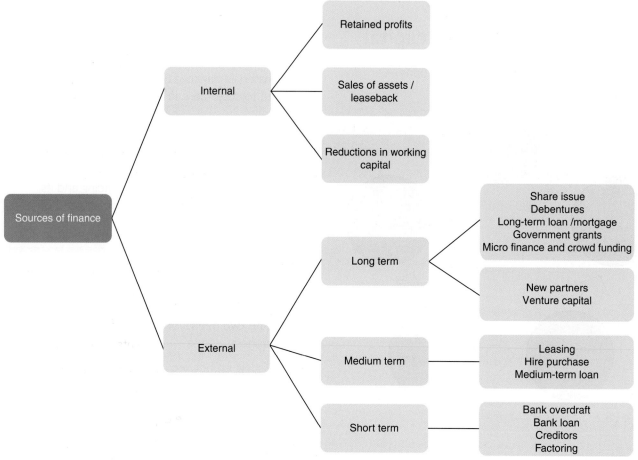

Figure 28.4 Sources of finance

28.7 Comparison of internal and external sources

Sources of finance		
Source	Advantages	Disadvantages
Retained profits (internal).	Source of permanent finance. No interest or other costs.	Not suitable for new businesses. Needs agreement of owners/ shareholders.
Sale of assets/leaseback (internal).	Useful for underemployed assets. Sale and leaseback may be possible.	May be expensive. Difficult to identify which assets.
Reduce working capital (internal).	Relatively easy, increases efficiencies.	One-off, likely to be small. Dangers of reducing too much.
Shares (external) • sell additional shares • convert to PLC.	Low risk – reduces gearing. Do not have to be repaid although shareholders will expect higher dividends.	Risks takeover. Can be expensive. Needs agreement of shareholders.
Debentures (external).	Similar to loans.	Similar to loans.
Long-term loans/mortgage, crowdfunding, venture capital (external).	Wide choice of types of loans to suit different situations. No loss of shareholder control.	May involve collateral. Interest payments may be high. May be risky – higher gearing.
Grants (external).	Do not have to be repaid.	Not widely available.
Leasing and hire purchase (external).	Avoids large cash payments. Leasing will reduce maintenance costs. One-off source, short term only.	Can be expensive. Less control over leased equipment.
Medium-term loan (external).	Straightforward way of borrowing from a variety of sources and a wide choice of types of loans.	May have stringent conditions. May not be available.
Bank overdraft (external).	Flexible. Easy to arrange.	Very expensive. Can be 'called in' – high risk to business.
Creditors (delay payments for purchases) (external).	Easy way of borrowing if suppliers agree.	May be a cost in terms of lost discounts for early payment.
Factoring (external).	Guaranteed income from debts.	One-off method. Can be expensive.
Find a partner (sole trader) or introduce a new partner (partnership) (external).	Cheap source of additional finance. Brings in expertise.	Dilutes ownership. Changes nature of business.

Table 28.1 Comparison of sources of finance

finance, investors will need to see a business plan (Chapter 40).

28.8 The choice of finance

The following are factors to consider in choosing a source:

- Timescale for the need – short/medium/long term.
- Need for flexibility – some sources not flexible.
- Use – is it for capital expansion, working capital or to solve a problem?
- Current financial structure – is it mainly debt or equity? If the balance changes then so does risk.
- Relative cost of raising finance – interest rates, state of stock market, charges, opportunity cost.
- Legal structure of business – can it raise equity finance? How much can it raise?
- Amount required.

Overdrafts can solve cash-flow problems in the short term but they do not solve liquidity problems. To raise

Progress check B

1. Explain the difference between short-term and long-term finance.

2. Why does a business have to be careful selling assets to raise finance?

3. State **two** drawbacks of overdrafts as a source of finance.

4. Why is trade credit a source of finance?

5. Why do retained profits appear to be a cheap source of finance?

6. Why might a new business decide to lease new equipment rather than buy it?

Factor influencing finance choice	Why significant
Use to which finance is to be put – which affects the time period for which finance is required.	• It is very risky to borrow long-term finance to pay short-term needs. Business should match the sources of finance to the need for it. • Permanent capital may be needed for long-term business expansion. • Short-term finance would be advisable to finance a short-term need to increase stocks or pay creditors.
Cost	• Obtaining finance is never 'free' – even internal finance may have an opportunity cost. • Loans may become very expensive during a period of rising interest rates. • A Stock Exchange flotation can cost millions of dollars in fees and promotion of the share sale.
Amount required	• Share issues and sales of debentures, because of the administration and other costs, would generally be used only for large capital sums. • Small bank loans or reducing debtors' payment period could be used to raise small sums.

Factor influencing finance choice	Why significant
Legal structure and desire to retain control	• Share issues can only be used by limited companies – and only public limited companies can sell shares directly to the public. Doing this runs the risk of the current owners losing some control – except if a rights issue is used. • If the owners want to retain control of the business at all costs, then a sale of shares might be unwise.
Size of existing borrowing	• This is a key issue – the higher the existing debts of a business (compared with its size), the greater the risk of borrowing more. Banks and other lenders will become anxious about lending more finance. • This concept is referred to as gearing and is fully covered in Chapter 35.
Flexibility	• When a firm has a variable need for finance – for example, it has a seasonal pattern of sales and cash receipts – a flexible form of finance is better than a long-term and inflexible source.

Table 28.2 Factors to be considered in making the 'source of finance' decision

28.9 Evaluating the appropriateness of a source of finance

TIP

You should be able to recommend appropriate sources of finance for businesses needing capital for different reasons recognising the legal structure of the business, the need for finance, gearing and by analysing the advantages and disadvantages of each source in a given situation.

Progress check C

1 Why would you not recommend shares as a source of finance for a partnership?

2 Give **three** sources of finance to meet long-term needs of a large public limited company.

3 Give **two** sources of finance suitable for short-term working capital needs of a sole trader.

4 Why is gearing important in considering the suitability of long-term loans?

Exam-style question

Paper 2

ABC

The ABC bus company started with just one bus five years ago. Joe, the owner, is a sole trader. The business has enjoyed rapid growth and Joe now owns four buses. There is the opportunity to expand into new routes which will require the purchase of three new buses – however, he does not have the money to buy them. Joe's profits grew steadily in the first five years, and all these profits have been re-invested to buy new buses. Next year he does not expect profits to be so great. Joe currently has no loans, although he is worried that his overdraft is getting higher – diesel prices have gone up rapidly and he has to pay his suppliers quicker than he used to. This is a worry to him. So far Joe has managed to run the business on his own. He is, however, finding it increasingly difficult to run the larger business, especially the personnel side of the business. Joe expects interest rates to rise following poor economic news. He was approached recently by a venture capitalist who was looking for opportunities to invest, however Joe did not really understand the proposal that was made to him. He did wonder about some wealthy relatives.

1 Evaluate possible sources of finance for Joe. [11]

Student's answer

Joe has two needs for finance. He clearly has a working capital problem and he needs long-term finance if he wants to expand his business with the new routes.

Dealing with the working capital problem first, Joe seems not to be handling cash flow well. Although the business is profitable he is unable to manage payments to his suppliers of diesel and his overdraft is increasing. We do not know the size of the overdraft relative to the business income but we do know it is a worry which suggests a significant problem. The overdraft does solve the immediate cash-flow problem but it does not solve the underlying problem. A solution might be to go to his suppliers and explain that their new credit terms have caused him a problem. They may then be prepared to re-negotiate their credit terms. If they fail to he could try other suppliers. If that does not work he will have to look elsewhere for an injection of capital.

As far as the long-term needs are concerned he needs a significant amount of finance to purchase three buses. He is a sole trader so that share issues are out of the question. A bank loan is possible because of the zero gearing ratio. However, the market seems uncertain and buses may not supply much security for the bank. The venture capitalist is a possibility but it would not be good for Joe to do something he is not comfortable with.

It is interesting that he is having problems running his expanded business and that he does lack certain skills. That suggests he needs some help so a new partner may be a possibility worth considering. He has some wealthy relatives who may be able to help, either through lending or by becoming a partner. The latter would depend on the skills they could bring, but if they had the right skills and could put a significant amount of money into the business that would seem an ideal way to grow for Joe.

Authors' comments

This is a good answer despite being brief. Not only has the student shown clear understanding of both long and short-term finance, this knowledge has been applied very effectively in context. The judgement at the end is largely convincing and seems very sensible given the situation of Joe's business.

Additional exam-style questions

Paper 1 Section A

1. a Define the term 'revenue expenditure'. [2]
   b Give **two** examples of external sources of finance. [2]
   c Explain the need for working capital. [3]
   d Explain the usefulness of debt factoring to a business selling electronic goods on credit. [4]

Paper 1 Section B

2. a Discuss suitable sources of finance for starting up a sole trader hairdressing business. [12]
   b Analyse the advantages and disadvantages of raising finance through loans for a public limited company. [8]

Costs

Learning summary

After you have studied this chapter you should be able to:

- ☐ understand the importance of cost information
- ☐ classify various types of cost
- ☐ explain problems allocating costs
- ☐ identify main uses of cost information
- ☐ understand and use break-even analysis
- ☐ evaluate results from break-even analysis.

29.1 Importance of costs

Cost information is important as costs it is central to most business decisions. For example, it is not sensible to set prices for a product or service without knowing the relevant costs. It is not possible to calculate profits without knowing costs. It makes no sense to invest in a major project without appraising the costs. The measurement of costs has to be accurate and relevant, otherwise decisions may be poor.

29.2 Classifying costs

Costs need to be classified for the purposes of analysis such as break-even, costing, pricing and other decisions.

TERMS

Average cost: total cost/number of items produced.

Direct costs: these are costs that can be clearly identified with each unit of production and can be allocated to a cost centre.

Indirect costs: costs that cannot be identified with a unit of production or allocated accurately to a cost centre.

Marginal cost: cost of producing the next item.

Fixed costs: costs that do not vary with output (in the short term).

Variable costs: costs that vary with output.

Total cost: fixed costs + variable costs.

TIP Direct costs are similar but not the same as variable costs. Not all direct costs are variable costs.

If a firm decided to produce a special order for a supermarket, and if the variable costs are $10 per unit and it costs $20 000 to change the packaging for an order of 20 000 units (i.e. $2 per unit) to change the packaging, then the direct costs are $12 per unit.

29.3 Problems allocating costs

Not all costs can be classified as either 'fixed' or 'variable'. This type of cost is described as 'semi-variable'.

- Purchase of equipment – fixed
- Raw materials – variable
- Promotion – usually fixed
- Rent – usually fixed
- Labour – can be either (fixed salaries + variable payments) – semi variable
- Energy – can be either (heating + powering machines) – semi-variable
- Internet services can be either.

Some costs can be shared over a range of products. For example, if you wanted to calculate the cost of running a Business Studies department there are costs that are shared with other departments such as heating and lighting as well as the salaries of exams officers, headteachers, caretakers.

Progress check A

1 Distinguish between fixed and indirect costs.

2 Give an example of a direct cost which is not variable.

3 Give **three** reasons why the manager of a shoe shop will be interested in cost data.

4 Give one example of a cost incurred at a school that is difficult to classify as fixed/variable.

5 A business produces 100 bicycles per month at a variable cost of $100 per bicycle and fixed costs of $5 000 per month. Calculate the total cost of a month's production, and the average cost of that production. What is the marginal cost?

29.4 Uses of costs in setting prices

As seen in marketing there are a variety of ways of setting prices, often related to market conditions. However, whatever the pricing strategy a price should usually be set so that at least the variable costs of production are covered. In the long term a business needs to cover fixed costs as well so that average costs are also important.

29.5 The other main uses of cost information

- Helping calculate profits.
- Whether or not to make a particular product (see Chapter 32).
- Whether to make or buy (see Chapter 32).
- Monitoring and improving business performance – by observing trends in costs, comparing outcomes with targets.
- Setting budgets (see Chapter 33).
- Deciding on resource use by comparing costs of competing resources.

- Making business decisions such as location, production method, investment appraisal.
- Calculating break-even (see next section).

29.6 Break-even analysis

Break-even analysis is a useful decision tool. Break-even point of production can be determined graphically and a typical break-even chart is shown in Fig 29.1:

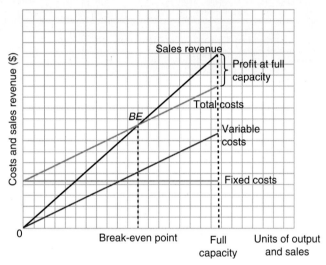

Figure 29.1 A break even chart

Or mathematically:

$$\text{Break-even} = \frac{\text{Fixed costs}}{(\text{Unit price} - \text{variable cost})^*}$$

* This is contribution per unit.

Note: Break-even is measured in units of production.

TERMS

Break-even point of production: the level of output at which total costs equal total revenue – neither a profit nor a loss is made.

Margin of safety: the amount by which the sales level exceeds the break-even level of output. If it is too low the business may struggle to become profitable.

29.7 Uses and limitations of break-even analysis

Break-even analysis	
Uses	**Limitations**
Price decisions	Assumptions may not be realistic
Purchasing new equipment	Costs etc. may not be linear
Choosing between locations	Costs difficult to identify for new projects
Performing 'what if' analysis	Costs difficult to classify
Which project to invest in	Assumes all units sold

Table 29.1 Uses and limitations of break-even analysis

Progress check B

1 Explain the term 'margin of safety'.

2 Explain why a business makes a loss at below the break-even production level.

3 A printing firm has fixed costs of $10 000. Each book costs $10 to produce and sells for $20. What is the break-even level of output?

4 A school has a break-even point of 200 students. Next year they plan to have 300 students and make a profit of $3000. What will be the margin of safety?

5 Discuss **two** benefits of the break-even technique.

6 Discuss **two** limitations of the break-even technique.

Exam-style question

Paper 2 (part question)

Luxo Cars (LC)

The board of LC is discussing whether to open a new factory, which will use the latest technology, in addition to their existing factory. The market for its luxury cars is growing and there is a great deal of potential for exports. The part of the country where LC want to build the new factory has high levels of unemployment and land costs are relatively cheap. However, the location is a long way from the country's cities and the nearest sea port is 300 kms away. The Board are discussing the following data:

	Existing factory	Proposed new factory
Fixed costs	$10 000 000 per year	$12 000 000 per year
Variable costs	$8 000 per car	$4 000 per car
Price	$16 000	$16 000
Break-even	1 250 cars per year	See part c

Table 29.2

1 a Define the term 'variable costs'. [2]

b Explain why the fixed costs for the new factory are likely to be higher than for the existing factory. [3]

c Calculate the break-even for the new factory. [3]

d Discuss the proposal to open the new factory. [11]

Student's answers

1 a Variable costs are costs which change with the level of output of a product or service. An example is the raw materials needed to manufacture a car.

b The new factory is going to include the latest technology. High tech equipment such as robots is likely to be expensive to buy and install and will need a modern purpose built building. So the fixed capital costs will be high even if output of cars is low. The existing factory will not have such high costs.

c b/e = – FC/(price – unit variable cost) = $12 000 000/(16 000 – 4 000) = 12 000 000/12 000 = 1000 cars per year d The new factory will be more efficient than the existing one because of the new technology. Robots are often used to make cars and these are more productive than labour intensive methods. This is why the variable cost per car is lower with the new factory and the break-even point is lower so it should be profitable at a low output level. Demand for LC seems to be strong and there is potential for increased sales through exports. These points suggest that the new factory is a good idea.

However, although labour costs might be quite low because of high unemployment, it is not clear whether workers will need expensive training to use the new equipment or not. Also, will the new technology mean that the brand loses an image about being 'handmade cars'? This could be important to some customers. The new factory is a long way from a seaport so exporting will be difficult and expensive. The extra costs of transport to the seaport might add to the variable costs of each car and cancel out the higher efficiency of the new factory.

On balance, LC can afford the new investment, the new factory could be a wise investment. Further research needs to be done on the demand for cars using high-tech equipment to make them. Also, it might be cheaper to increase output by modernising the existing factory and extra data about the cost of this and the impact on the break-even output would be needed before a final decision can be taken.

Authors' comments

l a, b and c are all correct.

d This answer makes good use of the evidence provided and these points are well applied to car manufacturing. There is a balance of analytical points made and there is a clear decision but this is conditional on the need for additional, relevant information. A very good answer.

Additional exam-style questions

Paper 1 Section A

l Explain the difference between variable costs and direct costs. [3]

2 Give examples of costs which are likely to be fixed at a school. [2]

Paper 1 Section B

3 'Marketing managers do not need to concern themselves with costs – it's the market that determines the price.' Discuss. [12]

Accounting fundamentals

30.1 Users of accounts and information they seek

The various stakeholders in a business have differing uses for accounts. Typically:

- Managers: Make decisions, monitor progress, set budgets, measure performance, compare.
- Suppliers: Is company safe to supply on credit? Is it able to repay debts?
- Government: How much tax due? How well is the industry/economy doing?
- Customers: Will the business survive? – important for spare parts, repairs etc.
- Banks: Is business secure enough to lend to? Is it safe to give an overdraft?
- Workers: Are jobs/wages secure? Could the business afford wage increases?
- Shareholders: What are the business prospects?

30.2 Income statement

This is a very important accounting record. It tells managers and other stakeholders whether a business is making a profit or not.

The major items on an income statement are:

Sales revenue

− Cost of sales

= **Gross profit**

− Expenses

= **Operating profit**

− Taxes, dividends

= **Retained profit**

TERM

Income statement: records the revenue, costs and profit (or loss) of a business over a given period of time.

Progress check A

In the year to 31/12/15, Metro Cola recorded the following (simplified) data on the company income statement:

	($million)
Revenue	30 990
Cost of sales	17 088
Expenses	11 671
Tax paid	1 040
Dividends paid	800

Table 30.1

1 Calculate the company's:

   i   gross profit

   ii operating/net profit

   iii retained profit.

2 Assess whether Metro Cola's stakeholders should be pleased with the company's recent performance if its retained profit was $4.9 billion in the year ending 31/12/14.

30.3 Statement of financial position

This tells managers and stakeholders what the 'net worth' of the business is. This can be compared with past years and other similar businesses.

What are the major items on a statement of financial position?

In Table 30.2 there is a simplified version of the statement of financial position for Metro Cola for year ending 31/12/15.

Progress check B

1 Why do you think the value of Metro Cola's intangible assets is so high?

2 Why do you think Metro Cola offers credit to its retail customers (creating debtors or accounts receivable)?

3 Do you think Metro Cola managers should be worried about the level of long-term loans taken out by the company? Explain your answer.

4 If Metro Cola made the following transactions during the year, indicate which category these would appear on in the statement of financial position. (The first has been done for you.)

   i   Purchase of property with a mortgage: non-current assets up and long-term liabilities up.

   ii Increased inventories financed by short-term loans.

   iii Sale of a trademark and the proceeds used to repay five-year bank loan.

Statement of financial position	
	$million
Non-current assets:	(fixed assets, kept for more than 1 year)
Property, plant etc.	8 425
Intangible assets	14 414 (not physical assets, e.g. trademarks)
Other assets	7 550
Total non-current assets:	**30 389**
Current assets:	(assets kept for less than 1 year)
Inventories	2 298
Trade receivables (debtors)	3 600 (money owed by customers)
Cash	6 816
Total current assets	**12 714**
Current liabilities	
Trade payables	5 651 (money owed to suppliers)
Short-term loans	7 518 (owed to banks etc., tax deferred)
Total current liabilities	**13 169**
Non-current liabilities	8 826 (e.g. loans, debentures)
Net assets	**21 108** (= total assets − liabilities)
Shareholders' equity	
Share capital	880
Retained earnings etc.	20 228 (owned by shareholders, not business)
Total shareholders' equity	**21 108** (balances with net assets)

Table 30.2 Metro Cola: statement of financial position as at 31/12/15

30.4 The need for ratios

Using ratios allows much easy analysis of company performance:

- Two values can be compared with each other, for example, current assets and current liabilities.
- Ratio results can be compared easily with past years.
- Ratio results can also be compared to those of other companies in the same or similar industry and with 'rule of thumb' values in some instances.
- Analysing accounts using ratios can indicate potential problem areas to focus on.

30.5 The current ratio and acid test ratio (liquidity ratios)

TERMS

Current ratio: liquidity ratio calculated by

$$\frac{\text{current assets}}{\text{current liabilities}}$$

1.5–2 regarded as 'normal' for many businesses.

Acid test ratio: liquidity ratio calculated by

$$\frac{(\text{current assets} - \text{inventories})}{\text{current liabilities}}$$

About 1 regarded as 'normal' for many businesses.

Liquidity: the ability of a business to meet its short-term liabilities with its short-term assets.

Note: many businesses survive without ratios at the 'normal' level. It is **trends** in ratios that are usually more important than the ratio at a given time.

Progress check C

1 Calculate the current ratio for Metro Cola in 2015.

2 Calculate the acid test ratio for Metro Cola in 2015.

3 Comment on this company's liquidity.

30.6 Profitability ratios

TERMS

Gross profit margin: $\dfrac{\text{Gross profit}}{\text{Revenue}} \times 100$

Profit margin: $\dfrac{\text{Operating profit}}{\text{Revenue}} \times 100$

TIP

When discussing ways in which a business might increase its profit margins do not forget to evaluate. For example: will increasing prices be a good idea if the demand is very price elastic? Will cutting the cost of sales by using cheaper materials lead to a lower quality product?

Progress check D

1 Calculate Metro Cola's gross profit margin for 2015.

2 Calculate Metro Cola's profit margin for 2015.

3 Discuss the usefulness of comparing these results with two other companies: Pepsi Cola and Ford.

30.7 Improving ratios

Liquidity ratio too high: inefficient use of financial resources, e.g. stocks too high – Solution: spend excess cash, reduce inventories.

Liquidity ratio too low: possibility of being unable to repay short-term debts, then might face liquidation (going out of business) – Solution: increase cash in the business by sale of redundant assets, slowing down spending plans, raising short-term finance by selling inventories, through long-term loans, debt factoring, share issues.

Gross profit margin too low: find lower-cost raw materials, increase price (but beware of impact on sales).

Profit margin too low: reduce operating costs (raw materials, labour), increase price (but beware impact on sales), reduce overhead costs (e.g. rent, promotion, organisational costs).

30.8 Limitations of accounts and ratios

Remember that:

- the 'latest' data might already be several months out of date
- the accounts might have been made to appear more attractive, i.e. window dressed
- different companies may have different 'year endings' so direct comparisons over the same time period become difficult
- the external environment can have a major impact on company performance decisions
- ratios differ between industries so difficult to compare
- ratio results may highlight problems – but they do not find solutions!
- the past may not be a good guide to the future.

Exam-style question

Paper 2

Tivoli Fashions (TF)

TF makes expensive wedding dresses. Each one is a unique design and they are all hand made using old fashioned sewing machines. Materials such as ribbons, semi-precious stones and silk are bought in from several suppliers. The Managing Director recruited two designers last year and this means that designs do not have to be 'bought in' from other businesses. For the first time the business promoted itself at a major wedding fair which was also attended by many of the growing number of rival businesses. Even though this was expensive for TF, there was much interest from potential customers. The following table shows an extract from TF latest accounts:

As at 31/5/16	$
Non-current assets	12 000
Current assets	7 000
Inventories	3 000
Current liabilities	8 000
For year ending 31/5/16	
Revenue	45 000
Cost of sales	15 000
Expenses	25 000

Table 30.3

1 a What is meant by the term 'non-current assets'? [3]

b Calculate for TF:

  i Gross profit margin [4]

  ii Net/operating profit margin [4]

  iii Current ratio [3]

  iv Acid test ratio. [3]

c Last year, the net profit margin ratio was 15 per cent. Analyse **two** likely reasons for the change in this ratio for the year ending 31/5/16. [6]

d Discuss **two** ways in which this business could improve its liquidity position. [11]

Student's answers

1 a Non-current assets are items that the business owns and tends to own for a period longer than 12 months. For example, vehicles, offices, factories, equipment, brand names.

b i Gross profit = $45k − $15k = $30k

  GPM = $30k/$45k × 100 = 66.7%

  ii Net profit = $30k − $25K = $5k

  NPM = $5k/$45k × 100 = 11.1%

  iii Current ratio = CA/CL = $7k/$8k = 0.875

  iv ATR = (CA − inventories)/ CL = $4k/$8k = 0.5

c The net profit margin has fallen from 15 per cent to 11 per cent. This means that on each $1 worth of sales the net profit earned has fallen by nearly $0.04 in just one year. Two possible reasons for this are expenses rising at a faster rate than sales or prices being reduced.

Expenses include overhead or fixed costs such as management salaries, rent and promotion costs. TF increased promotion costs in 2016 by attending a wedding fair, in order to increase demand, but this may have increased expenses by more than the increase in sales and then the net profit margin would fall.

If the selling price to retailers was reduced, perhaps because of the increased competition in this market, TF would have cut both its gross profit and net profit margins.

d The current ratio is 0.875. For a manufacturing business such as TF a comfortable current ratio would be in the range 1.5–2. We can observe that the business is lacking in liquidity. Looking at individual items it seems that inventories are quite high relative to cost of sales. The rest of current assets are likely to be receivables (debtors). $4k on sales of $45k seems a great deal for a product (individually made wedding dresses) sold to final consumers. Current liabilities are very high relative to cost of goods sold which suggests that either

TF is getting too much credit from suppliers or it is having to take out an overdraft to survive from day to day. The acid test ratio is 0.5 which is well below the 'comfortable' level of a business of this type confirming the comments made about the current ratio. Because inventories are removed from the ATR calculation this confirms the view that there are probably four possible solutions available:

- Reduce inventories: these are likely to be raw materials from a variety of suppliers and may be difficult to manage. Because the firm is using a job production approach, lean production techniques such as JIT are unlikely to work. If stocks could be reduced by selling more wedding dresses, then the cash raised could be used to reduce current liabilities and hence improve the ratios.
- Reduce receivables: it would not normally be expected to buy clothes on credit, particularly wedding dresses. The business needs to manage its customer credit more effectively. Reducing credit to new customers will increase cash which could be used to reduce trade payables or any overdraft.
- Reduce trade payables: the amount of trade payables is a concern, however, it is not an immediate problem if suppliers are not demanding payment. However, better promptness in payment will improve relations with suppliers. The question is, though, where would the extra money come from? If it

comes from short-term borrowing, then the liquidity position is unlikely to change much.

- Find some additional medium/long-term finance: this would enable trade payables to be reduced as well as short-term loans. Both of these would have an immediate beneficial impact on liquidity. However, it depends on whether the finance is available. Banks and equity financiers may not be keen on putting more money into a business with liquidity problems. Selling unused assets, or converting receivables to cash using a debt factor could release cash for reducing current liabilities.

Recommending a solution is difficult without further information. However, since it is unusual to offer credit for wedding dresses, and customers are unlikely to go elsewhere if credit terms are changed, then reducing customer credit seems a useful starting point.

Authors' comments

1 a to c The student clearly understands profit margins – two appropriate suggestions are made, these are both explained briefly and applied to TF Fashions.

d   The student clearly understands the ratios and has done an effective job interpreting them. Options for reducing the liquidity problem are identified and are discussed in context. The recommendation follows out of that analysis and is reasonably convincing, showing evaluation skills.

Additional exam-style questions

Paper 1 Section A

1   Define the term 'asset'. [2]

2   Explain the meaning of the term 'operating profit'. [3]

3   Explain why a food retailer may be able to operate with a low level of liquidity. [3]

Paper 2 Section B

4   Discuss the usefulness of published accounts to two stakeholders of a business. [20]

5   Analyse the usefulness of liquidity ratios to senior managers of a fresh fruit business. [8]

Forecasting and managing cash flows

Learning summary

After you have studied this chapter you should be able to:

- understand the purpose of cash-flow forecasts
- distinguish between cash and profit
- explain the uses and limitations of cash-flow forecasts
- construct, amend and interpret cash-flow forecasts
- recognise causes of cash-flow problems
- analyse solutions to cash-flow problems
- recognise the link between cash flow and working capital.

31.1 Cash flow

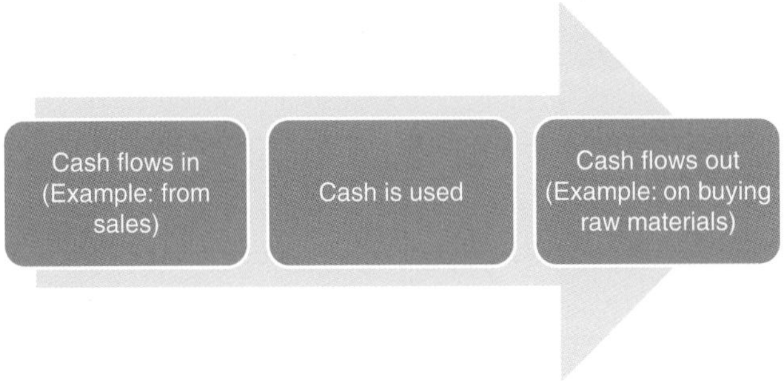

| Cash flows in (Example: from sales) | Cash is used | Cash flows out (Example: on buying raw materials) |

Figure 31.1 Flows of cash in a business

TERMS

Cash: money in the form of notes or coins or other methods of immediate payment such as cheques, banker's drafts etc.

Cash flow: the sum of cash payments to a business (inflows) less the sum of cash payments made by the business (outflows).

Cash inflows: payments in cash received by a business such as those from customers or from the bank (when receiving a loan).

Cash outflows: payments in cash made by a business, such as those to suppliers, employees.

Keeping a check on cash flow is important because employees and suppliers have to be paid, even though customers may not yet have paid for products they have bought.

Businesses need to hold cash in order to pay for everyday items. Businesses often receive cash as payment from many of their customers.

31.2 Difference between cash and profit

Cash = difference between money coming in and money going out.

Profit = difference between sales revenues and costs.

Products sold on credit are included in 'sales revenue' even though the cash has not been received.

Raw materials bought on credit are included in 'costs' even though they have yet to be paid for.

A firm can make a profit (it is earning more than it is spending) but may still become insolvent and face liquidation because of timing problems between cash inflows and cash outflows. This is the most common reason for businesses to fail.

TIP

When given the opportunity, emphasise the importance of having enough cash in the short term. Profit can wait to be earned in the long term – but cash payments always have to be made!

31.3 Uses and limitations of cash-flow forecasts

Uses:

- Planning when setting up a business.
- Convincing investors that an enterprise is worth investing in.
- Setting targets.
- Identifying possible future cash-flow problems.
- Aid decision making.
- 'What if' analysis can identify key issues.

Limitations:

- The future cannot be predicted with certainty, for example, competitors' new products might reduce the sales and cash inflow of a business.
- Unforeseen developments, for example, the credit crunch in 2008-09 made outcomes significantly different from forecasts.
- Only as good as initial assumptions.

TIP

Remember, cash-flow forecasts are forecasts, not actual amounts.

They are estimates based on assumptions.

They can neither be 'right' nor 'wrong' but they can be good forecasts or forecasts based on poor assumptions.

Progress check A

1 Why are cash-flow forecasts useful when setting up a business?

2 Why are assumptions needed for cash-flow forecasts?

3 Give **two** reasons why is it important to identify possible future cash-flow problems.

4 Why might a sudden change in oil prices affect the cash-flow forecasts of a taxi firm?

5 Explain how a business can have a cash-flow problem but still make a profit.

31.4 Construction, amendment and interpretation of cash-flow forecasts

Typically (although there are alternative presentations), a cash-flow forecast for a specified period shows:

Opening cash balance for the period

+ cash inflows (from cash sales, loans taken out, injections of owners' capital, payments by creditors for sales on credit)

− cash outflows (for cash payments for materials, labour, other variable costs, rents or leases, capital purchases, tax payments and other expenses)

= closing cash balance (= opening cash balance for the next period)

Easy to forecast (fixed or agreed)	Difficult to forecast
Owner's capital. Bank loans, property payments, capital purchases.	Cash and credit sales, labour, materials and other variable costs.

Figure 31.2 Forecasting cash flows

TERM

Cash-flow forecast: estimate of future cash inflows and outflows for a business.

31.5 Causes of cash-flow problems

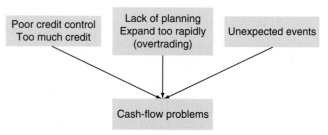

Figure 31.3 Causes of cash flow problems

Progress check B

1 What is meant by the term 'opening balance'?

2 What would happen to cash flow if a business bought its premises rather than renting them?

Progress check C

1 Explain how poor credit control can affect cash flow.

2 Give examples of unexpected events that might have an effect on the cash flow of a farm.

3 Explain how a recession might affect the cash flow of a car manufacturer.

TIP

Cash-flow forecasts do not solve cash flow problems, but they do help identify problems.

They are part of financial planning and can help prevent cash-flow problems from developing.

31.6 Improving cash flows

Progress check D

1 Explain how debt factoring could improve the cash flow of a steel manufacturer.

2 Explain why increasing credit given to customers will have an adverse effect on cash flow.

3 Explain how suppliers reducing their credit period would affect cash flow.

4 Give one reason why overtrading might cause cash-flow problems.

Method	Advantage	Disadvantage
Reduce credit terms to customers.	Immediate impact.	One-off method, will it upset customers?
Debt factoring.	Quick.	One-off, can be expensive, may send bad signals to creditors.
Delay payment to suppliers.	Immediate.	Could affect relationship with suppliers.
Sale of assets.	Could produce large cash inflows.	Are the assets needed? May take a while. Could be sold at a price lower than worth.
Sale and leaseback.	Still have use of the asset.	Loss of control? Loss of collateral. Long-term cost.
Overdraft.	Quick, easy.	Expensive, bank could withdraw facility.
Loan.	More security than an overdraft.	Increases risk to owners. Interest becomes future cash outflow.
Cut spending by finding cheaper raw materials.	Could improve profits.	Quality? How long would it take?
Cut spending by delaying capital purchases.	Reduces cash outflows.	Are the purchases needed? Would price go up?
Lease rather than buy.	No capital outlay.	Increased operating costs.
Increase sales.	Potentially quick way.	May be achieved by price reductions. Marketing costs could reduce inflows.

Table 31.1 Ways of improving cash flow

Just writing 'the firm should increase sales' does not demonstrate true understanding of the difference between sales revenue and cash flow – any extra sales would have to generate extra cash to help with a cash flow problem.

Any suggestion for increasing inflows or reducing outflows has to be thought about carefully in the context of the business. So a suggestion of 'reducing outflows by cutting staff costs' could well have a negative impact on output, sales and eventually future cash inflows.

31.7 Relationship between cash flow and working capital

Working capital and cash flow are closely related.

Cash flow describes the **flows** of cash in and out of the business. So, for example, a bank statement shows this for a bank account.

Working capital is the net **stock** of cash (and near cash) within the business for use in the day-to-day running of the business. A personal equivalent is a purse full of money able to be spent.

31.8 Managing working capital problems

Working capital too high means there is a stock of cash (and other near cash assets) tied up which the business could use more productively elsewhere.

Working capital insufficient means that the business has insufficient in its inventories of cash/near cash to meet its obligations – liquidation threatens.

Methods for managing cash flow will have an impact on working capital. So many of the solutions to cash-flow problems will also help working capital problems by:

- changing the amount of cash in the business
- changing the level of trade receivables
- changing the level of trade payables
- changing the levels of inventories
- changing the level of overdraft.

Progress check E

1   Explain the difference between working capital and cash flow.

2   Why might reducing the credit period for customers have a negative impact on the sales of a car retailer?

3   A holiday firm has excess cash at the end of the holiday season.

Give **two** examples of how this cash could be employed more effectively.

4   Give **two** disadvantages of using a debt factor for improving cash flow.

Exam-style question

Paper 2 (part question)

Enterprise Coal (EC)

Enterprise Coal (EC) has discovered huge reserves of coal in a remote region of the country. Coal has never been developed in this area before. EC is planning to develop a modern coal mine and has produced the following cash-flow forecast for this project for the next five years.

Cash-flow forecast for the coal mine project ($m)					
Year	2016	2017	2018	2019	2020
Opening balance	(10)	(90)	(95)	(85)	5
Sales of coal	0	0	20	100	X
Development costs	80	5	0	0	0
Operating costs	0	0	10	10	10
Closing balance	(90)	(95)	(85)	5	295

Table 31.2

l   a   Using the information in Table 31.2, calculate the value of X (the sales of coal in 2020). [2]

b   Comment on the usefulness to EC of this cash-flow forecast. [6]

Student's answer

l   a   Closing balance = opening balance + cash inflows − cash outflow

So +295 = +5 + X − 10 so X = 295 − 5 + 10 = $300 million

b   The cash-flow forecast shows the largest negative balance to be −$95 million. This shows, based on the assumptions used in the forecast, that the firm will have to arrange for a large amount of finance. After three years of production the firm is showing $295 million closing balance. This looks very favourable compared with the development costs of $85m. This helps the firm with the decision to go ahead with the project. However, the cash-flow forecast is only based on assumptions. It is very difficult to forecast for this type of project especially five years ahead. So although there are clear uses for the cash-flow forecast it ought to be compared with forecasts using other assumptions, most notably the price of coal which will affect the sales figures, and the development costs of a new, modern mine in a remote part of the country where coal has never been discovered before.

Authors' comments

l   a   The right answer is $300 million.

b   The student has clear understanding of cash-flow forecasts and their usefulness, and the answer uses the context effectively. A very good response.

Additional exam-style questions

Paper 1 Section A

1   Explain why it is difficult to forecast cash flows.
[3]

2   Explain why a business might have a cash-flow problem even though it is making a profit. [3]

3   Give **two** examples of cash outflows. [2]

Paper 1 Section B

4   a   Explain the importance of cash-flow forecasts to a new business. [8]

b   'You cannot solve cash-flow problems simply by selling more cars', said the MD of a car manufacturing business. Discuss. [12]

Paper 2

5   ABC taxis is hoping to get a loan from the bank for $8 000. The owner, Mike, has produced a cash-flow forecast for the first six months of his business (see Table 31.3; all figures in $):

a   Discuss the factors that the bank would take into account in deciding whether to lend $8 000 to Mike to help get the business started. [11]

b   The bank has said that it would be prepared to lend to Mike if the cash flows could be improved. Analyse **two** ways that Mike could use to achieve this. [8]

Month	1	2	3	4	5	6
Opening balance	0	(8 600)	(8 800)	(8 500)	(7 200)	(4 400)
Mike's capital	7 000	0	0	0	0	0
Sales	1 000	2 000	3 000	5 000	8 000	12 000
Capital expenditure	15 000	0	0	0	0	0
Labour	100	200	200	200	200	200
Other operating costs	500	1 000	1 500	2 500	4 000	6 000
Overheads	1 000	1 000	1 000	1 000	1 000	1 000
Closing balance	(8 600)	(8 800)	(8 500)	(7 200)	(4 400)	400

Table 31.3 Cash flow forecast

Costs

Learning summary

After you have studied this chapter you should be able to:

- [ ] understand the need for different costing methods
- [ ] understand the difference between full and contribution costing
- [ ] use costing methods to make decisions
- [ ] evaluate costing methods.

32.1 The need for different costing methods

Business managers need to know and understand costs to make a wide range of important decisions (see 29.1 Costs). Some of these decisions relate to the business as a whole, other decisions relate to part of the activities of a business often known as profit or cost centres.

TERMS

Cost centre: a section of a business, such as a department, for which costs can be identified and allocated.

Profit centre: a section of a business to which both costs and revenues can be allocated – so profit can be calculated (based on assumptions about overheads).

Although profits can only really be calculated for a business as a whole, it is useful to create cost and profit centres to provide:

- targets to work towards
- a way to monitor and control
- a method to assess performance
- a means to make decisions.

But:

- The concept of 'profit' applies to the business as a whole – many costs are overheads which are costs that apply to the whole business rather than to individual activities.
- Breaking businesses into separate 'centres' for costing purposes distorts the holistic nature of the business.
- Not all influences on a centre are within the control of the centre.

TERM

Overheads: an alternative term for indirect costs.

TIP

It is easy to confuse indirect costs (overheads) with fixed costs.

Indirect costs are costs that are shared with other parts of the business. Fixed costs may, or may not be shared. For example, a business studies teacher's salary is usually a fixed cost but it is not an indirect cost of the business studies course.

32.2 Costing methods

Decisions relating to products and profit centres can be made using a variety of costing methods.

Full costing/absorption costing

These methods attempt to allocate overheads to each individual cost or profit centre.

For a cost or profit centre:

Profit = Revenue for the centre − direct costs − allocated indirect costs

The profit for the business as a whole is the total of the profits for each individual centre.

Contribution costing

This method avoids allocation of overheads to cost or profit centres. It is sometimes known as marginal costing.

For a cost or profit centre:

Contribution = Revenue for the centre − direct costs

The profit for the business as a whole is the total of the contributions for each individual centre less the indirect costs.

Full costing versus contribution costing is shown in Fig 32.1:

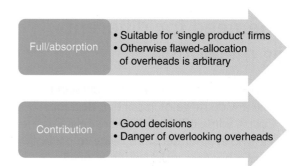

Figure 32.1 Different costing methods

Full costing	Absorption costing	Contribution costing
Allocates overheads in a simplistic, uniform way.	Allocates overheads in a more rational way.	Does not allocate overheads.
Easy to calculate and understand.	More work in allocating overheads.	*More difficult to understand as it appears to overlook overheads.*
But allocation of overheads will not reflect reality.	*But how do you decide a more rational approach? Floor space? Amount of machinery? Workforce?*	Does recognise that it is a **business** that makes a profit/loss and that a cost/profit centre makes a contribution to the overall business.
Enables 'profit' to be estimated at a detailed level in an organisation.		*Full costing better for single product firms.*
Particularly relevant to a single product business.		
Overhead costs do not risk being overlooked.		
Easy to use for pricing decisions if allocation of fixed costs is appropriate. If not, it is useless!		*Can be misleading when indirect costs (overheads) are confused with fixed costs (which are not necessarily overheads).*
But arbitrary allocation may lead to inconsistencies between cost/profit centres.		
Allocation has to be consistent over time, and may have to change if level of output changes.		

Table 32.1 Features and disadvantages of costing methods

32.3 Using contribution costing

Stop making product

Does it make a positive contribution? If so continue.

(If absorption costing were used it might show the product making a loss, but the allocated overheads would still have to be paid for by the remaining products.)

Does it make a negative contribution? If so:

- Is it an important part of a product range? Then maybe continue.
- Might there be a better future for the product? Then maybe continue.

Accept a contract or special order at below full cost/customary price

- Does it make a positive contribution?
- What might be the response of existing customers?

- Is there enough capacity to avoid adverse impact on existing products/services?
- Is a lower price consistent with brand image and other aspects of marketing?
- Is there a risk of resale into a higher price market?

If the answer to these is favourable, then accept.

Common example of special orders is producing 'own brand' products for supermarkets.

Sell a product/service at a discount to particular customers

Same process as accepting a contract.

Common examples:

- Discounted fares on trains and planes at off-peak times
- Discounted hotel room rates
- Cheaper off-peak electricity charges.

Make or buy in (outsource)

- Which makes the greater contribution?
- What would be the impact of 'buy in' on the workforce?

Exam-style question

Paper 3

iCos

iCos cosmetics have a range of products called iSkin. iSkin is a new product and little marketing has been done on it so far. It is designed to complement the range of products with one targeted at young people. The Chief Executive has been presented with cost information about the product range.

The Chief Executive responded to these figures by saying, 'These are bad results for the iSkin Junior range. I believe we should stop making this product immediately. This would increase our annual profit by $30 000.'

1 Do you agree with the Chief Executive that the company should stop producing the iSkin Junior cream? Use the quantitative data in Table 32.2, relevant calculations and qualitative data to justify your answer. [16]

2016 cost and sales figures				
	iSkin Junior	iSkin Cream A	iSkin Cream B	iSkin Cream C
Labour costs per 100 items	$40	$60	$30	$80
Material costs per 100 items	$200	$300	$100	$600
Allocated fixed factory and Head Office costs	$190 000	$250 000	$450 000	$350 000
Selling price per 100 items	$400	$500	$250	$900
Sales (boxes of 100 units)	1000	12 000	20 000	6000

Table 32.2

Student's answer

If iSkin Junior is stopped, lost revenue is $400 × 1000 = $400 000.

Direct cost savings are $(200 + 40) × 1000 = $240 000

So lost contribution would be $160 000.

The Chief Executive seems to have assumed that the allocated fixed and Head Office costs would also disappear giving the CEO's figure of a gain of $30 000. However, it is likely that these indirect costs would remain and have to be recovered by the remaining products.

I think it should not be cancelled because it makes a positive contribution and this would be lost, putting the firm in a worse position overall.

In addition, because it is a complementary product, stopping production may have an impact on other products. So, if consumers could not purchase this product, the other products in the same range may experience a fall in demand. It is also a new product

with little marketing. This suggests that if iCos spent money on informative and persuasive advertising and effective sales promotions, consumers would be more attracted to this new product. A significant increase in sales and revenue would then probably mean that an even higher contribution could be made.

So, the balances of quantitative and qualitative data suggests that the product should continue in production. I suggest that similar data is collected in 12 months' time and the future of the iSkin product could then be determined with more data to back up a final decision.

Authors' comments

In terms of quantitative information, the student has done very well, calculating contribution correctly and questioning the CEO's calculation. A good attempt is made to use the other evidence too and both quantitative and qualitative factors are used to support the overall conclusion. This is a good answer.

Additional exam-style question

Paper 3

The following information relates to the production of Midgets, one of a range of chocolate products made by Saturn.

	$ million
Revenue	440
Direct fixed costs	200
Direct labour	90
Direct materials	120
Management salaries (indirect cost)	50
Other overheads	20

Table 32.3

1 a Most of Saturn's other products make positive contributions. Advise Saturn's managers as to whether or not they should continue to make Midgets. [12]

b The directors of Saturn want Midgets to make a larger contribution towards Saturn's profits. Analyse methods that Saturn's managers could use to achieve this. [8]

Budgets

33.1 Why budgets are needed

A budget is a plan for the future, which an organisation aims to fulfil. It differs from a forecast in that a forecast is prepared based on assumptions.

Budgets are used to:

- plan
- allocate resources
- set targets
- coordinate
- monitor and control
- measure and assess performance
- improve plans.

TERMS

Budget: detailed plan for the future.

Budget holder: individual responsible for the initial setting and achievement of a budget.

Delegated budget: giving some delegated authority over the setting and achievement of budgets to junior managers.

TIP

Delegated budgeting ties in with motivational theories of Herzberg – making work more challenging and rewarding.

Progress check A

1   Explain the difference between a forecast and a budget.

2   Explain why a firm manufacturing shoes should prepare a budget.

3   Explain how a budget could be used to monitor performance in a hospital.

4   Why might a delegated budget improve motivation?

33.2 Types of budget

TERMS

Incremental budgeting: budgeting that uses last year's budget as a basis for the next year and adjustments are then made.

Zero budgeting: all budgets are set to zero and budget holders have to argue their case from a 'clean sheet'.

Flexible budgets: once set, expenses are allowed to vary as sales or production vary.

33.3 Stages in preparing budgets

Budgets are commonly prepared as follows:

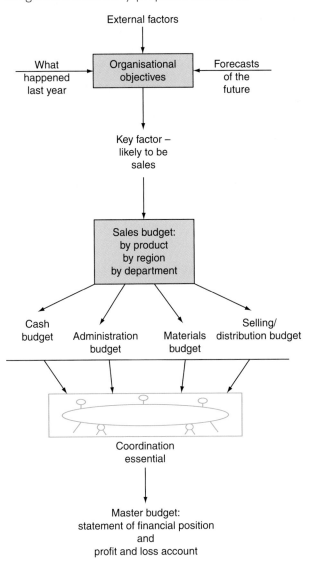

Figure 33.1 Preparing a budget

33.4 Benefits and drawbacks of using budgets

Benefits	Drawbacks
Provide a means of controlling income/expenditure.	May lack flexibility.
Allow for review of performance.	Focused on short term.
Clarifies responsibilities.	May lead to unnecessary spending.
Allow for delegation of financial responsibilities.	May require significant training.
Increase capital efficiency.	Difficult for new situations.
Help coordination between departments.	
Provide clear targets.	

Table 33.1 Benefits and drawbacks of budgets

TIP

Remember budgets are plans, not forecasts, although they may be based on, for example, sales forecasts. Budgets are targets for departments and people in the organisation.

33.5 Budgetary control – variance analysis

Variance analysis:

- measures differences between actual values and outcomes
- helps explain why the outcome is different from the plan
- helps in setting future budgets.

TERMS

Variance: the difference between a planned value and the actual outcome.

Progress check B

1   Explain **three** advantages to a new business of setting budgets.

2   Explain the benefits of setting financial targets to the manager of a supermarket.

3   Why might there be a need for training in a school for knowing how to produce and use budgets?

4   Why might setting a spending budget lead to more spending than necessary in a large organisation?

Favourable variance: the difference between actual and budget value that leads to a higher than expected profit, for example, sales are higher than budgeted or costs are lower.

Adverse variance: the difference between actual and budget value that leads to a lower than expected profit for a business, for example, lower sales or higher costs.

Progress check C

1   Distinguish between 'favourable' and 'adverse' variances in relation to costs.

2   Distinguish between 'favourable' and 'adverse' variances in relation to revenues.

3   Give one benefit of variance analysis.

4   How would knowing about variances help the manager of a hotel?

Exam-style question

Paper 3

Media International (MI)

MI produces and publishes a range of newspapers and magazines. Some titles have been doing well while others have struggled against competition. The following cost data has been collected.

1   Using the information in Table 33.2, analyse how, MI could use variance analysis to make decisions about its products.   [10]

Product	Budget ($)	Actual ($)	Variance ($)		Price relative to competitors
A	120 000	95 000	−25 000	Adverse	Very High
B	76 000	80 000	+4 000	Favourable	Same
C	55 000	56 000	+1 000	Favourable	Same
D	1 000	2 000	+1 000	Favourable	High
E	50 000	60 000	+10 000	Favourable	Low
F	100 000	110 000	+10 000	Favourable	Same
G	60 000	57 000	−3 000	Adverse	High

Sales Information for MI's publications

Table 33.2

Student's answer

The two products of immediate concern are the two with negative sales variances, products A and G. It is noticeable that both products have relatively high prices. It is also noticeable that the variance for product G is small, both relative to the sales and to product A. Product A has very high prices.

It is also notable that all the products that have positive variances have prices similar or lower than competitors except product D.

This strongly suggests that an important issue in determining the sales is the price of the magazine, which might be expected.

It may be that A and G have higher production costs, or simply that the price has been set too high. In either case, the business could take policy decisions to make the situation less adverse.

Product D behaves completely differently to the others and suggests a new product at its introductory stage which has done better than originally budgeted. It will be important to monitor this product to see if the positive outlook for the product continues.

At this stage there is no evidence to suggest stopping the production of any particular product but it would be useful to explore further pricing decisions for products A and G with particular emphasis on product A.

Authors' comments

The student clearly understands the concepts of favourable and adverse variances. The information has been used and analysed effectively. The answer demonstrates the usefulness of variance analysis in decision making.

Additional exam-style questions

Paper 3 (shortened case studies)

Paramount Café (PC)

The owners of the PC are concerned with the financial performance of their business. Having set a budget six months ago they are in a position to undertake variance analysis:

	Budget ($)	Actual ($)
Food sales	50 000	55 000
Other sales	4 000	3 000
Wages	16 000	20 000
Other variable costs	8 000	10 000
Overheads	9 000	12 000
Profit	21 000	16 000

Table 33.3

1 a Evaluate the usefulness of variance analysis to the owners of the PC. Your answer should include the calculation of adverse and favourable variances. [14]

b Discuss **two** possible ways in which the managers of PC could improve the performance of the business. [10]

Academy School (AS)

2 The AS is in the private sector. It charges fees to its students. The owners of the school aim to make a profit each year. The school has its budget set by the owners each year. They do not consult with the school's senior managers. The budget is set for the whole school. The headteacher wants to persuade the owners to set budgets for each individual department so that they operate more like profit centres.

Discuss the arguments the headteacher could use to encourage the owners to set departmental budgets. [16]

Chapter 34

Contents of published accounts

Learning summary

After you have studied this chapter you should be able to:

- ■ know why accounts are amended

- ■ understand the impact of key amendments on the income statement and the statement of financial position

- ■ explain the relationship between items on the income statement and the statement of financial position

- ■ understand the difficulties of valuing inventory

- ■ explain the role of depreciation in accounts

- ■ analyse the impact of depreciation on the income statement and the statement of financial position.

34.1 Why accounts are amended

Accounts often need amendment:

- New/revised data becomes available.
- Accounts are needed for a different time period.

Progress check A

I   Why is it important to start with the accounts for the end of the current year when producing accounts for next year?

34.2 Some key amendments to accounts and their interrelationships

Table 34.1 indicates the main ways in which the accounts are inter-related.

Cause	Impact on statement of financial position	Double entry
Sale of inventories for cash.	Inventories fall.	Cash increases (statement of financial position).
Creditors ask for early payment.	Accounts payable decreases.	Cash decreases (statement of financial position).
Additional shares sold and capital raised is used to buy property.	Share capital rises.	Fixed assets rise (statement of financial position).
Equipment depreciated.	Fixed assets fall.	Profits fall (income statement) and so shareholder equity (retained profits) falls (Statement of financial position).
Assets bought in part with a loan and in part with cash.	Assets increase (could be current or long term depending on nature of the asset).	In the statement of financial position, liabilities would increase by the extent of the loan and cash would decrease by the remainder amount.

Table 34.1 Common amendments to accounts

34.3 Problems valuing inventories

If an oil company bought a ship load of crude oil in October 2015 it may have paid $50 per barrel for the crude oil. In a very large crude oil tanker this would have cost about $50 million. By the middle of January 2016, three months later, the oil price had fallen to $25 per barrel meaning the oil from the tanker could only be resold for $25 million.

Should the inventory of oil in the tanker be valued at $50 million, $25 million or something else?

The principles governing accounts require the inventories to be neither under- or over-stated. This is usually achieved through use of either historical cost (cost when bought) or net realisable value, whichever is the smaller.

TERM

Net realisable value: the amount for which an asset (usually an inventory) can be sold minus the cost of selling it. It is only used on statement of financial position when NRV is estimated to be below the cost of purchase of the asset.

Progress check B

1. Explain why depreciation has an impact on shareholders' equity for an incorporated business.

2. Why does an increase in depreciation have an impact on the income statement?

3. A business buys a new lorry with a loan. The useful life is three years. Explain the impact of this event on the accounts of the business over the three years.

34.4 The role of depreciation

Most capital items such as machinery or vehicles have a limited life after which they have to be replaced. A business needs to reflect in the accounts that the asset is worth less each year and that provision is made for its replacement. This means reducing the value of the asset in the statement of financial position and reducing the profit of the business by the same amount recognising the need to provide for the eventual replacement of the asset.

34.5 Methods of depreciation

There are several methods of depreciation but at A Level you only need to consider straight line depreciation.

Straight line depreciation

In this method an asset is depreciated in equal amounts each year over its useful life.

Each year of the asset's life it is depreciated by an amount equal to:

$$\frac{\text{Original cost of asset} - \text{Expected residual value}}{\text{Expected useful life of asset (years)}}$$

Next year's net book value of asset = Current year's net book value of asset − Depreciation

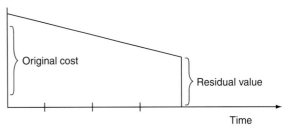

Figure 34.1 The impact of straight line depreciation

Depreciation of an asset has an impact on profit and value of assets but not on cash.

TERMS

Depreciation: the decline in the estimated value of a non-current asset over time.

Straight line depreciation: a constant amount of depreciation is subtracted from the value of the asset each year.

Net book value: the current statement of financial position value of a non-current asset = original cost − accumulated depreciation.

TIP

Other methods of depreciation are not tested by Cambridge.

Progress check C

1 Explain why fixed assets need to be depreciated.

2 Explain the difference between the useful life of an asset and its actual life.

3 Why does the process of depreciation lead to recorded profits being lower?

4 Explain why the amount paid for a new factory does not appear as an expense in the year that it is paid for.

5 A lorry cost $30 000 and is expected to last five years. After this its residual value is estimated to be $5 000. Using straight line depreciation, what is the annual depreciation of the lorry?

Exam-style question

Paper 3 (brief case study)

A business buys a piece of machinery for $70 000. The machinery is estimated to have a useful life of four years – after which it can be sold for $10 000.

1 a Calculate the annual depreciation charge using straight line depreciation. [2]

   b How much will the asset be worth after three years? [2]

   c What would happen to the accounts if the firm decided that the useful life was only three years, but with the same residual value? [6]

   d Explain the impact on the business's cash flow of changing the useful life. [2]

Student's answer

1 a The machine will depreciate by $60 000 over four years which is $15 000 per year.

   b After three years the asset will be worth $70k – $45k = $25k

   c If the firm decided the useful life was only three years, then annual depreciation would increase from $15 000 per year to $20 000 per year. The value of the asset in the statement of financial position would decrease by $5 000 a year more and reach $10 000 in three years. Correspondingly net profits would fall more quickly meaning $5 000 less each year would be put into reserves. So net profit would be lower, but the statement of financial position would still balance.

   d Depreciation is not a cash payment so there is no impact on cash flow.

Authors' comments

The student clearly understands depreciation and has given an excellent explanation, with correct calculations, of its impact on all parts of the accounts of the firm.

Additional exam-style questions

1 A supermarket business values its inventories of items for sale at cost price, its equipment is depreciated over two years and its buildings valued at market prices. Analyse the impact on its accounts of valuing assets in these ways. [10]

2 Discuss the view that because some assets are difficult to value the published accounts of a business are of limited use to stakeholders. [14]

Analysis of published accounts

Learning summary

After you have studied this chapter you should be able to:

- ■ calculate and interpret profitability ratios
- ■ calculate and interpret financial efficiency ratios
- ■ calculate and interpret the gearing ratio

- ■ calculate and interpret investor ratios
- ■ use ratio analysis to improve business performance
- ■ assess the practical uses and limitations of ratios.

35.1 Types of ratio

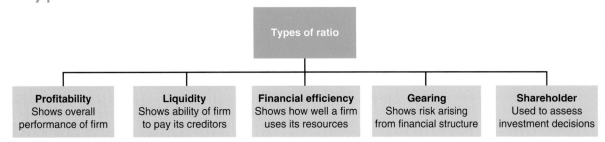

Figure 35.1 Classification of accounting ratios

The additional profitability ratio is:

$$\text{Return on capital employed (ROCE)} = \frac{\text{Operating profit}}{\text{Capital employed}} \times 100\%$$

Other profitability ratios and the liquidity ratios are discussed in Chapter 30.

35.2 Efficiency ratios

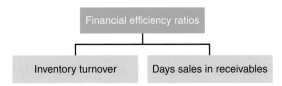

Figure 35.2 Financial efficiency ratios

These ratios are usually used when liquidity ratios have identified potential liquidity problems. Efficiency ratios help to determine the precise nature of the problem.

Financial efficiency ratios: used to assess the firm's ability to manage its current assets.

Days purchases in payables can also be calculated to explore the ability of a business to pay its suppliers.

Ratio	Formula	Interpretation	Comments	Methods to improve
Inventory turnover	$$\frac{\text{Cost of goods sold in time period}}{\text{Value of inventories}}$$	Unit: the number of times stock turns over.	Highly industry dependent. Reducing stock may impact on sales/customers. Days sales in stock sometimes used.	Improve stock control.
Days sales in receivables	$$\frac{\text{Accounts receivable} \times 365}{\text{Sales turnover}}$$	Too high then accounts receivable may not be managed well. Too low then customers might want more credit. Unit: days.	Varies for business to business and industry to industry.	Shorter credit terms. Improve credit control.

Table 35.1 Efficiency ratios

35.3 Gearing ratio

Financial gearing: used to measure risk associated with financing the business.

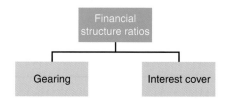

Figure 35.3 Financial structure ratios

Ratio	Formula	Interpretation	Comments	Methods to improve
Gearing ratio	$$\frac{\text{Long-term loans} \times 100}{\text{Capital employed}}$$ **Note:** There are several versions of the gearing ratio.	Over 50% = highly geared (relies more on loans than share capital). The higher the ratio, the higher the risk to investors. Low = safe and unambitious.	Owners' attitude to risk is fundamental.	Can be reduced by issuing more shares, or paying back loans.
Interest cover	$$\frac{\text{Operating profit}}{\text{Annual interest paid}}$$	The higher the ratio, the lower the risk to investors.		Reduce dependency on long-term loans. (Decrease gearing).

Table 35.2 Gearing and interest cover ratios

35.4 Investor ratios

Investor ratios: usually used by investors to assess the suitability of the firm for investment.

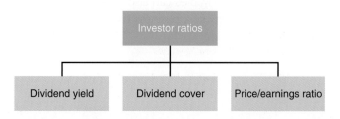

Figure 35.4 Investor ratios

Ratio	Formula	Interpretation	Comments	Methods to improve
Dividend yield	$\dfrac{\text{Dividend per share} \times 100}{\text{Current share price}}$	Can be used to compare with other investments, and interest rates. Trend is important. Unit: %	Highly dependent on: • volatility of market • company's dividend policy.	Day-to-day dividend management not possible. Could be managed with dividend policy but unlikely.
Dividend cover	$\dfrac{\text{Profit after tax and interest}}{\text{Annual dividends}}$	Compare with previous years to establish trend.	The higher the dividend cover, the more likely the firm is to be able to retain profits for investments.	Reduce dividends.
Price/earnings ratio	$\dfrac{\text{Current share price}}{\text{Earnings per share}}$	Compare with other similar businesses.	Could be influenced by general market movements, not related to the company.	Increase earnings per share.

Table 35.3 Investor ratios

Progress check A

1　Explain to a manager of a shoe shop what the liquidity ratios tell him about the business.

2　Why might a supermarket be able to do well with a very low current ratio?

3　How might the manager of a restaurant improve its profitability ratios?

4　Why would a bank be concerned if one of its business customers had a very high gearing ratio?

5　Last year Company A had a very low price/earnings ratio. There are rumours that it might be taken over by a competitor which has pushed the share price up. What would you expect to happen to the price/earnings ratio? Why?

35.5 Uses of ratios

Accounts are very detailed documents. Business decision makers want quick and easy ways of getting a 'picture' of the main financial features of a business. Ratios will tell them about:

• how good the business is at generating profits
• how effective the business is at managing its working capital
• how sound the business is going to be as a potential investment (both to potential shareholders and lenders)
• how risky the business is with regards to its financial structure.

The use of ratios, together with assessing trends, help in answering these issues. Strategies for improving ratios are included in the above tables.

Progress check B

(Also refer back to Chapter 31.)

1　Why might the owners of a car manufacturer want to analyse the accounts of a competitor?

2　How would ratios help the owners analyse the financial position of their competitor?

3　Give reasons why the accounts of a business are difficult to interpret.

4　How do ratios help people who are interested in the financial situation of a business?

35.6 Limitations of ratio analysis

- Accounts are historical. Forecast accounts are based on the past. The future may well be different from the past.
- Ratios cannot be looked at in isolation. Trends over time and within the industry need to be investigated.
- Firms in differing industries may well have very different 'acceptable' ratios.
- External events, for example, a recession, can have a significant effect on ratios.
- There is a range of different formulae for some ratios.
- Accounts can, within limits, be adjusted to make some ratios look favourable (window dressing).
- Accounts only contain items that can have a numerical value.
- Ratios can highlight potential problems but not solve them.v

Progress check C

1 The following is an extract from the published accounts of a car manufacturer.

$m	Year ending December 2015	Year ending December 2016
Revenue	800	700
Gross profit	100	70
Net operating profit	30	20
Inventories	60	80
Accounts receivable	40	30
Current assets	120	130
Current liabilities	80	130
Non-current liabilities	100	120
Capital employed	400	400
Number of shares issued	80m	85m
Share price at year end	$6.00	$3.00

Table 35.4

a Calculate the gross profit margin, net profit margin and return on capital employed for each year. Comment on the trend in the business's profitability.

b Calculate the current ratio, the acid test ratio, days sales in receivables and stock turnover ratio. Comment on the trend in the business's liquidity.

c Calculate the gearing ratio. Comment on the usefulness of this ratio to a potential lender to the business.

d Calculate the price/earnings ratios.

2 Explain how an increasing gearing ratio in a business affects the risk to a lender to the business.

3 Explain, with examples, why ratio results are often industry dependent.

4 How might having a sale to reduce inventories affect the current ratio?

Exam-style question

Paper 3

Sheila's Fashions (SF)

The Board at SF are anxious about the next AGM of shareholders. There has been considerable speculation in the financial press that investors, particularly large shareholders, are going to be critical of the company's performance. At the last AGM of this public limited company, many shareholders were disappointed with the falling profits. They were worried about the proposal to reduce dividends and the impact this could have on the share price of the company. Two of

SF's shops have recently been sold and leased back to improve liquidity and some suppliers are being kept waiting an additional two weeks for payment.

The decision to cut retail prices last year by five per cent on average had helped sales volume in the short term – but with the result of reducing profit. Because of relatively high unit costs, Sheila, the Managing Director, believes that the only way forward is through rapid expansion to reduce unit costs. The Board will be presented with the following financial information:

	2016	2017
Total dividends	$70m (paid)	$60.2m (proposed)
Dividend per share	$0.50 (paid)	$0.43 (proposed)
SF's share price at end of year	$5.00	$3.50
Operating profit	$200m	$150m
Capital employed	$1 000m	$990m
Retained profits	$45m	$15m

Table 35.5 Financial data on SF financial year ending 31st May

1 a Using data in Appendix A, calculate for **both** financial years 2016 and 2017:

   i the return on capital employed [3]

   ii the dividend yield. [3]

  b Discuss two ways in which SF's directors could improve the financial performance of the business, as measured by ratio analysis. [14]

Student's answer

1 a i 2016 = 20%   2017 = 15.2%

   ii 2016 = 10%   2017 = 12.3%

  b The dividend yield is up because of a fall in

share price – this is not necessarily a good sign and shareholders would prefer to see a higher dividend yield and a higher share price. The risk is that the share price could fall further if dividends are reduced again.

The ROCE results suggests that performance of business has declined. Perhaps this is the result of lower prices which have squeezed profitability. The question is: do directors want to reflect this decline in profitability in dividends or do they want to keep shareholders happy in the short term hoping that performance will soon improve?

With lower dividend payments, retained profit will increase and the liquidity of the business will also improve. If these funds are wisely invested, then future profitability is likely to increase. However, it could be that Sheila's plans are too ambitious in a difficult market.

If the dividend yield remained at ten per cent, i.e. $0.35 then SF would retain an extra $11.2m.

The final decision on dividends might depend on how important it is to stop shareholders taking drastic action at the next AGM. It is important that they are discouraged from selling shares as this will depress the share price and make the future use of additional share capital much less feasible. In the light of difficult trading conditions, it may be better to keep shareholders happy than expand using the funds kept in the business from a dividend reduction.

Authors' comments

The student uses all of the calculated ratios to build up effectively a picture of the present financial position of the firm. The student has also recognised the key attitudes of shareholders as well as the current economic situation of the firm. The student proceeded to make a judgement which is supported by earlier analysis.

This is a well balanced answer with a supported conclusion.

Additional exam-style questions

Paper 3

1 Discuss the usefulness of ratio analysis to any two stakeholder groups of SF apart from shareholders. [14]

2 Discuss the idea that a high level of gearing is not advisable. [14]

Investment appraisal

36.1 Investment

Investment is spending money now with the hope of an improved return in the future. In this context it could be spending on new machinery, new factories, major marketing campaigns and so on. Investment appraisal provides the tools for assessing such decisions.

> **TERM**
>
> Investment appraisal: evaluating the profitability or desirability of an investment project.

36.2 Factors involved in investment decisions

A key issue is that of risk. The essence of an investment is that it is planned to bring in future returns. Inevitably the future is uncertain as a result of both factors beyond the control of a business (e.g. competitors' behaviour) or within the control of the business (such as unexpected delays). Investment appraisal compares the forecasted net cash flows of an investment project with the original investment. However, uncertainty does not rule out investment appraisal techniques – 'what if' analysis' can explore the impact of a range of uncertain outcomes.

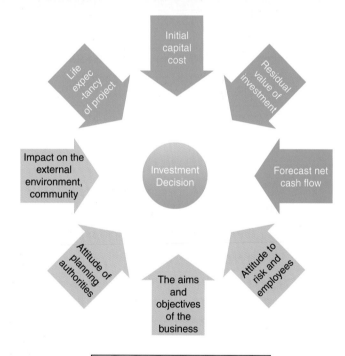

| Dark green arrow: | Quantitative factors |
| Light green arrow: | Qualitative factors |

Figure 36.1 Factors that influence an investment decision

> **TERM**
>
> Forecasted net cash flows: forecasted cash inflows less forecasted cash outflows directly related to a particular project.

Progress check A

1 Is spending money on staff uniforms an investment? Explain your answer.

2 Give **three** examples of likely investments by a software company.

3 Explain the term 'annual net cash flow' in the context of a new piece of machinery.

4 Explain why actual annual net cash flows for a new oil refinery might be different from those forecast.

36.3 Investment appraisal: payback and accounting rate of return (ARR)

TERMS

Accounting rate of return (ARR): measures the profitability of an investment as a percentage of the initial investment (see table for formula).

Payback: length of time it takes for the net cash inflows to pay back the original cost of the investment.

Criterion rate: the minimum rate set by management for investment appraisal results for a project to be accepted.

Method	How calculated	Advantages	Disadvantages
Payback	Length of time it takes for the net cash inflows to pay back the original capital cost of the investment.	• Easy to compare projects. • Will want short payback if borrowing for project, maybe less than criterion level. • Short payback reduces opportunity cost. • Long payback increases uncertainty, risk. • Quick, easy to calculate, understand. • Widely used.	• No discounting of the future. • Simplistic. • Disregards cash flow beyond payback period (focuses on short term rather than long term).
Accounting rate of return (ARR) – sometimes known as average rate of return.	$P/C \times 100$ where P is annual average net cash flow of project and C is capital cost of project.	• Compare with ARR of other projects, prevailing interest rates. • Some businesses set a minimum acceptable rate for projects, the criterion rate. • It focuses on overall net cash flow. • Easily understood, relatively easily calculated and compared to criterion rate.	• Ignores timing of cash flows. • Includes cash flows from towards the end of the life of the project – more uncertainty. • No discounting of the future.

Table 36.1 Payback versus ARR

36.4 Discounting the future

There is always an opportunity cost in investing in a project. This is reflected in the discount rate.

The following are reasons for discounting the future:

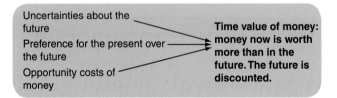

Figure 36.2 Reasons for discounting

36.5 Net present value (NPV) and discounted payback

> **TERMS**
>
> Net present value: Today's value of the estimated net cash flows resulting from an investment.
>
> Discounted payback: Uses the same method as payback but the cash-flow forecasts are discounted. Little used method.

How to discount the future is shown as follows:

Figure 36.3 Calculating NPV

Net present value

Advantages	Disadvantages
It considers both size and timing of cash flows.	Some managers find it difficult to understand.
Discount rates can be chosen for different economic circumstances.	Depends on choice of discount rate. What should it be?
It considers the time value of money which includes an element of risk.	May be difficult comparing projects with different capital costs.

Table 36.2 Advantages and disadvantages of net present value

Progress check D

1 Explain what a positive net present value means.

2 A project lasts five years. In a cash-flow forecast, a business has been optimistic about the residual value of an investment at the end of the five-year period. Explain the impact on net present value if a more realistic forecast is used.

3 The future for the retail sector has become less predictable due to long-term economic conditions. Should the discount rate for a retail business increase? Explain your answer.

4 Why might a business use a criterion rate rather than the prevailing interest rate?

Discounted payback

Similar to payback but instead of using cash flows the calculation uses discounted cash flows. This method recognises that cash flow may overstate future benefits of a project because of the time value of money.

36.6 Internal rate of return (IRR)

An NPV of zero indicates the point of indifference:

Greater than zero: the project is worth considering.

Less than zero: the project is not worth considering.

The discount rate that gives a zero NPV for a project is known as internal rate of return (IRR).

The question then becomes 'Is the IRR acceptable to the business?' You will not be required to calculate IRR.

Advantages	Disadvantages
The IRR can easily be compared with prevailing interest rates or the criterion rate.	The calculation is more complex than other methods.
It avoids the need to choose an actual discount rate.	It is more difficult to understand.
It is easy to compare different projects.	It might give a false sense of precision – other factors are involved in the decision.

Table 36.3 Advantages and disadvantages of IRR

TERM

Internal rate of return: the rate of discount that gives a net present value of zero – the higher the IRR the more profitable the investment.

Progress check E

1 Project A has an IRR of ten per cent while project B has an IRR of 20 per cent. All other things being equal, which project would you chose? Explain your reason.

2 What would happen to the IRR for a project if all future net cash flows for a project were projected to increase?

36.7 Limitations of investment appraisal

- Numerical methods only consider 'measurable' features of a decision. There are other important factors to consider.
- Calculations are only as reliable as the data used. Forecasts can only be, at best, opinions about the future.
- Each method has its own shortcomings. Results between methods may give contradictory messages.
- Risks are difficult to assess and attitudes to risk can vary considerably both within an organisation and between organisations.

TIP

Unless the question only asks for calculations, it is important to consider the non-numerical features of an investment decision as well as the strengths and weaknesses of any technique you use. Of particular importance is to recognise which aspects of forecasts are critical to the decision and how different assumptions about these might affect the decision.

Progress check F

1 Explain how the views of a local community might affect an investment decision.

2 Explain why qualitative factors might influence the decision of a newspaper to replace its printed version with an online version.

3 What qualitative factors would be involved in the decision to replace software in a retail outlet?

Exam-style question

Paper 3

GGJ Perfumes

New factory location could reduce costs

GGJ has always manufactured its products in Country P. However, wage rates and land prices are at least 50 per cent higher than in Countries R and S. The directors plan to establish a new factory abroad to manufacture products under the 'Lavender Fragrance' brand. This would lead to the closure of one of the two existing factories in Country P. The Operations Director had produced a report about two possible factory sites – one in Country R and one in Country S. Here is some of his report.

* The employment laws in Country R are the same as in Country P.
* Country R is in a large free-trade area with many other countries and is a well-known tourist destination.
* The opportunities for joint ventures and accepting sub-contracted work are likely to be higher in Country S due to the huge perfume industry already based there. This would offer opportunities for economies of scale.
* The initial investment in Country R for the factory capacity required would be at least $3.5m, based on a five-year lease of the property.

The expected cash inflows from the Country R location over this time period are forecast to be ($m)

	Year 1	Year 2	Year 3	Year 4	Year 5
Expected cash inflows	2.5	2.5	3.0	4.0	6.0

Table 36.4

* Cash outgoings are expected to be 50 per cent of cash inflows in any one year.

Results for Country S are

ARR	Payback	NPV	Capital cost
40%	3 years	$3.6m	$8m

Table 36.5

1 a Calculate for the Country R location:

    i Average rate of return (ARR) [3]

    ii Payback period [3]

    iii Net present value (NPV) at ten per cent discount rate. [4]

  b Using your results from part (a), data in Table 36.5 and other information, recommend the country in which GGJ Perfumes should locate its new factory. [14]

Student's answer

1 a i Net cash inflows are only half of the cash inflows in the table because cash outflows are half of the cash inflows. So net cash inflow = $9 m, total net cash flow = $5.5 m. ARR = ($5.5 m/5)/$3.5 m × 100 = 31.4%.

ii Payback: in the first two years there is a net inflow of $2.5 m, so there is a need for a further net $1 m to make up $3.5 m. That can be earned in two-thirds of the third year. So payback = 2 years 8 months.

iii

Year	Cash flow ($m)	Discount factor	Discounted cash flow ($m)
0	(3.5)	1	(3.5)
1	1.25	0.91	1.1375
2	1.25	0.83	1.0375
3	1.5	0.75	1.125
4	2	0.68	1.36
5	3	0.62	1.86
			NPV = 3.02

Table 36.6

b This is an important strategic decision which will be difficult to reverse. It is very important that GGJ make the right decisions. Country R has lower capital cost and quicker payback, which is important for this business with falling profits, although no actual evidence for falling profit is given. Lower ARR for the Country R location is a worry for GGJ, however it is still high, as is required with quite a high risk venture into a foreign country.

Country S offers a higher ARR with potential for further profits from economies of scale in future. The higher capital cost could be a problem for GGJ, if profit is falling but government grants are available. It would be useful to know how large these are and for how many years they are offered.

Qualitative factors are also important in location decisions. Which location represents more of a culture shock? Are managers prepared to move to either location? Answers to these and other non-numerical questions would influence the final decision. Country R might be more attractive to managers if tourists find it appealing. Language and distance problems need to be considered but, again, not enough information is provided. The huge perfume industry in Country S could give cheap components. However, Country R will ensure no trade restrictions, unlike Country S location, and this will be important if GGJ plans to export a higher proportion of 'Lavender Fragrance'.

The final decision would have been made more accurate if more information had been provided, for example, the estimated unit costs in each location.

Based on my results and the other data, I would recommend Country R because of the key issue of falling profits at GGJ and higher capital cost in Country S which makes financing more difficult.

Authors' comments

1 a The student obtained the correct answers and it is pleasing that they showed their workings. This is important in case they make a mistake.

b The student answers this in a very logical way with sound analysis of some of the factors relevant to each site. There is a clear and supported decision – an excellent answer.

Additional exam-style questions

Paper 3

1   Evaluate the likely limitations of the investment appraisal used by GGJ Perfumes.   [12]

2   Cheery Chocolates is currently losing market share to its main rivals. The directors of Cheery Chocolates believe that a new marketing campaign is needed. This would cost five per cent of turnover for the next three years. Discuss the factors, other than the results of an investment appraisal calculation, that the directors would need to consider.   [12]

Unit 6
STRATEGIC MANAGEMENT

What is strategic management?

37.1 What is meant by 'corporate strategy'?

A strategy is a 'way of achieving an objective'. The importance of corporate aims and objectives was revised in Chapter 4. This chapter assesses the meaning and importance of corporate strategies.

> **TERM**
>
> Corporate strategy: a long-term plan of action for the whole organisation aimed at achieving a particular corporate objective.

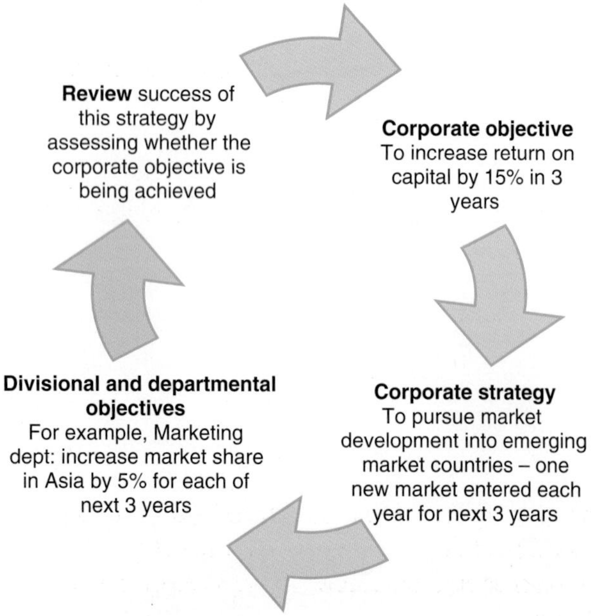

Review success of this strategy by assessing whether the corporate objective is being achieved

Corporate objective
To increase return on capital by 15% in 3 years

Corporate strategy
To pursue market development into emerging market countries – one new market entered each year for next 3 years

Divisional and departmental objectives
For example, Marketing dept: increase market share in Asia by 5% for each of next 3 years

Figure 37.1 The corporate strategy cycle

Influences on strategy formation

Corporate strategic decisions are influenced by:

1 Corporate objectives (see Chapter 4).

2 Resources available – a small business may not have the finance or skilled management required to develop a high-technology product.

3 Competitive environment – are competitors innovative? Are they entering new markets? Are they cutting costs to be more competitive? A business is likely to respond to each of these situations with a different strategy of its own.

4 Strengths of the business – focusing on existing strengths to develop new strategies is likely to be more successful than trying to develop new strengths.

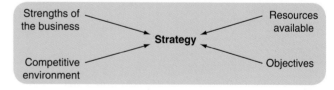

Figure 37.2 Factors influencing corporate strategy

37.2 Strategy and tactics – what are the differences?

> **TERM**
>
> Tactical decision: short-term decisions aimed at meeting a specific part of the overall strategy.

The key differences between strategic decisions and tactical decisions are shown in Table 37.1.

	Strategic decisions	Tactical decisions
Time period	Long term	Short term
Resources required	Many (usually)	Few (usually)
Taken by	Directors/senior managers	Middle/junior managers
Reversing the decision, for example, if it is a bad one	Difficult	Relatively easy
Impact usually on	Whole organisation	One department

Table 37.1 Differences between strategic decisions and tactical decisions

Progress check A

1 'We intend to improve returns to our shareholders over a five-year period'. Quote from a company CEO.

    Is this an objective or a strategy? Explain your answer.

2 'We will focus on research and development of new products to create more consumer interest'. Quote from a company CEO.

    Is this an objective or a strategy? Explain your answer.

3 'Our aim is to penetrate the markets we are in to gain further market share'. Quote from a company CEO.

    Outline one strategy that the business might adopt to achieve this objective.

4 Outline the difference between a marketing strategy for the launch of a new product and the marketing tactics that might be used to apply the strategy.

5 'The furniture company today announced that it will offer three special discount deals for customers as well as a trial of a new colour material for its dining chairs.' Quote from a newspaper article.

    Are these tactical or strategic decisions? Explain your answer.

37.3 The need for strategic management

TERM

Strategic management: the role of management when setting long-term goals, taking and implementing strategic decisions that should enable a business to reach these goals.

Senior management in any business needs to develop strategies for the future.

Each stage of strategic management brings benefits to the organisation (see Table 37.2).

Stage of strategic management	Benefit
Analysing current position of business – strategic analysis (Chapter 38)	Helps in the process of making appropriate decisions – identifies strategic opportunities.
Setting appropriate objectives (Chapter 4)	To give the business focus and direction.
Taking the appropriate strategic decision(s) (Chapter 39)	Effective decision making should choose the 'best' option for the business.
Implementing the decision(s) (Chapter 40)	Integrating and coordinating departments, allocating sufficient resources – should increase chances of strategic decision being successful.
Evaluating success of decision(s) against the pre-set objectives	Have the objectives been met? If not, another decision may be necessary.

Table 37.2 Benefits of strategic management

37.4 How strategy can influence organisational structure?

Chandler considers that 'structure follows strategy'. This means that the organisational structure of a company should be based on the strategies it is following.

You might want to revise organisational structure again – refer to Chapter 14. Three clear examples of how organisational structure depends on strategies being followed are outlined in Table 37.3.

Strategy	Impact on organisational structure
Rationalisation (for example, cost cutting to gain competitive advantage).	Delayer the organisational structure. By removing layers of 'middle managers', overhead costs can be reduced and communication improved.
Market development – expansion into other countries' markets.	Geographical divisions with considerable decentralisation; for example, S.E. Asia, USA, Europe, Rest of World. Locally-made decisions may be more effective than centralised decisions.
Expansion into different product areas.	Divisional structure so that each range of products has its own divisional head and becomes a profit centre of the business.

Table 37.3 'Structure follows strategy'

If organisational structure does not 'follow strategy' then the wrong structure may be used, possibly leading to:

• higher overhead costs
• no separate and accountable profit centres
• centralised decision making when decentralisation might be better.

Progress check B

1 Why do you think it is important for a manager to follow the stages of strategic management when developing a range of new products?

2 Why do you think it is important to implement an important strategic decision carefully?

3 Why is it important to review the impact of a strategic decision against the original corporate objective?

37.5 Competitive advantage – what is it and how to achieve it?

Competitive advantage means that a business has a clear benefit over its rivals – increasing the chances of sales and profits growth.

Michael Porter states that competitive advantage can be gained in one of two ways and that this decision is a central component in a firm's competitive strategy:

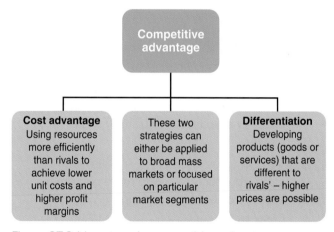

Figure 37.3 How to gain competitive advantage

Progress check C

1 Outline how a computer manufacturing company's decision to attempt to become the lowest-cost producer in the industry might impact on its organisational structure.

2 Why might it be an advantage to create a decentralised organisational structure when a company starts operating in more than one country?

3 Explain, with business examples, the difference between the two approaches to competitive advantage: cost advantage and differentiation advantage.

Exam-style question

Paper 3 Section B (which also assumes knowledge of Chapters 38–40)

Read the case study at the end of Chapter 9 (TeePrint).

Additional case study material:

Several months after this decision was taken, a major multinational clothing business announced plans to open a large factory in Country A. It intends to sell the clothes it produces in its own retail shops in both Country A and in other countries. This business will mean greatly increased competition for TeePrint and Ahmed and the other directors plan to respond with strategies that will establish a competitive advantage for the company.

1 a Analyse why competitive advantage is important to TeePrint. [10]

 b Evaluate the importance of strategic management to TeePrint as it attempts to establish a competitive advantage. [20]

Student's answer to 1(b)

Strategic management means setting long-term objectives and deciding on strategies that should best meet these objectives. Ahmed aims to keep the business competitive – in a world which is growing increasingly competitive because of globalisation. He will be able to measure the success of his attempts to achieve this aim in future years by measuring sales success against other similar businesses in the markets that TeePrint operates in. If sales of TeePrint continue to grow, and particularly if it gains market share, then it is likely that the objective of 'competitiveness' will have been achieved.

TeePrint has, according to Porter, two main ways of achieving or maintaining competitive advantage. It can either try to reduce costs to some of the lowest in the industry and use this low-cost base to drive prices below those of rivals. Alternatively, it can try to differentiate its products sufficiently to allow higher prices to be charged as consumers are prepared to pay to buy this 'difference'. Both of these strategies require effective management to be successful.

The global clothing industry is very competitive with many businesses offering very low prices with products made in the lowest-cost countries in the world. Some use very unethical practices to obtain low costs – such as using suppliers who pay little attention to health or safety or employment laws, for example, often employing school age children.

Other businesses – such as Burberry – have a well-established brand name for style and quality and emphasise the differences between their clothes and those of rivals. High prices lead to high profit margins – which can be a very profitable strategy but one which will be at a serious disadvantage during an economic recession due to the high income elasticity of demand for these branded products.

Ahmed needs to undertake strategic analysis to research TeePrint's own internal environment (SWOT) and the external business environment (PEST). This analysis will allow the directors to identify those strategic directions for the business that might experience less competition and which build upon TeePrint's strengths. Strategic analysis is perhaps the most important part of strategic management because when it is done well it can avoid poor decisions from being made as the environment in which the decision will take effect has been so well understood.

Strategic choice means choosing between the different options identified through strategic analysis. By using the tools of strategic choice – which can include investment appraisal – the most effective option can be forecasted. Other techniques include Ansoff's matrix, decision trees and force field analysis. The latter two techniques have the benefit of putting quantitative values into decision making and these can help Ahmed take objective decisions not based on opinion. However, the figures that these techniques need are often based on forecasts or judgements and no strategic choice technique can 'guarantee success', partly because the external environment can change so rapidly.

Once a decision has been made Ahmed and the other directors will have to put it into effect – and this is called strategic implementation. If the decision is made to opt for a 'differentiation strategy' then this will need to be implemented very carefully. The focus on design, fashion and quality will require employee recruitment and training and this will have to be handled sensitively to avoid disturbing existing workers who were originally employed just to 'print T-shirts'. Ahmed will need to establish a

→

new vision for the business and communicate this to all workers and he should also explain clearly the reasons for the change in direction of the business. A differentiation strategy could fail badly if the workforce is not fully in support of the changes that need to be made.

So strategic management will be vital to TeePrint as it attempts to gain and keep a competitive advantage. The question is whether Ahmed and his other directors have enough business experience to introduce the strategic management stages of analysis, choice and implementation. If they do not, then other more experienced directors might need to be recruited. Alternatively, a joint venture with a small differentiated clothing producer with TeePrint contributing some finance and knowledge of large-scale production techniques might be the best way of

ensuring that the strategy of differentiation to achieve competitive advantage might be effective.

Authors' comments

Can you identify the strengths of this answer? There is excellent understanding of strategic management and nearly all of the points made — and the concluding paragraph — are applied to TeePrint. The stages of strategic management are well analysed — but perhaps more detail could have been given on the techniques referred to and their benefits and limitations. There is sound evaluation, e.g. in the final paragraph and in some other references, e.g. the briefly explained limitations of quantitative choice techniques.

This is well on the way to becoming an excellent answer!

Additional exam-style question

Paper 3

I   Answer part (a) for the TeePrint case study above.

Strategic analysis

Learning summary

After you have studied this chapter you should be able to:

- [ ] understand what strategic analysis is
- [ ] understand how to undertake, interpret and evaluate SWOT analysis
- [ ] understand how to undertake, interpret and evaluate PEST analysis
- [ ] evaluate the importance of vision and mission statements
- [ ] understand how to undertake, interpret and evaluate Boston Matrix analysis
- [ ] assess the significance of Porter's Five Forces and core competencies as frameworks for business strategy.

38.1 How strategic analysis helps a business

TERM

Strategic analysis: conducting research into the business environment and the business itself to help form future strategies.

By undertaking effective strategic analysis a business should obtain answers to three important questions.

1 Where is the business now – in terms of its products and main markets?
2 How might external events impact on the business?
3 How could the business respond to these events?

The answers to these questions will help business managers decide on the most effective future strategies the business could adopt.

38.2 SWOT analysis

This is part of the process of determining:

| Where are we now? | → | Where do we want to be? |

TERM

SWOT analysis: a form of strategic analysis that identifies internal strengths and weaknesses and external opportunities and threats.

Benefits

- SWOT analysis is useful to managers when planning a new strategy. It helps to match the firm's resources and strengths to the opportunities available – whilst identifying the major external risk factors.
- The process of undertaking the SWOT analysis can promote discussion and cooperation between senior managers.
- Inexpensive – it is usually undertaken by business managers, not expensive external consultants.

Limitations

- Often over simplified – it can just lead to lists being created with no priority or quantitative measure given to each factor.
- Much more detailed analysis of each strength, weakness, opportunity and threat will be needed – especially before a major strategic decision is taken.
- Often based on analyst's subjective views. Another manager might arrive at a different SWOT list.
- Different managers will give issues different levels of importance.

TIP

Strengths and Weaknesses should be internal, Opportunities and Threats are external.

Progress check A

1 Explain why SWOT analysis is important when considering new strategies.

2 Should a business decide to take advantage of every 'opportunity' identified? If not, why not?

3 Undertake a simple SWOT analysis of a well-known business in your country that is planning to expand its operations.

4 Explain why your SWOT analysis might be different from someone else's SWOT analysis of the same business.

38.3 PEST analysis

The macro-environment means the important external issues that affect business performance and future strategies. Some business analysts refer to PESTLE analysis by separating out two further external factors: legal and environmental.

An example outlining PEST analysis for Toyota setting up operations in a country for the first time is shown in Figure 38.1.

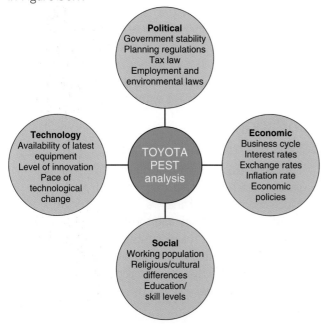

Figure 38.1 Factors influencing Toyota's PEST analysis

TERM

PEST analysis: the strategic analysis of a firm's macro-environment – political, economic, social and technological factors.

Benefits

- Provides an understanding of wider business environment.
- Encourages analysis of the business environment in setting future business objectives and strategies.
- Helps to identify future problems and take action to avoid them or minimise their effects.
- Different PEST analyses for each country a business operates in will highlight political, economic, social, cultural and legal differences.

Limitations

- Not much use if it is just a list of points – they need further critical analysis.
- May need to be updated regularly given the pace of external changes.
- Some information may be based on inaccurate forecasts, e.g. economic changes.
- Only considers the external environment.
- Judgements still need to be made about the relative importance of each factor to the business.

Progress check B

1 Why might 'political' factors (including legal factors) be different in differing countries?

2 Explain how the 'economic' environment might change quickly.

3 Suggest **three** 'social' factors for a multinational soft drinks business to analyse before starting operations in your own country.

4 Give examples of businesses likely to be greatly affected by technological change in the next few years – examples should include both negative and positive effects.

38.4 Vision statements and mission statements

Benefits

- Help provide decision makers with focus and direction – 'will this new strategy help us achieve our vision/mission?'
- Sense of purpose is provided to decision makers – 'we may need new strategies if we are to attain our vision/mission'.

Limitations

- Often rather general and ill-defined so of limited use when taking specific decisions.
- May need to be constantly reviewed to meet changing circumstances and new challenges.

38.5 Boston Matrix analysis

The Boston Matrix in Fig 38.2 shows:

- Four products sold by one business.
- The size of each circle represents the value of sales for each product.
- The four products are in different markets with different rates of sales growth.
- The products have either high or low market share.

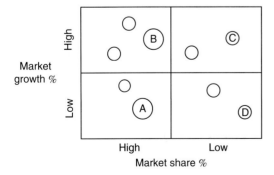

Figure 38.2 Boston Matrix

The four Boston Matrix product classifications are:

Product A – 'Cash cow' – low market growth but high market share

Product B – 'Star' – high market growth and high market share

Product C – 'Problem child' (or question mark) – high market growth but low market share

Product D – 'Dog' – low market growth and low market share.

Uses of Boston Matrix analysis

- Analyses the performance and current market position of existing products.
- Encourages managers to take strategic decisions about existing products, such as:
  - (i) 'Divest' dog products.
  - (ii) 'Build' problem children, for example, with cash obtained from 'cash cows'.
  - (iii) 'Hold' or support a star product to lengthen the period of its success.
- Encourages managers to take decisions about developing new products, for example, to replace a 'dog'.

Limitations of Boston Matrix analysis

- Provides information and some analysis but it does not explain why a product is in the position it is.
- Cannot forecast what might happen with each product – other information might be needed, such as market research.
- Assumes that high market shares are always more profitable than low market shares – may not be the case if a higher profit margin is made on a low volume product.

38.6 Porter's Five Forces

By understanding the forces that determine competitive rivalry, the following types of strategic decisions could be made more effectively.

• Which markets to enter and what are the potential barriers?
• Do we stay in existing markets?
• What actions can be taken to improve our competitive position?

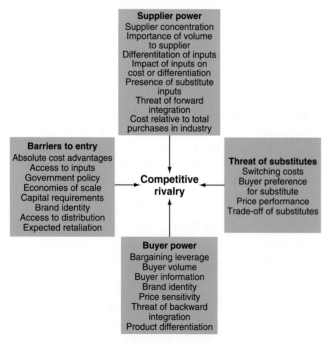

Figure 38.3 Porter's Five Forces model

38.7 Core competencies

Core competencies include unique sets of skills or production techniques. Examples include:

• Microsoft – set of software patents and skills that are difficult for other firms to duplicate.
• Toyota – hybrid technology engines that can be adapted to many types of vehicle.
• Walmart – low-cost logistical system that gives the firm a substantial cost advantage for entering new markets.

To be of commercial value to a business, a core competencies should:

• be able to offer recognisable benefits to consumers
• not be easy for other firms to copy
• be applicable to a range of products and markets.

Once a core competence has been established, it opens up strategic opportunities for developing new core products and consumer products. It raises the question: should businesses only pursue strategies that build upon their core competencies?

> ### TERMS
>
> Core competencies: an important business capability that gives a firm competitive advantage.
>
> Core product: a product or process based on a firm's core competence.

Exam-style question

Paper 3

Timber Products (TPC)

TPC is a public limited company. It owns forests in several low-income developing countries. It cuts down trees to produce timber (cut wood). Most of this timber is sold to other users but TPC also has a factory producing wooden furniture, using its own wood.

This furniture is traditionally designed and is sold through 'low price' retailers. Consumers' incomes have been rising in recent years and demand for imported furniture has increased. Imported furniture is often made of new technology materials such as plastics not wood and is based on modern designs. Lower import tariffs and an appreciating exchange rate have made imports more competitive.

Several pressure groups are angry that TPC destroys large areas of woodland each year – often in areas of great natural beauty. TPC has responded by stating that they plant one new tree for every one cut down. The organisational structure of TPC is a hierarchical one – in the factory, for example, there are seven levels of hierarchy with an average span of control of three.

All of the company's sawmills are operating at full capacity – reflecting the high level of demand for its timber which is sold at very competitive prices. The company recorded a return on capital employed of 14 per cent in the last financial year.

The directors of TPC are about to choose one of two strategic options for expansion:

- Option 1: Takeover of a large Asian furniture manufacturing firm. This might lead to economies of scale in wood furniture making and allow TPC to import furniture from a low-cost factory.
- Option 2: Exploitation of other primary products. Much of the land where the forests were is still owned by TPC. This land could contain metals such as copper and lead. These could be mined to earn additional revenue. TPC has no experience of this industry and mines would lead to local residents being relocated.

1   a   Evaluate the importance of both SWOT and PEST analysis to TPC's directors as they consider future strategic options for expansion. [20]

b   Discuss the usefulness of the Boston Matrix and Porter's Five Forces model to TPC's directors as they consider the two options for expansion. [20]

Student's answer to 1(a)

SWOT and PEST are forms of strategic analysis. These can be undertaken by a business to learn more about the business environment and its own strengths and weaknesses before forming new strategies. SWOT assesses the firm's internal strengths and weaknesses and external opportunities and threats. TPC is profitable which can be useful when financing further expansion. Retained profits, if held in cash, are internal finance so TPC will not have to pay interest charges on this source of finance. TPC also seems to own a lot of land – both forests and land that used to have trees and this land could be used to extract metals. Weaknesses of TPC seem to include a tall organisational structure which leads to high fixed costs of management salaries and limited scope for delegation. This weakness could be quite easily overcome with delayering of middle managers – and some of these managers could be given roles in the expansion option which is finally chosen.

The opportunities for TPC include using its land for alternative uses although this will require managers skilled in these activities. It could also use its furniture making resources to make a wider range of higher quality furniture which might yield higher profit margins than the existing styles. It might be quicker and more effective to take over another furniture maker – which is being suggested in Option 1.

Threats come in different forms. Firstly, economic conditions are making it cheaper to import foreign furniture and probably timber and metals too. This represents a serious threat to TPC's future business unless actions are taken to reduce costs – or possibly differentiate its furniture output to make the demand for it less price elastic.

Using PEST analysis will include an assessment of environmental, economic and social issues. It should make it clear to TPC how its actions are creating a poor image because of environmental concerns. Its activities are causing local residents great concern and extracting metals might lead to relocation. If any of these activities are shown to be illegal, then TPC will have huge expenses to pay. Technological changes in furniture making and materials used could make wooden furniture less and less popular and market conditions may become less favourable for this division of TPC. Higher consumer incomes suggest that TPC could usefully 'go up market' with its styles of furniture to appeal to consumers with more to spend.

Strategic analysis is important to TPC because it plans to expand. The analysis helps to identify the most likely strategies which would lead to successful expansion by identifying the key factors the directors should consider. It appears that the directors have formed Option 1 and 2 strategies without undertaking serious strategic analysis. Option 1 does not seem suitable given the continued focus on wood furniture. There is no reference to other materials – which are becoming more popular – or more exclusive styles. Focusing on price may not be appropriate given the external conditions that have now been analysed.

Option 2 has been identified but no consideration seems to have been given to environmental, social or legal issues – all important external environment factors. Perhaps TPC might consider selling the land that no longer has trees to a mining company which will have the competencies required to extract metals. Not having these competencies is a weakness

for TPC. The company could then use the finance raised to take over a furniture maker that specialises in quality designs in a range of materials. This would help to diversify TPC as a business, at a time when cheaper timber imports could threaten its wood business.

So strategic analysis is vital to allow TPC to consider a wider range of options than the two in the case study. These forms of analysis are rather subjective and need to be updated frequently to be effective, for example, the currency could depreciate quickly which makes imports more expensive again and allows TPC to be more competitive with its wood exports. TPC should also consider using the Boston Matrix and Porter's Five Forces model in its strategic analysis and the information gathered would then allow a much more detailed consideration of alternative strategies for expansion.

Authors' comments

This is a well-focused answer. The student makes a very good case for using strategic analysis in this case. There is a good attempt to analyse some of the SWOT and PEST issues relevant to TPC and explain how they might influence future strategies. There is scope for further evaluation/judgement of the techniques themselves but this is well on its way to being an excellent answer.

Additional exam-style question

Paper 3

1   Answer part (b) for the Timber Products case study above.

Strategic choice

39.1 What is meant by 'strategic choice'?

Strategic choice means deciding between future strategies.

Strategic choice is necessary because:

- limited resources mean that a business cannot pursue all possible strategies
- even if there is only one possible new strategy, the choice still exists of not pursuing it.

Strategic decisions can be vital to the future success of a business so the choice of which one(s) to pursue is very important.

39.2 Ansoff's Matrix and making strategic choices

> **TERM**
>
> Ansoff's Matrix: a model used to show the degree of risk associated with the four growth strategies: market penetration; market development; product development and diversification.

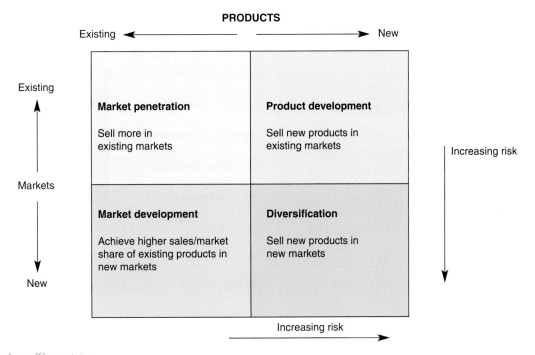

Figure 39.1 Ansoff's matrix

According to Ansoff, the main classifications for different growth strategies that a business can choose are:

1 Market penetration – as both the product and the market are known to the business this is the least risky strategy.
  Tactics that can be used as part of this strategy include: lower prices, increased advertising and sales promotion, development of brand image.
2 Market development – the existing products are well known to the business but there might be substantial differences between existing and new markets. For example, business customers may have different requirements to those of consumers. Consumers in different countries may have different tastes and cultural influences.
3 Product development – the existing markets are offered new products – or developments of existing ones. This requires research and development and there is often a considerable risk that this could prove to be unsuccessful or ineffective if competitors launch an even better product.
4 Diversification – often the riskiest strategy in the short term because both the performance of the product and the exact needs of consumers in new markets are unknown. This might be the strategic option chosen by a business that has uncompetitive products in markets that are either saturated or experience high levels of competition.

Progress check A

1 Why is it often quite risky for a business to enter new markets?

2 Why is the result of research and development into a new product never certain?

3 Give an example of a diversification strategy that could be adopted by a banking business operating in your country.

4 A supermarket chain in your country wants to pursue a market penetration strategy. Explain **two** ways in which this could be carried out.

TIP

Although Ansoff's Matrix can be useful in assessing risk, and helping to choose between strategic options, remember that it is only a starting point for strategic choice – detailed use of quantitative techniques such as investment appraisal and decision trees are needed to give more depth of analysis.

39.3 Force-field analysis and making strategic choices

TERM

Force-field analysis: identifies and analyses the positive factors (driving forces) that support a decision and negative factors that restrain it.

Kurt Lewin suggested using this model before making important strategic decisions. If the restraining forces are much more significant than the forces for change, it could be better not to take this strategic decision. If, however, management action can reduce the restraining forces and/or increase the forces for change, the decision might be worthwhile. A force-field diagram is shown in Fig 39.2:

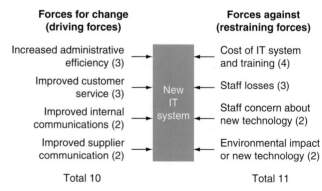

Figure 39.2 An example of force field analysis

Steps to take

1 Analyse current business position and where it 'hopes to be'.
2 Identify all restraining forces and driving forces.
3 Allocate a number to them indicating the significance of each force (1–10).
4 Total both sets of scores – decide whether to proceed with the strategy.
5 If the strategy is decided on but restraining forces still exceed driving forces, how can restraining forces be reduced and driving forces increased?

Limitations of force-field analysis

• Not all of the restraining/driving forces might be identified.
• Numerical values are entirely subjective.
• Gives a numerical result which seems to suggest great accuracy in assessing success/failure of the new strategy.

Progress check B

1   Identify **two** possible driving forces and **two** possible restraining forces in a decision to relocate production of computers to a low-cost country.

2   Suggest numerical values for these forces (scale: 1–10; where 1 = very weak) to indicate their relative strength/weakness.

3   If the total numerical value for restraining forces is greater than driving forces, suggest any **two** actions managers might take to reverse this.

39.4 Decision trees and making strategic choices

TERMS

Decision tree: a diagram that sets out the options connected with a decision and the outcomes, probabilities and economic returns that may result.

Expected value: the likely financial result of an outcome = probability × forecast economic return.

Constructing a decision tree

1 Information required
  • All possible outcomes from a decision
  • Estimated probability of each outcome occurring
  • Estimated economic return from each outcome.

2 Method of construction
  • Work from left to right
  • Square nodes for each decision point
  • Round nodes for each set of outcomes
  • Add in probabilities and economic returns.

3 Calculating expected values
  • Work from right to left
  • Multiply each probability of an outcome by its economic return
  • Add these results at round nodes
  • Take the best result at each square node
  • Subtract cost of decision to calculate the best expected value and therefore the most beneficial decision.

Progress check C

Forecasted probabilities and economic pay-offs from alternative marketing strategies:

	Probabilities of success/failure	Forecasted economic pay-off
Option A	0.70 probability of success	$12m gain
Capital cost $5m	0.30 probability of failure	$2m loss
Option B	0.50 probability of success	$10m gain
Capital cost £3m	0.50 probability of failure	$1m loss

Table 39.1

1   Draw a decision tree based on this data.

2   Calculate the expected monetary values of Option A and Option B.

TIP

You may be asked to calculate expected values from a decision tree given to you – but you may also be asked to draw the decision tree first.

Limitations of decision trees

- High margin of error (especially with 'one-off' projects) as the probabilities and economic returns are estimated or based on assumptions.
- Qualitative factors – such as objectives of the business and ethical considerations – are not allowed for on a decision tree.
- The results obtained are 'average' results that would be obtained if the decision was taken on several occasions. The expected monetary values will not be the exact results from making a decision once.

Strengths of decision trees

- Systematic approach that requires managers to consider all options and outcomes.

- Identifies key aspects of a decision.
- Can be used to assess key assumptions through 'what if' analysis. Example: by changing probabilities.

Progress check D

1 Explain what is meant by 'expected monetary value'?

2 Explain why decision trees might have limitations when being used to help make a choice between two strategies that have never been adopted before.

3 Give one example of a potential decision that becomes a riskier option, after a decision tree has been constructed, as a result of an economic downturn/recession.

Exam-style question

Paper 3

YouthMag (YM)

YM publishes several magazines for teenagers. They focus on music, fashion and sport. There is great competitive rivalry in this market sector. The owner of YM, Jed, wants to produce a magazine aimed at a different market segment. He has decided to use the decision tree technique to help him make the choice between launching a new magazine for 20–35 year olds or a new magazine for 56–70 year olds. The decision tree he constructed shows the forecast probabilities and possible pay-offs from the magazine (see Fig 39.3). If the printed magazine is successful then Jed will launch an internet-only version too as he believes that this is the future for magazine publishing. In addition to the decision tree in Fig 39.3,

he has undertaken some secondary market research and the results of this are shown in Table 39.2.

	2017	2018	2019
% increase in consumer spending by 20–35 year olds	6	4	2
% increase in spending by 56–70 year olds	6	5	5
% of population aged 20–35	10	11	11
% of population aged 56–70	15	18	19

Table 39.2 Market research data for the country (2018 and 2019 are forecasts)

The decision tree constructed by Jed to help make the choice between the two magazines (all financial data in $000s) is as follows:

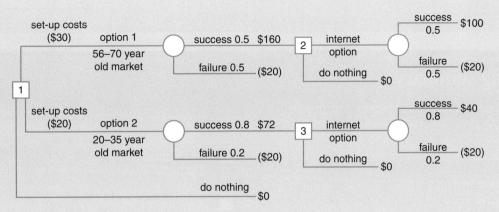

Figure 39.3 Jed's decision tree

1 a   Use the decision tree to calculate the expected monetary values of the two magazine options. [10]

   b   Which age range should the new magazine be produced for? Use your results to part (a) and any other information to support your recommendation. [16]

Student's answer to 1(a)

(All values in $000)

Value at Node 2 = (0.5 × $100) + (0.5 × −$20) = $40

So, if the magazine for 56–70 year olds is decided on, the internet version will also be profitable so this expected value can be added to the pay-offs of the paper-based magazine.

Value at Node 3 = (0.8 × $40) + (0.2 × −$20) = $28

So, if the magazine for 20–35 year olds is decided on, the internet version will also be profitable so this expected value can be added to the pay-offs of the paper-based magazine.

Value of Option 1 before subtracting set-up costs

= (0.5 × $200)* + (0.5 ×−$20) = $90

Value of Option 2 before subtracting set-up costs

= (0.8 × $100)* = (0.2 × −$20) = $76

*These pay-offs include the expected values from the internet options which have already been calculated as $40 and $28 (all figures in 000s).

Expected monetary values at Node 1 after set-up costs deducted = $60 Option 1

$56 Option 2 (all figures $000)

Authors' comments

A correct and very well laid out answer. Excellent.

Additional exam-style question

Paper 3

1   Answer part (b) for the YouthMag case study.

Strategic implementation

40.1 Strategic implementation

Once strategic decisions have been made action needs to be taken to put them into effect. This is what strategic implementation means – ensuring the organisation is prepared to accept and carry out the major decisions that have been made.

TERM

Strategic implementation: the process of allocating and controlling resources to support chosen strategies.

Factors that need to be considered within strategic implementation:

- Plan of action
- Adequate resources
- Preparing workforce for change
- Appropriate business culture and leadership style
- Control and review system – is the chosen strategy leading to the desired results?

40.2 Business plans

Starting a new business, or developing a new strategy for an existing business, should be planned for. Planning should always be the first stage of the strategic implementation process.

TERM

Business plan: a document describing a new business or a development of an existing business, its objectives and strategies, the market it is in (or plans to be in) and financial forecasts.

Figure 40.1 Content of a Business Plan

Entrepreneurs setting up a new business will be asked by potential investors for a detailed business plan.

Existing businesses use business plans too when planning to implement major strategic changes.

Progress check A

1 Why would a potential investor – such as a bank – be unlikely to invest in an entrepreneur's new business if a business plan had not been written?

2 Why would an existing business be advised to develop a business plan for a strategic decision such as entering an export market for the first time?

40.3 Corporate plans

Corporate plans are the route map that a business intends to follow over the medium to long term (more than one year). Typically, corporate plans include details of:

1 Long-term objectives of the business – SMART aims for the next few years.
2 The business strategies to be introduced to achieve these objectives.
3 The department/divisional objectives and strategies based on those for the business.

Benefits of corporate plans

- Managers have to consider the strengths and weaknesses of the business and how to implement the strategic decisions made in drawing up the plan.
- Clear plans provide focus, direction and a clear plan of action to managers for the coming years.
- Help to coordinate the work of all functional departments towards commonly agreed goals.
- Provide a control and review stage to allow checking of performance against original targets.
- Most useful when flexibility and contingency planning are built into the plan.

Limitations of corporate plans

- Based on forecasts of the future (for example, interest rates, GDP growth, company sales and competitors' actions) that may prove to be unrealistic.
- Take time and resources to develop – for example, these may be in short supply for small businesses.

- Managers can become so 'tied to the plan' that they fail to adapt and respond to changing internal and external circumstances.

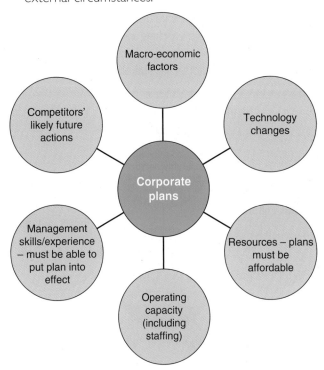

Figure 40.2 Factors affecting corporate plans

Progress check B

1 If corporate plans have to be often changed – due to external and internal forces – is there any point in preparing them? Explain your answer.

2 Why would it be important to coordinate the work of all functional departments when developing a corporate plan?

3 Explain how any one external economic factor could affect the corporate plan of a large exporting business operating in your country.

40.4 Corporate culture

Difficult to measure and define – but every business has one! How does a business really operate? What standards and ethical position does a business take? How are workers treated and managed? Once all of these questions have been answered it is possible to have an idea about a firm's corporate culture.

TERM

Corporate culture: the values, attitudes and beliefs of the people working in an organisation that control the way decisions are taken and how the business interacts with stakeholders.

Figure 40.3 Types of corporate culture

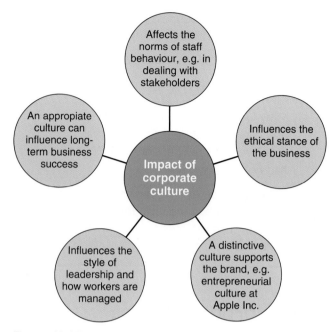

Figure 40.4 The importance of corporate culture

40.5 Changing corporate culture

Changing culture is often essential following strategic decisions, e.g. to take over another business or to become more socially responsible. Changing corporate culture can result in changes to senior staff, job descriptions, ethical stance of the business and working practices.

Some key steps that managers should follow are:

• Focus on developing the positive aspects of the business.
• Obtain full commitment of senior staff to the change – their behaviour and attitudes are crucial.
• Establish new objectives and mission statement.
• Encourage participation of all staff in changing culture.
• Train staff in new procedures.
• Change the staff reward system – appropriate behaviour under the new culture should be appropriately rewarded.

Progress check C

1 Government departments and organisations often operate with a role culture but research and development companies (for example, in I.T.) often operate with task or entrepreneurial culture. Explain the possible reasons for these differences.

2 If a family owned food retailing business, with loyal staff and a 'person' culture, is taken over by a large public limited company with the objective of driving through major changes, do you think that a change in culture might be necessary? Explain your answer.

3 The major shareholders in an oil producing company with a poor environmental and ethical record want to change the company's ethical stance and attitude to social responsibility. What changes might have to be made within the business to achieve this?

TIP

As with leadership styles, there is no one 'perfect' corporate culture for all business organisations and at all times.

40.6 Change management

Change management: planning, implementing, controlling and reviewing the movement of an organisation from its current state to a new one.

Major change is an important feature of modern business life.

- Changes can be slow and occur over a period of time – incremental change.
- Some changes are much more sudden and significant – revolutionary change.
- Dramatic, revolutionary change often causes more problems to business than incremental change.
- It cannot be prevented – some forces external to any business are always greater than the power of the business to prevent them.
- Change has to be planned for – hence the need for corporate planning – and it needs to be prepared for.

Change management – other factors

- Lead change – do not just manage it.
- This means that managers should not just 'get resources ready for change' but should be dynamic and proactive in selling the benefits of change and making sure that the whole organisation accepts it.
- Use project champions and project groups to help drive change forward.

TERMS

Project groups: these are created by a business to address a problem – such as a major change – that requires input from different specialists.

Project champions: a person assigned to support and drive a new project forward – they explain the benefits of change and support the project team putting change into effect. They also promote the need for and advantages of change at every opportunity.

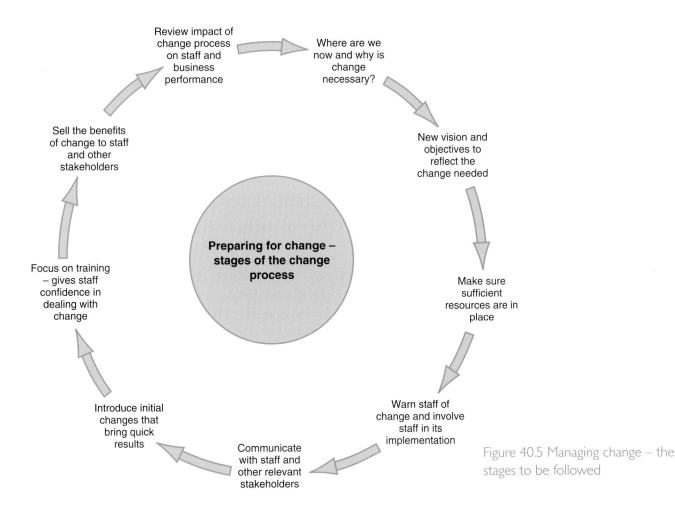

Figure 40.5 Managing change – the stages to be followed

Despite the best efforts of leaders promoting change management, there could be resistance to change due to:

- fear of the unknown, for example, new technology
- fear of failure, for example, not being able to cope with new work techniques
- losing something of value such as the previous business culture
- lack of trust, for example, if managers have not been open and communicated well
- inertia – some people just do not like change!

> **TIP**
>
> There is scope to refer to leadership styles when discussing management of change – who would make more effective 'change managers' – autocratic or participative leaders?

Progress check D

1 What do you think the main difference is between 'managing change' and 'leading change'?

2 Give **two** examples of incremental changes that have affected businesses in your country.

3 Give **two** examples of revolutionary changes that have affected businesses in your country.

4 Assume that your school or college is aiming to relocate to another part of the city/country. Explain how this major change could be managed most effectively.

40.7 Contingency planning

> **TERM**
>
> Contingency planning: preparing an organisation's resources for unlikely events.

Disasters and other unforeseen events occur – fires, floods, IT 'crash', oil tanker explosions and so on – and if businesses did not plan to cope with these there could be major problems.

- Bad publicity – because the business was not ready with resources or people to deal with the emergency.
- Loss of worker and consumer confidence, for example, lack of safety equipment or no response to dangerous products being sold.
- Business is unable to continue operations for long period of time, for example, premises destroyed.
- Legal claims – because damage caused to other people or businesses.

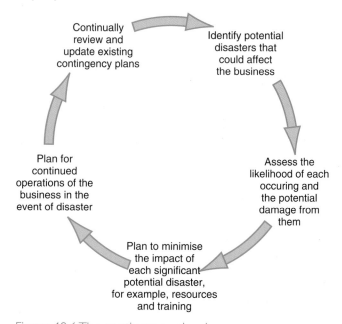

Figure 40.6 The contingency planning process

Limitations of contingency planning

- Time-consuming to identify each potential risk and assess the likelihood of occurrence and potential impact on business.
- Must be constantly updated – to take new risks into account and to take account of new developments, for example, in fire-fighting techniques.
- Cannot always identify or assess the degree of risks involved.
- Staff training costs increase if labour costs are high.

Progress check E

1 One form of contingency planning is sometimes referred to as 'business continuity planning'. Explain what this means.

2 Explain why not all business risks can be planned for.

3 Explain, with an example, how contingency planning might give workers and consumers greater confidence.

4 Explain, with an example, how contingency planning could reduce the bad publicity for a business following a disaster or accident.

Exam-style question

Paper 3

Africa Clothing (AC) – cost reduction strategy

AC manufactures quality fashion clothes for women and girls. Employees in its six factories receive wages above the legal minimum and they have excellent conditions of employment and good communication with managers. Employees are allowed to make complete garments as this encourages them to take pride in their work. Quality is high but so are production costs. AC's profitability is falling as the company's Marketing Director has recently been forced to lower prices to two of AC's largest retail customers. Competition in the retail sector is increasing from online businesses that avoid the high fixed costs of shops.

AC's directors have decided on a cost reduction strategy to attempt to restore profitability. Three factories will be closed. Finance raised from the sale of these will be used to expand the other three and equip them with the latest technology machinery for material cutting and sewing. Factory employees will have to focus on just one task and train in the use of the new equipment for that task. The machines are very fast and cost-effective but potentially dangerous for operators unless they are fully trained. Many middle managers will lose their jobs too. Rumours about these changes have spread quickly amongst the workforce. AC's directors are meeting tomorrow to discuss how these changes could be most effectively implemented without damaging the reputation of the business or the quality of products.

Crisis at AC

Last year a batch of cloth was received from a supplier that was wrongly marked: 'Fire resistant – ideal for children's clothes'. However, it was just ordinary cotton cloth. AC used it to make children's clothes and then disaster struck. A child was badly burned when she stood close to a fire wearing one of AC's skirts that caught alight. The newspapers condemned both AC and the shop. AC followed a pre-prepared plan and withdrew all similar clothes, offering shops and consumers compensation. AC paid for the girl's medical treatment and donated $1m to a children's charity. The cloth maker was removed from AC's approved suppliers list. Sales of AC's clothes fell by only three per cent over two months and then increased again.

1 a Discuss ways in which the proposed changes within AC could be managed effectively. [20]

b Evaluate the importance of contingency planning to AC's future success. [20]

Student's answer to 1(a)

Effective management of change is a key factor to help the business succeed in future. The proposed cost reduction strategy will require careful and effective management of change for it to result in increasing AC's profitability. This is a major change which will result in redundancies, a huge retraining programme, possible relocation of some workers and changes in working methods. The rumours are already circulating and this is a bad sign as informal communication about major strategic change can often cause employees to worry and become anxious, resulting in lower motivation. AC's directors must act quickly to ensure the changes are introduced as effectively as possible although it is likely that some employees will still be negatively affected by them.

AC must be honest and open about the need for these changes. Explaining why they are necessary to all stakeholders is important, but especially employees. The fact that the business may not have a future at all if the decline in profitability is not reversed would help to justify the changes that are going to be made. A clear vision for the future of the business, once the changes have been introduced, will be essential to reduce fear of the changes and help most employees to accept them. The decision about which factories to close will have to be taken by directors – this could not be taken participatively as workers will be very unlikely to support the closure of the factory they work in.

Once the decision has been made it should be clearly announced with no room for rumours. Managers should then hold meetings with trade union or other representatives of the workers to discuss redundancy payments, relocation payments for workers who might be needed in the other three factories once they are expanded and the retraining programme. Workers may propose that only voluntary redundancies are used, especially if there are several older workers who would be willing to leave work early for a generous redundancy payment. This would help protect the jobs of other workers. Involving workers or their representatives will help to give them a sense of control and ownership of these changes. The alternative is just to force all of these changes on to workers in an autocratic way and this is very likely to lead to opposition and possible industrial action. This is particularly important in this case as workers used to have excellent employment conditions and good communication with managers.

Project teams could be allocated tasks in the changeover period such as helping to plan the extensions and selecting the suppliers of the new machinery. Project champions could be appointed from well-respected employees to help convince their colleagues of the need for these changes.

The change in working practices could be demotivating and employees may push for some relaxation in the 'one worker one task' requirement.

Organising work in the three remaining factories in teams would help to give some variety in the work being performed and some control over working lives.

A big retraining programme can be unsettling to workers too as some might think that they will not be able to learn the new skills required. Off-the-job training will be needed as the machinery has not been used within AC before. Bonuses for successful completion of training programmes might be effective in motivating workers to undergo the training but AC must be careful to keep the cost of the changes low as the whole aim is to increase profitability.

If AC can make the changes in ways that employees are prepared to accept and be positive about then productivity should improve and unit costs fall. This will help to restore AC's profitability. If, however, managers use an autocratic approach and use little communication, relying on rumours to spread news of the changes, then the future for AC will not be good. Upset and resentful employees may not increase productivity, even with the new machines, and the fall in profitability might not be reversed.

Authors' comments

Good effort. The student clearly understands the concept of change management. It is well applied to the changes AC is proposing so the answer is in context. The points made are well explained and analysed, especially about the potential impact of using an autocratic approach to change management.

The student also demonstrates the skill of evaluation because different approaches to change management are assessed. The student uses evaluative expressions such as 'must act quickly', 'essential' and 'particularly important in this case' and these are all attempts to show judgement. There is a sound overall conclusion – again in the context of the case study business. An excellent answer!

Additional exam-style question

Paper 3

l   Answer part (b) for the Africa Clothing case study above.

Answers

The following are outline answers only; these are not the full answer.

All exam-style questions and answers that appear in this publication are written by the authors.

Chapter 1

Progress check A

1   Special chairs, hair dryers, possibly a computer for keeping record of appointments.

2   Where there is likely to be a large number of potential customers walking by – main street in town centre? But expensive to locate there too.

3   Truck drivers, truck mechanics to maintain vehicles, workers to load the trucks, office worker to take customers' orders.

4   The business has created additional value because, assuming the clothing is sold for the same price, the cost of bought-in materials will now be lower.

5   It could be bought by a final end user or consumer such as a student or it could be bought by a business to help with the business accounts (it is then a capital good).

Progress check B

1   Managing and leading workers will be an important role for an entrepreneur – appropriate leadership style could help to motivate workers.

2   Setting up a new business venture is always going to be risky – especially if the entrepreneur has no or little business experience.

3   The most successful new business start-ups are often by entrepreneurs who have a new idea for a product or a new way of delivering a service. Being creative can increase the chances of success.

4   The entrepreneur might run out of cash – if he/she has miscalculated the amount of capital required to set up the business; new competitors might enter the market; the external environment might become very negative for new businesses, e.g. higher interest rates.

Progress check C

1   New enterprises create employment and they add to a country's total value of goods and services produced (GDP). They can help to reduce unemployment.

2   Many people might agree with the objectives of a social enterprise and want to work for it.

3   These enterprises are not 'charities' and they need profits to continue to expand and to offer their socially responsible product to customers.

4   Social objective, e.g. supporting disadvantaged groups; environmental objectives.

Additional exam-style questions

1   Taking decisions that lead to more added value – a bigger difference between the cost of bought in materials and the price a product is sold for.

2   Buying the new vehicle involves using scarce resources which cannot now be used to buy other items. The lost benefit of the next most desired item becomes the opportunity cost.

3   a   Three objectives: financial, e.g. making a profit; environmental, e.g. recycling materials; social, e.g. helping disadvantaged groups.

    Not the same as charities – social enterprises are trying to create value – as other enterprises do – but they aim to do so without damaging the environment and by working with and benefiting certain disadvantaged groups in society.

    b   New enterprises usually have limited resources so are more vulnerable to factors that can lead to business failure than well established businesses:

    Lack of finance; lack of management experience; vulnerable to dynamic business environment; competition from larger business (perhaps with lower costs).

    Discuss these and other likely causes of failure – possibly by using examples.

Which factors are likely to be most important? Perhaps lack of management experience – this experience might have led to the entrepreneur responding effectively to competition and not external environment changes; perhaps lack of finance – additional finance would allow a business to survive longer and build up stronger relationships with customers for future success.

4 a i   Risk taking and decision making undertaken by an entrepreneur.

      ii Resources needed by Linda's business to start up and survive – land, labour, capital and her enterprise.

   b i $560–$280 = $280

      ii She can use the added value to pay for other costs – like the rent on her workshop – or, once all costs have been paid, she can earn a profit.

   c   She will need to show creativity, e.g. to design innovative new plates and bowls and to sell these in ways that attract new customers.

       She will need to be multi-skilled because she will not only need to be a good potter – as the quality of her plates and bowls will be important to customers – but she will need to be good at record keeping and keeping accounts so that her business does not run out of finance.

   d   Raising the price – this will perhaps indicate to customers that Linda's products are creative and of high value – however, if competitors' prices are much lower, then Linda's sales could fall and she might create less value than before.

       Reducing costs of bought-in materials might mean lower quality products – higher added value of each item might be cancelled out by lower sales if customers think the product is not worth the price charged for it due to lower quality materials.

       Overall, this should be a supported recommendation; a conclusion is necessary.

Chapter 2

Progress check A

1 Student's own answer.

2 Secondary as it is processing raw materials into a finished product.

3 High consumer incomes lead to high levels of spending on 'luxury' services that could not be afforded in a low or middle income country such as tourism, beauty treatments, restaurants etc.

4 Student's own answer.

Progress check B

1 Sole trader; partnerships.

2 This gives potential shareholders confidence that if they purchase shares in the company they can lose no more than this original investment if the company fails. This makes it easier for the company to sell shares.

3 Wants to keep complete control and independence in operating the business; does not want to share profits.

4 Owners might not want to have full disclosure of accounts or to run the risk of losing control if too many shares are sold to new shareholders.

5 Joint venture is when two businesses agree to start a new business operation, sharing the financing and the risks – and profit if it is successful. A franchise business exists when there is a sale of a licence to operate using the name and business model of the franchisor.

6 By becoming a franchisor, the business will be able to sell licences to other businesses or new entrepreneurs and this will expand the franchisor's operations more quickly and with less investment than if the business opened more shops itself.

7 The joint venture could be with a business already established in the country. This business would have local knowledge and be aware of consumer tastes and local cultures. This could reduce the risk for the other business of expanding into the country.

8 Reduces the risk of the investment – can only lose the value of the initial investment if the business fails.

9 Cost of the conversion, e.g. complex documents have to be prepared and the shares offered for sale.

   Danger of loss of control if other shareholders buy up a high proportion of the issued shares.

Additional exam-style questions

1 a Business that has only one owner, although it might employ workers.

b To increase the amount of capital to be invested in the business. The owner of a sole trader business might have limited capital.

2 a It limits shareholders' liability to their initial investment. It encourages new investors as they know the maximum that they could lose.

It therefore increases the chance of new private limited companies raising share capital they need.

It means that existing public limited companies might be able to raise capital for expansion from a new issue of shares – an important source of finance.

b Joint venture – new business set up between two existing businesses, e.g. to operate in another country or to research into new products.

Spreads the risk and the costs of expansion. Might allow a better promoted and financed launch of operations in the proposed country.

In-country knowledge provided by the business already operating there might be very important, e.g. market conditions, consumer tastes for retail products and laws controlling the type/quality of retail goods that can be sold.

May be arguments and disputes.

Which company controls the joint venture?

Profits have to be shared.

Overall decision needed – might depend on the financial resources that the business considering expanding abroad has and 'how different' market conditions are in this country.

3 a i Business that has separate legal identity from owners and sells shares but not to the public via the Stock Exchange.

ii Comprises businesses owned and controlled by individuals or groups of individuals – as opposed to state-owned businesses in the public sector.

b Primary – extracting raw materials from the earth, growing food, fishing – in this case mining minerals.

Secondary – using raw materials to process them and make products for sale to consumers/ other businesses. In this case, processing minerals, e.g. into cement.

c It would mean that Spanish Minerals were involved in the new ROC operations – rather than just trying to compete with them.

They could contribute local knowledge, e.g. health and safety laws for mining operations in Spain – and gain a share of the profits of the new operations.

The minerals mined could be used in the Spanish Minerals' processing operations, e.g. cement making. This would give a reliable source of supply.

d Yes: raise finance to expand and compete more effectively with ROC, e.g. buy best sites for mining.

Could use the finance for a joint venture with ROC.

Sale of shares would make Joe and Pablo richer.

No: reduces control of Joe and Pablo – ROC could even buy out the newly formed plc and take Joe and Pablo out of the business completely.

Cost of going public.

Overall judgement/conclusion needed based on preceding analysis.

Chapter 3
Progress check A

1 This is often a problem with this form of measuring business size. It is best to calculate 'full-time equivalent' (fte) number of employees.

Co. A therefore has 50 fte employees and Co. B has 30 – so Co. A is larger using this measure.

2 Electricity generation is very capital intensive with relatively few workers employed – the exact opposite of an office cleaning business.

3 No issued shares on the Stock Exchange – therefore no 'share price' which is used to calculate market capitalisation.

4 It could be – especially if they sell cars of similar price. However, comparing a maker of luxury cars which could sell for hundreds of thousands of dollars with a manufacturer making small city cars would give a misleading image of relative size.

Progress check B

1 Student's own answer.

2 Shortage of capital – limited capital will make expansion difficult.

No benefits of large-scale buying of supplies – so costs per unit might be higher than for larger business.

3 Poor communication – it is difficult to communicate effectively with a very large workforce.

Poor coordination – large businesses with many divisions operating in different countries might find it difficult to ensure consistent and coordinated decisions are taken.

Additional exam-style questions

1 a Market capitalisation; value of sales.

b Small businesses often give good customer service and the owners can usually deal with most customers themselves. Many customers who go to hairdressers want personal service and they might feel that they would not get this in a large hairdressing business. Therefore many hairdressing businesses remain small.

2 Family businesses are owned and operated by the members of, usually, one family. This might lead to some problems:

- Succession: who is going to take over once the current managing director retires?

- Will they be a good manager just because they are a son/daughter or other relative? Favouritism can lead to the best manager not being appointed.

- The family might prefer to aim for 'keeping control' rather than 'growth of the business' so opportunities for expansion and increasing output/employment are not taken.

- Some family businesses do not act quickly to respond to new threats or opportunities – 'the family has always done it this way'. This might be especially true if the founder of the business has very fixed views on how 'his/her' business should be operated.

3 Small firms, typically, employ relatively few people and have little capital invested in them. They are more common in some industries than others. They frequently offer:

Innovation; new products and new ideas; essential supplies for larger businesses; competition for larger businesses; employment to workers; they might expand and become larger in future.

However, they are often less important to an economy than larger businesses as they might have higher unit costs; they might not be very efficient; they might be at greater risk of failing than larger businesses as they are usually less diversified and have fewer customers.

On balance – often very important, especially in certain industries – but governments should not overlook the importance of larger businesses too.

4 Purchasing benefits – able to order sports equipment/clothing in large quantities – helps to reduce costs per unit (economies of scale) and keep shop prices low. Major reason for success of business

Able to negotiate with property companies from position of strength – keeps rents/leasing costs low of JT's 35 shops. Reduces fixed costs and increases profitability of JT

5 Joe has driven the business to success – but are his children able to carry this on? Lack experience? Lack interest? May use inappropriate management style/methods (workers appear to be dissatisfied). Family businesses often have succession problem – Je might not have prepared/trained his children well enough. Professional/external managers might do a better job.

Joe's children can benefit from Joe's experience still. They may share his motivation and commitment – want to have pride in continuing a successful business. May want to pass successful business on to own children.

Balanced discussion needed – plus a conclusion based on points made. Many factors will determine future success of JT – can the younger members of the family deal with these effectively?

Chapter 4
Progress check A

1 Not specific, measurable or time specific.

2 Helps to measure success or failure, e.g. after first year; useful for investors to judge how realistic the entrepreneur is.

3 To achieve a six per cent increase in market share in Asia within two years.

4 Gives a much clearer focus to managers when deciding on appropriate objectives; able to measure success or failure more accurately.

5 They would not have a clear direction or sense of focus.

6 To be national market leader in food and drink retailing within three years.

Progress check B

1 It is more of a mission statement than an objective – it is not SMART.

2 To ensure that the appropriate strategies of these departments are chosen which will increase the chance of the overall objectives being met.

3 Not necessarily – unless requested by investors or other key stakeholders. Only when it is important to publicise the mission statement to stakeholders would one need to be carefully devised. On the other hand, a mission statement can help determine the overall objectives so some entrepreneurs will focus on a mission statement really early on in the life of the business.

4 It might change ownership, e.g. from private to public limited company and the new owners/directors might want to change from 'satisfactory profit' objective to 'rapid growth in sales' objective to increase market share and power over retailers/suppliers.

Also: economic boom or recession – original objective(s) might be inappropriate and the objective might not become 'survival'.

Progress check C

1 As the original owners (perhaps a family business) are now losing control, the key objective might now be 'growth' or 'profits' rather than, say, continuity or ethical values.

2 In a boom, business growth is likely to be a realistic objective; in a recession it might be wiser to set the objective of 'survival'.

3 Children may be too young to make rational decisions and they might put pressure on parents to buy toys – that some families might not be able to afford.

4 Local people to be treated fairly and compensated during disruption caused by drilling for oil.

Government ministers/officials not to be bribed for drilling licences.

No misleading claims or adverts made about how 'clean and environmentally friendly oil and gas products are'.

Additional exam-style questions

1 a An objective or aim that is specific, measurable, achievable and time specific.

b Ethics means following a code of conduct which results in 'doing the right thing'. A business might incorporate ethics into its objective because the culture of the management is focused not just on profit but on not harming other groups or interests in society, e.g. a business may choose to pay a good living wage even though this may not be a legal requirement.

2 a Define all three terms. Mission statement makes clear the long-term aim for the business in ways that will motivate employees and attract stakeholders. Objectives and the long-term targets that a business sets – these should be SMART to be really effective. Objectives should be set with reference to the mission statement. Strategies are the plans that a business adopts in order to achieve its long-term objectives.

For example: Mission: To be the world's favourite airline.

Objective: To increase market share in the business air traveller market.

Strategy: Purchase or lease planes that have the biggest section for business travellers.

b Define business objectives. Explain what is mean by 'successful' – may be in terms of survival, profits, growth etc.

Clear objectives – especially if they are SMART – provide focus, a form of measuring progress and a framework for future strategies.

Should help a book retailing business pursue strategies that are likely to help it survive and be more profitable.

However – even most appropriate and clearest objectives may be insufficient to achieve success if competition is too powerful (Amazon book sales), technology changes too rapidly (e-books) or economic conditions make running a retail business more difficult (higher taxes on consumers).

3　A measure against which performance can be assessed – profit max (in this case) can be judged by comparing past profits with current profits and profits of similar businesses in same/different businesses. Will indicate to Liam whether his objective is being reached.

Gives focus and direction to all employees and to business strategies – e.g. the decision taken by Liam are designed to increase (short term) profits.

4　Define ethical business behaviour. Refer to each of the 3 examples. Is putting pressure on suppliers – especially small ones – unethical? Could it drive them out of business? Ethical or just "good business"? Being tough on new employees by taking away job security for 1st year – exploiting workers or just making sure the best workers stay? "Making payments" to secure contracts – is this bribery? Is it illegal in JT's country? If it isn't, is it still unethical? Is Liam putting the future good name and long term success of the business at risk to gain short term profits? No overall conclusion is possible – but all round discussion and weighing up of ideas needed.

Chapter 5

Progress check A

1　When making important decisions, the managers/owners of the business do not just consider the likely impact on profit but also consider the effects the decision might have on all stakeholders.

2　New jobs – especially important if the region has high unemployment.

Extra traffic and possible pollution from factory – might worsen air quality in the area.

3　If they are being sold at much lower prices – and they are made aware of the quality of the item, e.g. food close to its 'best before' date.

Progress check B

1　Fulfill all of is legal obligations, e.g. ensure that workplace safety is up to minimum legal standards.

To pay wages/salary regularly at the rate previously agreed between employee/employer.

2　Fulfill work requirements contained in the contract of employment.

Not to steal or act unethically at work.

3　Student's own answer.

4　Students/parents – school fees are likely to rise substantially (especially if school is popular).

Teachers (employees) – might be expected to work longer hours or teach more classes for no or little additional pay.

Additional exam-style questions

1　a　Owners are just one of the several groups of stakeholders. Stakeholder groups often have different objectives, e.g. customers – good value, reliable products; suppliers – to be paid promptly; workers – job security and competitive pay. Businesses often aim to satisfy these objectives as well as satisfying the owners' objectives for growth/profit. 'Satisfied' stakeholders can lead to customer loyalty; suppliers keen to supply reliably and on time; well-motivated workers – other examples can be given too. Satisfied stakeholders can help business achieve long-run success.

　　b　Objectives of stakeholders can conflict – customers want lowest possible prices but owners want profits and workers aim for high wages. Steelmaking can be polluting so although the local community wants jobs and incomes – it does not want an unhealthy environment. Steel making business may have to prioritise objectives, e.g. growth of output and creation of more jobs may be more important than a very clean environment. The business might become more profitable if it meets some of its stakeholders' objectives, e.g. motivated workers are more productive and satisfied customers will show more loyalty and buy products in the future.

A more profitable business might then decide to satisfy other stakeholder groups aims, e.g. investing in local community projects; paying suppliers promptly; researching cleaner production methods. So, in the long term a successful and profitable business might be able to reduce the potential conflict between stakeholder objectives.

An overall conclusion to the answer is required.

2　a　Although the **local community** might benefit from increased job vacancies, it could also be affected by dust, noise and pollution from the mine. This could affect local people's health. The water supply might be polluted from waste from the mine workings. The new road would mean trucks and other vehicle movements – creating further air and noise pollution. Local people may have to relocate.

The **government** might receive more tax revenue – but it might have to spend more on local roads and other infrastructure as the heavy mine vehicles will damage the existing roads.

b Short term – conflict likely, e.g. between jobs/incomes and the environment. Customers may want low prices but the mine company might have to pay very low wages to keep its costs/prices down.

Long term conflict might be reduced in the profits of the mining company and the tax revenue received by the government are partly used to compensate 'losers', e.g. people affected by pollution or by being forced to relocate. Depends on whether business/government decide to use resources in these ways.

Chapter 6
Progress check A

1 Student's own answer.

2 Student's own answer – will vary from country to country.

3 Student should explain that with certain products, e.g. cars or cell phones, there is much more choice because many of the models available to consumers are imported – trade increases consumer choice.

Progress check B

1 Will price of water rise or fall? Will clean water be more or less widely available? Will jobs be created or lost? Will private companies invest profits in improving supplies?

2 Student's own answer.

3 Likely to be: access to wider market; government incentives; lower costs than in other countries etc.

4 Likely to be: jobs and incomes; exports of output from MNC; inward flows of capital; increase competition for local firms forcing them to become more efficient; tax paid to government.

5 Is tax be to paid or do MNCs avoid tax? Local businesses might be forced out of business – jobs could be lost; MNC may have too much influence over government, e.g. in gaining planning permission for new operations in environmentally sensitive areas.

Additional exam-style question

1 Define privatisation first.

Three years since National Minerals and other private businesses were created from privatisation of mining industry. Profits have increased – but are they kept in Country X? Profit tax should have increased **but** do companies avoid tax? Jobs have fallen – but would they have been lost if the mines were still state owned? Efficiency has risen – makes the industry more competitive against, e.g. ROC – but are workers under too much pressure/Is this a cause of the accident number rising? New investment increased – shows good prospects for industry's future? Overall judgement needed.

Chapter 7
Progress check A

1 The businesses currently operate in different industries.

2 It is forward vertical integration as the farmer is taking over a business that operates 'closer' to the market/consumers.

3 Profits should increase compared to the combined profits of the two formerly separate businesses if costs are cut, e.g. closing branches/offices in towns where both banks currently have offices, to avoid duplication.

4 Yes: if services are improved, e.g. the new, larger business can afford the latest IT equipment to offer online banking services.

No: closing bank branches/offices might make it less convenient for some customers to travel to a branch.

5 Lack of synergy – different business cultures between managers/directors of the two countries may make decision making very difficult and objectives might differ substantially. Also, cost savings might not result if costs rise due to diseconomies of scale especially when the new business had operations in more than one country.

Progress check B

1. Joint venture occurs when two businesses agree to form another company together to manage a specific expansion project. Strategic alliance does not create a separate company but is a legal agreement to work together to achieve a common objective.

2. To benefit from each other's strengths. The plan could be to develop a computer system that will appeal to both consumers (Apple's strength) and to business users (IBM's strength).

3. May have been problems over control – which company's management has the greater decision-making power, could have been a clash of business culture/leadership as Russian businesses are often managed and led in different ways to those common in most UK-based businesses.

4. Student's own answer.

5. May have been inadequate financing for expansion; senior managers might not have had the skills or experience needed to operate a rapidly growing business, e.g. dealing with many employees.

Additional exam-style question

1. This horizontal integration was between two businesses with different objectives, different product ranges and operating in different markets – all of these factors make lack of synergy very likely.

   Culture clash between directors/managers of the two businesses as their approaches seem to be so different – this makes decision making very difficult.

   Costs per unit might not fall if diseconomies are greater than economies of scale.

   Was the merger given long enough to succeed? Did managers have enough experience of operating a large business? How could the problems of labour turnover and customer complaints have been tackled?

Chapter 8

Progress check A

1. Probably not! It might lead to health problems for customers and it might result in the restaurant failing to meet government health standards as outlined in law.

2. Employees would be able to check that they are receiving the correct pay rate and conditions of service as laid down by the contract.

   Employers might benefit from more motivated employees as they now have more job security.

3. Large firms might insist that customers only buy from them by refusing to supply essential products; they could also charge very low prices to force the small firm out of business and then raise prices.

4. To protect consumers who are unaware of the quality of the product – perhaps for technical reasons – which could make it dangerous to use.

5. If the business pays low wages, it will be forced to pay wages up to the minimum level set by the government law. This will increase costs and reduce profits unless the business is able to motivate the workers to produce more.

Progress check B

1. Higher fixed costs of buying/leasing the machinery.

   Higher costs of training and possibly maintenance too.

   Lower labour costs due to increased labour efficiency.

   Lower wastage costs as the machinery is likely to be very accurate and reliable.

2. Word processing; data storage/handling.

3. Online secondary market research; e-commerce by selling through web pages.

4. E.g. analyse the exact requirements; evaluate different systems available and compare to requirements; plan for introduction, e.g. training; monitor performance of IT against original requirements.

5. A small customer service business such as a hairdressing salon or café.

6. E.g. mobile/cell phone business – to keep pace with technological developments of rivals and to try to create a USP.

Progress check C

1. Average age is rising; higher proportion of the population over 60 years.

2. Try to retain older employees, e.g. by retraining or offering flexible working hours.

Develop and market products aimed at older generation e.g. a construction company might build more retirement apartments and not large family houses.

3 Student's own answer.

4 Research customer needs of the ethnic groups migrating to the country; develop a range of products suited to these needs, e.g. special foods or clothing products.

Progress check D

1 To help fulfil its CSR aims/obligations; to project a responsible image of the company; to report to stakeholders on the wider social/environmental impact of the business, i.e. not just financial accounts.

2 Using less oil, e.g. by purchasing a more efficient heating system, will reduce costs of operation and reduce pollution from emissions.

3 Business can now more easily promote itself as a sustainable and environmentally friendly one and this will attract customers who want to buy environmentally friendly products.

4 Yes: any reduction in costs will help to make the business more competitive and keep prices low.

No: any short-term gain in competitiveness might be cancelled out by bad publicity from this unethical decision.

5 Estimates of efficiency gains might be from the manufacturer of the machine – will these be accurate? Cost of energy in the future can only be forecast and is not known for sure; other costs of buying and operating the machine need to be included – will it cost more to maintain than existing machine?

6 Marketing benefits: to be able to promote the business as a socially responsible and environmentally friendly business.

Financial benefits: potential investors might be more encouraged to invest in a business that acts in a socially responsible way – these 'ethical' investors might not want to be linked to companies that produce dangerous goods in an environmentally damaging way.

7 Consumer boycott hits sales substantially.

Bad publicity resulting from pressure group activity damages the reputation/image of the company.

Additional exam-style question

1 Consumer protection: will make existing products illegal unless safety equipment is improved. Making the necessary changes to existing models will add to production costs and AMG may have to raise prices.

Employees rights will include employment contract. This will make employees more motivated and may increase labour efficiency but AMG will have to revise its HR strategy to avoid breaking the law.

Chapter 9
Progress check A

1 The total value of a country's output of goods and services has increased, after adjusting for the effect of inflation. This is known as 'economic growth'.

2 They are likely to increase – and this will lead to an increase in demand for income elastic products.

3 Inferior goods have negative income elasticity of demand – as incomes rise, so demand falls. During a recession, average incomes fall so the demand for inferior goods will increase.

4 Demand is rising rapidly and prices of products and assets (such as land and property) will be increasing.

5 Increase – a recession means that demand for most products is falling so output will fall – and less output means fewer workers will be employed.

Progress check B

1 They might have skills which are no longer demanded or live in regions that are not benefiting from the general economic growth of the rest of the country – frictional unemployment.

2 Not necessarily – businesses that produce goods or services with high price elasticity of demand would be unwise to increase prices substantially during a period of inflation – but it might depend on what competitors are doing with their prices.

3 Higher raw material costs and higher wages paid to employees.

4 Labour pay rates might fall as there are more workers looking for jobs than jobs available – this should reduce average labour cost.

5 As there are few alternative job opportunities employees will be discouraged from leaving the job that they currently have.

Progress check C

1 Reduce taxes such as income tax, sales tax (value added tax) and profit (corporation) tax.

   Increase government spending, e.g. on schools or welfare benefits.

2 If these businesses produce goods and services with low income elasticity of demand, the sales of them will not change much if consumers' disposable incomes rise.

3 It will make the MNC less likely to invest in the country as it will be able to retail a lower proportion of any profit that it makes.

4 House construction as most people buy houses with borrowed money (mortgages). An increase in interest rates will now make buying a house more expensive.

5 When inflation is rising above the government's target for price rises. Higher interest rates should reduce demand for goods and services and reduce the rate of inflation.

Progress check D

1 Assuming a UK student:

   £1:$1 changes to £1:$1.20

   This shows an appreciation of the £ as one unit of the currency can now buy more dollars than before (so the $ has depreciated).

2 Assuming a UK student:

   £1:1 Euro changes to £1:0.9 Euro

   This shows the value of £ has depreciated as 1 unit of it buys less Euros than before the change (so the Euro has appreciated).

3 A currency appreciation will mean that imported components become cheaper in the local currency. A currency appreciation will mean the exports will have to be increased in price (in terms of foreign currency) to earn the same amount of local currency as before the appreciation. This could reduce the demand for them.

4 It will be able to sell its products in foreign markets at lower foreign currency prices – making exporting potentially more profitable.

Progress check E

1 Student's own answer, e.g. firearms or other dangerous products.

2 It may reduce incentives to other businesses to become more efficient as their managers/owners might also expect government financial support.

3 Some businesses will be reluctant to train employees in case they are then 'poached' by other employers. Government finance to support training will help prevent the lack of training that results from this market failure.

Additional exam-style question

1 Economic growth is slowing (but economy is not forecast to be in recession). Consumer incomes will not rise as fast in 2019 as 2017 – so demand for printed dresses and shirts will not be increasing much – but depends on income elasticity of demand. Higher inflation – this will raise costs for TeePrint so it may have to raise prices of its T-shirts and the proposed new products – impact on revenue will depend on price elasticity of demand.

   Higher unemployment – this will mean some consumers' incomes will fall as they lose their jobs but labour wage rates might also fall as there will be less demand for workers.

   Currency forecast to depreciate – raising imported T-shirt costs but making it possible to lower export prices.

   So, this information is very useful but other information needed before final decision about new products/markets is made.

   What proportion of total costs is made up from imported T-shirts? What percentage of sales does TeePrint make in Country A? Is the government planning to use expansionary fiscal policy to reduce unemployment and increase growth – will this make inflation worse? Expansionary fiscal policy could encourage consumers to increase demand if their disposable incomes rise.

Chapter 10
Progress check A

1 Incorrect decisions, inaction, poor leadership.

2 Objectives are needed to help direct, monitor and control.

3 Setting objectives for future levels of sales; organising the deliveries of products for selling; delegating tasks to employees; ensuring resources are available for busy periods; appraising employee performance.

Progress check B

1 Directors, worker representatives.

2 Responding to change, threats, opportunities.

3 The nature of the task – customer comes first; the skills of the workforce – fairly low level; the policies of the company – fairly tight.

Progress check C

1 Indecision, lack of clarity.

2 Desire to succeed – essential for motivating employees; ability to think beyond the obvious – identifying new opportunities; multi-talented – must inspire, solve problems, be creative; incisive mind – able to recognise and solve problems quickly.

3 De-motivated employees which might affect productivity, poor decisions which could lead to poor business performance.

Progress check D

1 Where instant decisions are required; where the workforce is largely unskilled; where it matches the culture of the business.

2 Research is an activity that requires freedom to develop in whatever way the research suggests. It is unlikely to follow a predictable pattern. It follows, that with a highly qualified team, leadership should be one that enables the research to develop. Leadership that allows personal and team development would be appropriate, possibly laissez, faire, paternalistic or democratic.

3 Decision making might be slow. Democratic decisions may not be the best.

4 Democratic.

5 In any business situation there will be some decisions that require an immediate response. Here autocratic leadership might be appropriate. There are other situations when it is best that a wide range of views help the decision process. Here democratic leadership might be better.

Progress check E

1 McGregor categorises management attitudes towards employees rather than categorising employees. Hence it is wrong to say that McGregor claimed there are two types of employee.

2 Theory Y sees managers as recognising that employees respond well to responsibility.

3 Theory X suggests that the manager does not fully trust employees and sees employees as needing motivation. These ideas are consistent with autocratic management.

Progress check F

1 Leadership style depends on the situation, the personality of the leader, the nature of the task, the nature of the workforce. Given any particular situation there might be a variety of styles of leadership that work.

2 Democratic leadership requires time for decisions and a range of views. Quick decisions do not allow for either of these possibilities. Hence autocratic leadership might be better.

3 Employees will instinctively react against change and be suspicious of how change is going to affect them. It is important, therefore, that employees are involved in decisions relating to change. This can best be achieved through democratic leadership or possibly paternalistic. Autocratic leadership will be unhelpful in most 'change' situations.

Progress check G

1 Only formal leaders have formal authority. The authority of informal leaders derives from their personality and efforts rather than formal responsibilities.

2 Charisma, enthusiasm, commitment.

Progress check H

1 Lack of understanding of others, lack of social awareness, lack of social skills.

2 Understands the needs of others, aware of social developments, skilled in self-management.

Additional exam-style questions

1 Emotional intelligence refers to the ability of managers to understand their own emotions and those of the people they work with. This can help business performance.

2 Mintzberg's leadership functions are: interpersonal, informational and decisional.

3 Autocratic leadership: leader takes all decisions; one-way flows of information; employees not involved

and little delegation. However, decisions can be made quickly, can react more quickly to unexpected changes and there is certainty about peoples' roles.

Discuss the leadership needs of today's competitive business environment.

- The need to manage and lead change, for example as a result of a change in competitors' marketing or the arrival of important new technology.

- The global nature of markets and increased competition which means businesses have to be able to compete more effectively.

- Increased expectations of workers, for example, the need to be involved or consulted at work is becoming more prevalent.

The importance for leaders to respond to different situations is clear. However, the leadership style should adjust to a given situation (a change in competitors' behaviour or an unexpected disaster could require an immediate leadership response whereas new technology would need a much more considered response with employee input). So, for example, respond rapidly to change brought about by a competitor or market (autocratic?), introduction of new working practices (democratic?), dealing with people of different cultures etc. (autocratic unlikely to be best here?).

It can be concluded that it is not possible to support the view in the question in all circumstances.

4 Analysis should include: skills of the workers; willingness to accept responsibility; whether workers can discuss and agree on the job losses; whether a quick decision needs to be taken.

Chapter 11

Progress check A

1 Examples of poor motivation include high absenteeism, low productivity, high labour turnover.

2 Managers will want to achieve efficiency and to achieve targets related to productivity. Motivated employees are more likely to be efficient (better attendance, less labour turnover) and these will translate into higher productivity.

3 Lower costs, higher customer satisfaction, lower absenteeism, lower labour turnover, all of which are relevant to the activities of a supermarket.

Progress check B

1 Taylor seemed to be suggesting more work for the same pay which is not what the employees want. Taylor also relies on work study and nobody likes being watched.

2 Taylor encouraged recruitment of people with relevant skills to improve productivity.

3 Human beings seek more than just money. People like to be praised and like to have a sense of achievement. Needs change over time.

Progress check C

1 Mayo suggested employee motivation could be improved by: consulting with employees; working in teams; empowering employees. Managers could use these ideas.

2 Taylor saw money as a key motivator, Mayo thought that money had little impact on productivity.

3 Workers' welfare could be seen as part of helping employees to take an interest in their jobs. This is one of Mayo's motivators.

Progress check D

1 Self-actualisation is a state of achieving one's ambitions. It is likely to be a temporary state as once achieved ambitions are likely to be extended or changed.

2 One possibility is that once needs are met then needs become greater.

3 Managers have the responsibility of getting the best out of their employees. Improved motivation is the best way to achieve this. Satisfying needs improves motivation.

4 Employers can help employees meet physical needs through a fair level of pay. Safety needs can be met though providing good (safe) working conditions. Social needs can be met through teamwork. Esteem needs can be achieved through rewarding employees with praise. Self-actualisation can be achieved through providing employees with opportunities.

Progress check E

1 Achievement, recognition, interesting work.

2 If employees think that they are not paid enough or are not getting a satisfactory pay increase they can feel that the business does not recognise their importance/achievements and so could become demotivated.

3 Good leadership can motivate, however changing the leadership style may not have as big an effect on motivation as, for example, being given responsibility.

Progress check F

1 Affiliation is probably a stronger need for employees than managers or leaders.

2 Entrepreneurs have to be self-motivated. The best way for this is through achievement since teamwork or praise are unlikely to motivate them and other needs are likely to have been met.

3 McClelland recognised that people are different and intrinsically motivated in different ways. Maslow assumed that employees are motivated by the same things but that people are at different stages.

Progress check G

1 Piece rate pay encourages people to work faster. It is unsuitable for lorry drivers because faster lorry drivers could be dangerous drivers and endanger the safety of the public.

2 Company cars, insurance, pension schemes.

3 Profit sharing depends on the performance of the business as a whole in terms of the profit it has achieved. Performance-related pay could be applied at levels smaller than the whole business such as department or section.

Progress check H

1 Empowerment, teamwork, job rotation.

2 Piece rate depends on the quantity of work completed, e.g. the number of items produced. Performance related pay is similar but is measured in terms of achieving targets which need not be units of output (e.g. reducing the number of complaints from customers).

Additional exam-style questions

1 A hygiene factor is a feature of Herzberg's motivation theory. It is a factor which does not directly motivate but an absence of the feature could demotivate.

2 Performance-related pay, profit sharing.

3 Empowerment is the process through which employees are given the responsibility to make their own decisions and have control over the tasks they undertake.

4 BQS is considering:

- Delaying a pay increase which means that pay will be less than that for competitors. Likely to demotivate employees and therefore they seek jobs elsewhere. They will have committed levels of spending and there might be problems if they do not get a pay rise.

- Introducing flexible working contracts so that employees will not get paid if they are not needed. This might suit a few employees but could upset many, particularly those who require full-time work.

- Greater staff discounts on goods purchased by staff. Staff might like this as they are likely to buy their family food and other products from the supermarket.

- Payment of a bonus in the form of shares if the business does well. This might provide an incentive to work harder and could make up for the loss of a pay rise. However, it is income that is unpredictable.

- Longer working hours with no extra pay. Employees will not like this at all and it could be demotivating.

Perhaps the most important is the loss of future pay rises since a satisfactory level of income is essential to every family.

Chapter 12
Progress check A

1 Supermarkets are very labour intensive and so they rely on people for their success. The idea of an HRM department is to have a team that aims to bring the best out of the employees. In this way the supermarket would benefit directly from the HRM department through recruitment of the best people

for the job, effective training and a focus on welfare issues. Effective workforce planning would also help.

2 HRM issues in a small business are likely to be fairly simple as there will be few employees. Usually managers or owners should be able to sort out most of the problems. Where problems cannot be easily solved it may be better to outsource (subcontract) the HRM issues as it would be more expensive to set up and run an HRM department.

Progress check B

1 A global downturn is likely to have an impact on most businesses as customers (businesses or final consumers) are likely to have less income to spend. In most instances, sales of a business will fall and the business may have to cut down on production and employees. In some instances, the business could benefit, for example shops that focus on products for low-income people. In these instances they will have to plan for a possible increase in the workforce. The business may also benefit from cheaper raw materials, which may help it compete.

2 A new factory would require a workforce which would probably have to be recruited (and in addition, possibly transferred from other factories). The business would need to have an idea of how many people are needed, what skills are needed and where the skills are available e.g. through training.

3 Possible skills shortages.

Possible shortages of people.

Possible excess of people.

Progress check C

1 Product development is an area of the business that needs new ideas. Externally recruited people might be best to bring in new ideas either because they are new to the business and not 'set in their ways' or because they bring ideas across from their previous employer.

2 Banks are organisations that rely heavily on procedures. Customer care is also very important. Internal appointments will be familiar with the bank's procedures and customers.

3 A job description will have details of tasks to be done in a particular job. The person specification will have details of the skills and qualities that the person doing that job should have.

4 Labour turnover = 5/50 × 100 = 10%

Progress check D

1 Most employees will not be used to flexible working. In a traditional car factory they will only know about their own job. They will also be used to working set hours within tightly controlled procedures. Flexible working will be a completely new way of operating and they will need to be trained into working in a different cultural environment. Car manufacturing is complex so employees will need to be trained in a wide range of skills.

2 Staff development can help an employee feel valued, through improved skills the employee could get more fulfilment, with greater skills may come greater responsibility. All these relate to Herzberg's motivators.

3 Induction training is a type of training designed to make a newcomer to a business familiar with the way that particular business operates. The training is likely to be highly specific to that business so is likely to take place within the business. 'Off-the-job' training, in contrast, is usually more general in nature and can take place off the site of the business.

4 Employee development should be directed towards the aims of the business as well as the needs of the employee. Managers are usually in the best position to judge both of these.

5 Businesses with large IT departments may have a leading role in the process of upgrading the computers. They would be the best people to undertake the training. In most other organisations it is best if the business that supplied the hardware/software upgrades provides the training.

Progress check E

1 Fashion goods are usually considered as luxuries. In a global downturn there is a general reduction in incomes. When people have lower incomes they spend less on luxuries, which means that fashion shops will have lower turnovers and may have to make employees redundant.

2 A business can only make an employee redundant when their job is no longer required (i.e. it is a job-related decision rather than an employee-related decision). An employee can be dismissed for breaking the conditions of their contract, incompetence or a breach of discipline (i.e. it is an employee-related decision rather than job-related).

3 The business needs to make sure it cannot be taken to court for unfair dismissal. In addition, it would not want to face media criticism or other bad publicity. In addition, it needs to think about the morale of the remaining employees.

4 Redundancy can be expensive, it can affect the general level of morale, it could lead to the loss of valuable skills/experience. Redeployment avoids these.

5 Theft, incompetence.

Additional exam-style questions

1 Two roles of a Human Resource Manager are to oversee recruitment and training.

2. 'On-the-job' training is training that takes place in the workplace in relation to a specific job unlike training that takes place at a training establishment.

3 Workforce planning could enable managers to identify what jobs are needed, what jobs are no longer needed, what training needs will help increase workforce skills.

4 The role of HRM includes: recruitment, selection, training, advice, workforce planning. It is important that a school recruits and trains quality teachers and support staff. It is important that teachers get paid on time. The welfare of staff at school will also be important. A school can be a complex organisation with ever-changing needs. Workforce planning will help the school prepare to meet those needs.

5 The answer should cover the benefits of training to a business and its employees, as well as its costs and implications for grants, company tax etc. The question, though, really hinges round why people would take their skills elsewhere and so should focus on how it would keep its employees, concluding that it is probably not a waste of time.

Chapter 13

Progress check A

1 For most businesses human resources are the most important resource. People work, come up with new ideas, sell products/services, work with machinery and solve all sorts of problems. Without improving employee performance, the business will not do as well as it could.

2 The most effective way would be to measure sales in relation to the number of employees.

3 Inefficient workforce, lack of training, lack of resources.

4 Continuity is important in education. It might divert resources having to recruit. Labour turnover is often a sign of low morale – not good at a school.

5 Total days lost through absenteeism $= 10 \times 10 = 100$

Total possible days worked $= 10 \times 200 = 2000$

Absenteeism $= 100/2000 \times 100 = 5\%$

It is not advisable to perform the calculation 'per person' although in this instance it can be done.

Progress check B

1 Hotels rely on good customer service. Training could help employees provide better customer service and that would be a way of improving employee performance.

2 Absenteeism is usually a sign of low morale. Teamwork could increase morale. Also, teamwork could result in peer pressure to stop people absenting themselves.

3 Giving employees a stake in any business is likely to motivate them which will improve labour productivity. Poor productivity is likely to be reflected in poor customer service which is bad for an airline. With a stake in the business, airline employees will see the need to improve their own performance in relation to customer service and hence productivity.

Progress check C

1 Improved class attendance, improved examination results.

2 Improved results depend as much on the students as the teachers.

3 There might be external factors influencing the results. The targets might be too ambitious.

Progress check D

1 To protect employees. To set standards for business behaviour. Because it is what voters wanted.

2 To prevent coercion.

Progress check E

1 Happy workers are good workers. To attract the best people to work for the business. To avoid bad publicity.

2   More efficient, better industrial relations.

3   There could be different outcomes in each of the locations leading to complex arrangements. Could be communication/management issues.

Progress check F

1   Legal protection, getting pay increases, getting better conditions of service.

2   A strike would be disastrous for society if there was no police protection.

3   Relative strengths of the two groups. Views/support of the public/customers. The reason for the dispute, what is being sought and what is being offered.

4   They may not be against it! However, it could reduce the power of individual unions.

Additional exam-style question

1   Define workforce planning. Difficult in this industry – variable demand, interest changes and technology. Effective workforce planning helps to ensure enough people (not too many either) of the right skills. Helps to reach output and cost targets. New factory will need sales forecasts of EU demand to plan the workforce. Will need to consider EU employment laws, e.g. redundancy and security of jobs. So, workforce planning very important but cannot ensure success. Has SSE estimated the higher costs of operating in the EU accurately? Will communications with Head Office be effective? Joint venture might have been a wiser move – local knowledge of the partner could have helped with workforce planning too. Success will also depend on product design and suitability for EU market.

Chapter 14
Progress check A

1   So that people know who does what, to define communication channels, to clarify responsibilities.

2   Large organisations tend to have a large number of employees, many with highly specialised roles. These need clearly defined departments with clearly defined responsibilities. Small organisations are usually more informal, often with employees and managers multi-tasking, doing tasks as and when needed, rather than keeping to one clearly defined role.

3   For a particular piece of information the employee will need to know what area of the business is responsible for that activity and who in that area (department) is likely to have the information. So, for example, if the employee needs to know recent sales data the employee should be able to identify the person in the sales department who keeps records.

Progress check B

1   They make communication between departments more difficult, communications are slower as they have to go all the way up the hierarchy, the more levels then the more scope for distortion of communications.

2   Employees will feel comfortable when their role is clearly specified. They will find it easier to communicate with other areas of the business.

3   Most countries and most markets are highly competitive and if businesses do not respond quickly to change, they will be left behind by competitors.

Progress check C

1   Teams are multi-skilled so can draw on a range of skills. It encourages cooperation.

2   Through teams drawn from different subjects, e.g. a tutor system that is non-subject based.

3   Because it is multinational there would be communication difficulties if teams are drawn from around the world. Skills may be too diverse.

Progress check D

1   Because information flows will be quicker, easier and easier to circulate so that the structure may not have to be so rigid or clearly defined.

2   Banks are highly regulated and staff must adhere to clearly defined procedures. Teachers have some autonomy in the classroom in terms of how the curriculum is delivered and discipline.

3   A wide span implies a wide range of responsibilities. A manager may not be able to fulfil or monitor all of those responsibilities so will have to delegate as they cannot do everything.

4   Large businesses tend to be more complex so communication channels and responsibilities have to be clearly defined.

Progress check E

1   The headteacher and governors cannot possibly be expected to take an interest in and manage every teacher and every lesson so they have to delegate some responsibilities to teachers.

2   Instructions may not be clear, people think and behave differently, instructions could be ignored.

3   Authority is the power assigned to a manager. Responsibility means being accountable or answerable for actions. You can give someone the authority to do a particular task but you retain the responsibility that the task will be done.

4   Authority is the power assigned to a manager, accountability is the requirement to be answerable for anything to do with the power that is exercised.

Progress check F

1   Global markets require efficiency, rapid communications and the ability to change quickly. Multi-layer organisations do not meet these requirements. Delayering will make the business more effective in these respects.

2   There will be too many people involved in decisions, slow communications and more resistance to change.

3   Scientific experts, lawyers, market researchers.

4   It depends on the food and the business. If regional taste is an important factor then decentralisation would help the business respond to local taste. If the culture of the business is for centralisation then decentralisation may not work.

Additional exam-style question

1   Define centralised structure. Analyse possible benefits of centralisation in this case, e.g. same policies used in all countries SSE produces and sells in; less chance of different HR policies being used which could lead to employee problems (one set of factory workers with better conditions than others). Consistent marketing strategy determined by Head Office might make it easier to establish same global brand image and keep marketing costs down.

Analyse possible disadvantages of centralisation in this case: EU factory needs different HR policies and trained technical employees will expect more delegation/decision-making authority. Selling in

EU markets might benefit from decentralised decision making to allow for appropriate localised marketing strategies. R and D team and other new employees developing new products might work more creatively with considerable delegation/ decentralisation.

Overall conclusion and evaluation needed, e.g. keep some functions centralised, e.g. finance, as expansion will be expensive and SSE needs to control spending because of this; but could decentralise HR and marketing.

Chapter 15
Progress check A

1   It is important that students know what is happening. For example, students will want to know the dates of school holidays. It is also important that school managers know how students are performing, so exam results, for example, should be widely circulated for decision-making purposes.

2   Effective communication is communication that achieves its purpose. So, for example, a business might communicate with its customers through and advertising campaign. It will be effective if customers change their buying behaviours.

3   Large shops may have problems if one department does not know what another is doing, if employees do not know about changes to policy, if managers do not know what is happening on the 'shop floor'. Each of these problems could be a result of poor communication so problems can be avoided through effective communication.

Progress check B

1   Quick, cheap if the equipment already exists, easy to communicate with many people.

2   There is no permanent record of the conversation.

3   Offering employment to an applicant; confirming the details of a contract.

4   Advertisements, labels on products, placing of products within the shop.

5   There needs to be a record of the discussion, the discussion will need to be available to a range of people, and there has to be the possibility of feedback.

Progress check C

1   Language, choice of medium, skills of the communicators.

2   Jargon is vocabulary that is known and used by a select group of people, e.g. teachers. Using jargon could exclude those that are not in the group from understanding the messages.

3   Each intermediary used increases the risk of misunderstanding.

Progress check D

1   Feedback happens when the receiver of a communication responds to the communication, for example by saying that the message has been understood.

2   Feedback can act as confirmation that the message has been understood, alternatively seeking clarification if the message has not been understood. Either way it helps to ensure the best chance that the message is understood.

3   Messages get distorted with intermediaries. The shorter the communication channel, the fewer the intermediaries so the smaller the chance of distortion.

Progress check E

1   Horizontal communication might be difficult. They might not understand each other's language (e.g. marketing jargon or accounting jargon).

2   Employees may be more prepared to talk to each other than to their managers.

3   Informal communication can become negative and undermining.

4   Employees will understand better what is going on and what they are to achieve. This will make them feel more confident and so more motivated. Good communication also improves the employees' sense of belonging which also helps motivation.

5   It involves staff participation which appears in several motivation theories and also relates to teamwork which also features in the theories.

Additional exam-style question

1   Post and telephone seem to be used (shareholders and suppliers/customers).

Post – slow and expensive especially for large book of accounts/report. Telephone – may not be answered, no visible contact, no physical record.

Alternatives – managers – video conferences? Cheap to set up; some face-to-face contact. Two-way communication – discussion might lead to better decisions. However, is senior management in SSE prepared to be seen and encourage participation in this way? Shareholders – online reports/accounts and follow up with more regular meetings with shareholders (not just AGM perhaps). Keeps them better informed of latest company developments. However, some shareholders may not have IT and prefer to read paper documents. Expensive for them to print out web version. Suppliers/ customers – company website for orders and technical queries (customers) and suppliers' websites/email for suppliers. However, some queries might need a discussion/direct contact with SSE staff. Web-based communication too impersonal?

Recommendations to be made in all cases based on preceding analysis.

Chapter 16

Progress check A

1   Researching markets; communicating with production department about the products consumers want to buy; preparing adverts for products; (other tasks could be suggested).

2   Making decisions using information about consumer tastes and needs is likely to lead to a more successful business.

3   Increase market share; increase sales by ten per cent each year (other objectives are possible).

4   • Apple's corporate objectives

To ensure that the marketing objectives, if achieved, will help the Apple company achieve its overall corporate objectives.

• Objectives of other departments within Apple

There should be communication between departments within Apple to ensure that objectives are coordinated, e.g. to increase sales by ten per cent each year will need the operations department to increase output too.

5 Market led (or oriented) businesses will use market research to help decide what products to produce. Product led businesses do not do this so they might have to spend a lot on advertising to sell the products they have made.

Progress check B

1

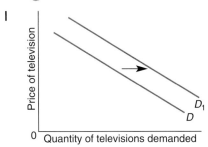

2

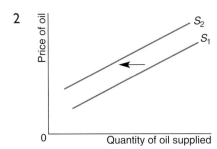

3 Rise in both cases – show this by putting a supply curve on Q1 diagram and demand curve on Q2 diagram and note what happens to the equilibrium price.

4 $20m/$90m × 100 = 22.2%

5 Year 1: $30m/$90m × 100 = 33.3%

Year 2: $35m/$110m × 100 = 31.8%

6 $230m × 0.15 = $34.5m

7 The business could use a high market share in its advertising such as: 'The country's most popular breakfast cereal'. It will also make it easier to encourage retailers to stock the cereals as they will be asked by consumers for this particular brand.

Progress check C

1 Present the products in an attractive and appealing way, e.g. not wrapped in a lot of plastic so the meat/vegetables cannot be seen effectively.

Give consumers information about how the products were produced ('organic'; 'locally produced' etc.).

2 Computers for school students (relatively low price and easy to carry); computers for low-income developing countries (low price and easy to repair); retro/vintage computers (there are many collectors of old computers now!); small tablet computers.

3 Able to focus on the products needed by a particular section of the market – avoids development costs of computers to meet all consumers' needs; able to focus marketing on the selected niche market.

4 Family oriented cars – for families with children; luxury sport cars – high income, unmarried consumers; farmers – rugged vehicles with four wheel drive.

5 Farmers – products will be developed for farmers' specific needs – less comfortable but more rugged than normal vehicles so should be more reliable and break down infrequently; able to focus marketing/selling efforts on farmers, e.g. at agricultural shows.

Additional exam-style questions

1 Dividing one large market into smaller sections based on different consumer profiles e.g. the cinema market into films for children and films for senior citizens

2 Simple, easy to use camera for young consumers, using cheap materials – sold at relatively low prices

Expensive, advanced technology digital camera with interchangeable lenses supported by brand name and promotions for high income groups greatly interested in photography – made using expensive materials

3 Total value of sales [possible number of total units sold] made by all businesses in the market during a time period – usually one year

4 Last year: $4m/$32m × 100 = 12.5%

This year: $4.6m/$35m × 100 = 13.1%

Change is up by 0.6 percentage points (accept 0.6%).

5 The increase in market share means that although the market grew last year HiQ's sales grew even faster. This suggests that the products of the business are becoming even more popular – other retailers might want to stock HiQ's products that it buys in.

6 By income group of consumers: famous branded sport clothing for high-income group consumers.

By type of user, e.g. professional athletes will demand a much higher level of product performance (running shoes, for example) than casual sports players will.

7   Yes: shops already exist; fixed costs already incurred so may be cheaper than using another channel of distribution; quicker than setting up new retail outlets; may encourage parents buying clothing for children to also buy sports clothing for themselves.

No: shops do not appear to be well organised or to have a good image; adults might expect higher standards of presentation than children; if well-known brands of adult sports clothing are to be sold then a much higher quality image of retail outlet would be advisable.

Overall supported conclusion needed.

Chapter 17

Progress check A

1   Knowing about the market and market trends can help in product, pricing, promotion and place decisions.

2   Customer needs and tastes are very important in affecting the demand for a product – knowing as much about these as possible will help to make the product a success.

3   New product development (NPD) can be very expensive and take a long time. Before committing time and money to NPD, a business will increase its chance of success if it has researched market trends and consumer needs first.

Progress check B

1   Specific to needs of the business; up to date; results not accessible to other businesses.

2   Data from secondary research (e.g. if market size is falling) can help managers decide whether it is worthwhile spending time and money on primary research.

3   For a completely new product or market where no previous data exists.

4   It gives information which cannot be easily put into a number format, e.g. the influences behind consumers' decisions such as 'Explain why you preferred Product A to Product B'.

Progress check C

1   Ad hoc; judgemental; snowball; convenience.

2   Convenience: small business or new start-up; finance limited; quick results needed.

Snowball: when other respondents are hard to identify or contact, the names suggested by those who have undertaken the research will be useful.

3   It reduces cost and time spent on primary market research – and the whole 'population' might not be known or accessible to market researchers.

Progress check D

1   They can be difficult to analyse statistically.

2   Sampling bias; questionnaire bias; respondent bias, e.g. when convenience sampling is used amongst friends.

3   Cheaper form of data collection than interviews.

4   Sample too small; unrepresentative sample; respondent bias – they might try to 'please' a member of their family.

Progress check E

1   Mode – result is a whole number (size) and represents the most popular size bought by customers.

2   By one extreme high or low result.

3   The range indicates the maximum and minimum dress sizes likely to be bought by customers; the IQ range will indicate the mid-range of sizes which 50 per cent of customers will buy.

Additional exam-style questions

1   a   i   Information that is not in number form – it contains consumers' opinions and views.

ii   Information that is expressed in a number format and can be analysed statistically. For example, 'the number of doctors who would be prepared to use NCH facilities at a certain price'.

b   Reduces risk of wasting government finance on facilities that will not be demanded – this finance will have an opportunity cost.

Increases the chance that the most appropriate facilities will be constructed – those that will be in most demand from private sector doctors and other private sector health providers. This will raise more finance for the hospital.

2   Random sampling gives all members of the 'population' an equal chance of being selected. No grouping of the population is made.

Stratified sampling may use random sampling but first the population is divided into groups or strata based on one factor, e.g. age. The number chosen in the sample from each strata will depend on its relative importance to the whole population.

3   Finance likely to be limited – so secondary research will be essential.

Cheaper than primary, readily available to a new entrepreneur and could help him/her decide whether to go ahead with primary research and what form this research should take.

Primary research might be best undertaken amongst family/friends etc. rather than amongst the wider population – this will be more convenient, quicker and cheaper – but will it be as accurate?

Quantitative data – 'the prices charged by other food retailers' will help the entrepreneur make key decisions.

Qualitative data – 'explain why you buy food from this retailer and not the larger one in the town' will help the entrepreneur decide on key issues about location, layout etc. of new food shop.

Cost-effectiveness will be essential – finance limited.

Overall judgement about the relative advantages of the different methods/type of data needed – in context of a new entrepreneur.

Chapter 18
Progress check A

1   Student's own answer.

2   By using customer relationship marketing, e.g. loyalty vouchers; better communication, e.g. email to customer as birthday approaches; allowing online bookings.

3   a   Difficult to differentiate the basic services that banks offer – and it is now increasingly easy to switch accounts from one bank to another – therefore CRM very important to retain loyalty of existing customers.

   b   Mobile phone providers operate in a highly competitive market and it is easy to switch (once contract period has ended) so any CRM activity which keeps customers loyal is likely to be cheaper than advertising for new customers.

Progress check B

1   Not necessarily – the performance of the product and whether it meets customer expectations will be more important. Advertising might be necessary to attract new customers; reinforce brand image and inform consumers of new features/price levels.

2   See Fig 18.3.

3   For example: iPad: more powerful processor; more capable camera; promotion of the product towards business users not just consumers.

4   Launch: informative advertising to let potential customers know about the product/price/where it can be bought etc.

Growth: supportive advertising reinforcing the brand image; advertising the initial success of the product.

Maturity/saturation: possibly less advertising and more focus on CRM instead.

Decline: advertising of special offers or, if extension strategies are used, advertising which informs customers about these product updates. If the product is just going to be withdrawn, then no advertising at all.

5   Not necessarily a good predictor of what will happen as estimating the length of each stage is very difficult.

In practice, it is difficult to know which stage a product is in – if sales have stopped growing, is this definitely the maturity/saturation stage or is it a temporary phase (maybe due to economic factors) before sales start to increase again?

Progress check C

Original price	New price	Original demand	New demand	PED	Comment
$5	$6	1500	1050	−1.5	Demand is elastic and revenue should fall if the price is increased.
$1000	$1050	300	270	−2	Demand is price elastic and revenue should fall if the price is increased.
$1	$0.95	5000	6000	−4	Demand is price elastic and revenue will increase if price is reduced.
$10000	$11000	200	195	−0.25	Demand is price inelastic and revenue should rise if the price is increased.

2 If the same price change was applied to both goods (in per cent) then the quantity demanded of X would change by more than the quantity demanded of Y.

3 Demand curve would be flatter for D than for C.

Total revenue would rise for C but fall for D (as demand for D is price elastic).

4 Number of close competitors.

Proportion of consumers' incomes spent on the product.

Whether product is a necessity or not.

Progress check D

1 Mark up expected = 25%

Variable cost per unit = $10

Weekly fixed costs = $1000

Units sold per week = 500

Fixed cost per unit = $2

Total cost per unit = $12

Price = $12 + 25% = $15

2 If spare bedrooms exist for tomorrow night, important to fill them with guests paying a positive contribution. Calculate variable cost of guest per bedroom and add on a contribution = price charged to customer.

3 When there are a number of competitors with very similar products; when it is easy for new competitors to join the market.

4 Charging different prices to different groups of consumers for the same product, e.g. adult and child prices at a cinema.

5 Skimming – high price for new products to gain high profit margin – price lowered as competitors enter the market.

Penetration – low price to gain market share and customer loyalty – gives opportunity for higher price some time after launch.

6 a Skimming – when there is no competition, e.g. for a product with a USP.

b Penetration – when market share is important, e.g. to gain special treatment from retailers.

7 When consumers associate high price with quality and exclusive brand image, e.g. TAG watches.

Additional exam-style questions

1 a i Market share % = $\dfrac{\text{Sales of Redgate}}{\text{Total market sales}} \times 100$

ii Selling a product below cost of production or bought-in costs – to gain market share and 'put a squeeze' on competitors – as with supermarkets charging very low prices for bread and this makes it difficult for Redgate to compete.

b i Total cost per cake = $35
Price = $35 plus 20% = $42

ii Total cost per unit = $32
Price = $32 + 20% = $38.40

d Yes: competition is high in selling bread and it might be easy for supermarkets or other local bakers to enter the market for specialist cakes and start under-cutting Redgate's prices.

Important to retain customer loyalty by focusing on 4Cs.

In this case: high quality products (do not buy in cheaper materials!); communicating better with customers, e.g. encourage online orders; Twitter and other social media to make customers feel more involved with business.

Offer free delivery to improve the total 'offering' to customers.

No: it is successful as a cake maker and customers might be loyal due to good products and good reputation; quite difficult for other cake makers to establish a quality image quickly; better to spend marketing resources on advertising and promotion to encourage new customers to buy from Redgate.

Overall, justified conclusion needed.

2 a CRM aims to increase customer loyalty; use of the 4Cs – give shoe retailer examples; will be cheaper than gaining new customers; shoe retailing highly competitive – need to retain customers, interest and make them feel involved with the activities and success of the business.

   b Definition – also a sketch diagram might make the rest of the answer clearer to follow.

Soft drinks can pass through a product life cycle as tastes change and competition launches new products – perhaps Coke and Pepsi are exceptions.

Can use the plc to help determine appropriate marketing mix decisions at each stage – apply to soft drinks.

The model can also be used to help build a balanced portfolio of products at different stages of their plcs.

However, difficult to use plc to make sales predictions as so many factors will affect demand for any one brand of soft drinks, e.g. increasing concern about sugar content of them; difficult to tell which stage a product is at; marketing mix decisions will also depend on competitors' actions – not just the estimated stage of the plc a product is at.

Chapter 19
Progress check A

1 To inform potential customers and to entice them to try it for the first time.

2 To attract new customers; to support the brand image; to retain customers; to sell to other segments of the market.

3 Direct mail – focused mail shots to people who have already been identified as potential customers.

Sponsorship, e.g. of sports stars – gains TV and other media coverage when that star is playing.

Press releases – positive news about the company and its products is released to the press/media.

4 The financial amount to be spent on advertising/promotion in a given time period.

5 Not necessarily. It might try public relations or other below the line promotions, e.g. sponsorship, which are not directly paid for communications. Social media/online advertising might be cheaper than traditional media. Business needs to assess what potential customers are likely to find most appealing.

6 To help make future promotion decisions. It is pointless spending money on advertising and promotion if no assessment of its 'success' is attempted. If it has been unsuccessful, but no record is kept of this, then similar expensive promotion mistakes might be made in future.

Progress check B

1 Computer games bought only by young consumers – they tend not to watch mainstream TV channels.

2 New washing machine – able to demonstrate its style and performance to mass market at peak viewing times.

3 Impulse purchases, e.g. bars of chocolate. An attractive display might stimulate demand.

4 Launch – heavy informative advertising.

Growth – brand differentiation advertising/promotion.

Maturity – retain customer loyalty promotions.

Decline – use extension strategies supported by advertising/promotions.

5 Increase market share; increase sales; increase brand awareness; improve customer loyalty.

Progress check C

1 Projects a quality, professional image. Helps to add value to the product. Many consumers have little knowledge of jewellery so need expert advice.

2 B2B – expensive product, not many sold at each transaction; expensive to hold inventory for channel intermediary; expert technical knowledge required – best obtained from manufacturer.

3 Factory may not be close to population centres; expensive to retail to consumers, e.g. holding inventory so manufacturer wants other businesses to bear this cost; many consumers want to see and try before buying.

4 Cheap product sold in small quantities; national sales coverage required; expensive to own shops; wholesaler will break bulk for small retailers.

5 Student's own answer.

6 Through viral marketing with informal consumer reports and reviews on products; tweets with image; Facebook with images of the product.

Additional exam-style questions

1 a Advantages: global reach; potential for increased sales; cheaper than opening shops; no profit margin for clothing retailer; prices can therefore be more competitive.

Disadvantages: very competitive – how can business get its website viewed before those of rivals? Consumers cannot see, try it, feel it (important for clothes?) or gain fashion advice from shop assistant; transport costs – cost of handling returns from dissatisfied consumers.

2 a i Paid for communication with consumers to inform and persuade, for example, TV and cinema advertising.

ii Use of social networking sites or SMS text messages to 'spread the word' about a brand and to sell products. This is becoming more common and it might be particularly effective for hi-tech product bought by younger consumers.

b i 2% of $120m = $2.4m

10% of $2.4m = $240 000

ii By value of sales in comparison to total camera market in the country – market share, especially as HTC's marketing objective is in terms of market share.

c Global coverage – 50 shops cannot provide this. Internet sales will allow HTC to become less dependent on sales of cameras in just one national market.

Lower cost – savings from not paying the fixed costs of the shops will allow HTC to invest more in developing new cameras with a USP.

d Define the 4Ps and explain that they should be consistent with each other. Lightpix is a unique product (claims HTC) and is likely to have a high price. It will need careful packaging for online delivery. Promotion is 'high tech' social media and not traditional with no TV, cinema, newspaper advertising. Will this matter to the potential buyers of Lightpix? They are not necessarily all going to be younger consumers with access to social media and online advertising. Is online selling the best way to sell cameras? Helps to make the price competitive (but how price elastic will the demand for Lightpix be?). Perhaps consumers want to see, feel, try a camera first before buying?

Conclusion: for the younger generation perhaps this does seem like an integrated/consistent mix. But what proportion of potential customers will be young? Is HTC missing out on other types of consumers? For these the proposed mix is not integrated or consistent with the quality/high price image of HTC and Lightpix.

Chapter 20

Progress check A

1 No, external factors could change greatly in an unforeseen way, so a plan should have some flexibility built into it.

2 If a strategy is decided first, e.g. 'develop new markets in other countries' and then the objective 'increase market share in our existing markets', the strategy is just not suitable or appropriate. Remember: objectives before strategy!

Progress check B

1 C appears to be an inferior good – more of this should be produced if there is a recession as consumers are likely to buy more of it.

D is a normal good but with low income elasticity – it might be a 'necessity' product so demand will not vary much with booms/recessions.

E has high income elasticity – a luxury good. More of this will be sold during a boom period when consumer incomes are rising.

2 C up; D not much change – slightly down; E down significantly.

3 Each extra 1 per cent of advertising spend increase sales of B by 3 per cent but sales of A by only 1 per cent.

4 How old are they? Results might be different now. Will depend on the effectiveness of promotion campaign – not just how much is spent.

5 P and R are substitutes; P and S are complementary goods.

6 External factors might change, e.g. a new competitor or an existing rival might have a very effective new advertising campaign.

Progress check C

1 Brainstorming; feedback from customers via sales employees; R and D department.

2 Eliminates those ideas with least chance of success – it might be too expensive to develop all new ideas into final products.

3 If the product fails it will have cost less to market in a test market than launching the product in the whole market.

4 Nature of the products/consumer expectations.

5 a To research into more efficient and lighter cars that need less power.

b Newly launched powerful sports cars might now be less successful.

6 Offensive: develop new products before competitors.

Defensive: respond to the new products developed by other companies – perhaps trying to improve on them.

Progress check D

1 Where change in one variable, e.g. advertising spend, occurs and another variable also increases, e.g. sales.

2 When the total seasonal variations of each time period, e.g. quarter, are added together and divided by the number of results.

3 When a newly developed product is being considered for which there is no past sales data.

4

Quarter	Sales $000	Trend (quarterly moving average) $000	Seasonal variation $000
1	56	63	−7
2	67	66	+ 1
3	80	70	+10

5 Likely to be income elastic products especially the expensive models, so variations in the business cycle will lead to sales rising/falling.

6 New competitor enters the market; unforeseen economic changes, e.g. increases in government taxes on the product.

7 Cyclical – occur over time period of more than one year.

Seasonal – occur within one year.

Additional exam-style question

1 b Marketing strategy: a coordinated objective, budget and marketing mix.

Clear objective – 5 per cent market share. Not a mass market product – can price skim – as RCC also need to earn their investment in R and D back.

Budget of $1m – not large – public relations; viral marketing using social media etc.; sponsorship, perhaps of sports stars, should be used rather than traditional above the line media – these methods are likely to appeal to 'young people'.

Mix – high price – above those of competitors' products which do not have the USP of Sunsafe Junior. High income elasticity – and rising incomes in Country P – consumers will demand higher status products (will parents or young people themselves buy this product?).

Viral marketing – aimed at young people; brand forming; sports stars' or pop stars' sponsorship.

Attractive and exclusive looking packaging – supporting the RCC brand as well as being informative about the product.

Increase up-market retailers – beauty salons or exclusive pharmacists to support its 'health and natural' image.

Mix must be integrated – to give consumers consistent message.

Need to review progress towards market share target towards end of the year and adjust the mix if necessary. All recommendations must be explained/supported/integrated with each other.

Chapter 21
Progress check A

Globalisation benefits	Globalisation drawbacks
a New markets open up.	**b** More foreign competitors in home market.
c Costs may be lower in foreign markets (if locating there).	**d** Cultural differences exist in foreign markets (when selling overseas).
e Increased competition can force a business to increase efficiency.	
f Integration with foreign businesses more likely.	**g** Takeovers by foreign businesses more likely.

Progress check B

1 Student's own answer based on: population size; GDP; GDP growth; openness to trade etc.

2 Some foods are not accepted in some societies/cultures, e.g. pork to Muslims; beef to Hindus.

3 Large market; rapidly growing market; relatively small domestic car industry (although this is changing quickly).

Progress check C

1 Existing markets might be saturated/facing more competition; large and growing middle class in India with spending power.

2 Pan global – although the promotions used might be changed and geared towards local market trends/features.

3 Products, e.g. health and safety regulations; pricing – might be maximum price controls; promotion – advertising directly to children forbidden in some countries.

4 Product – many products are age related so produce clothes for middle-aged people in Japan but fashion clothing for young consumers in Brazil! Promotion techniques/media and the message used might vary due to different age structure of population; place – online selling likely to be more common in countries where average age is low.

5 Gain local market knowledge (important for food products); benefit for established and trusted brand name (important for food); share costs of the venture.

6 Lower costs of marketing than global localisation; establishes consistent brand/product image globally.

Additional exam-style questions

1 a Define globalisation; MB has benefited from being able to put supplies from 'lowest cost providers' in several different countries. This allows it to be a low-cost provider and helps it be profitable despite pricing meals 'competitively'.

It has expanded internationally – as a consequence of lowering/ending of trade barriers. It can move capital to the countries it plans to expand into – benefiting from rapid expansion of many countries. Giving economies of scale and global reach.

It has a diverse workforce – globalisation allows it to employ restaurant workers from many countries and it has a wider choice of good workers – able and willing to offer the quick service MB is well known for.

Chapter 22
Progress check A

1 The main resource would be the crude oil which is the raw material. In addition, oil refineries have large amounts of machinery and equipment for refining the oil and delivering to customers. Some labour is required for maintenance and management.

2 Cement manufacturers usually sell most of the production to the construction industry.

3 A shoe shop will need premises, people to serve, electricity to light the showroom and equipment such as tills, chairs.

4   Land includes buildings such as factories, shops, offices. It also includes physical land in the examples of farming or mining.

Progress check B

1   Consumer needs are usually determined through the use of market research.

2   Quality is a feature of a product. If the quality does not meet the requirements of the customer it means that there are ways that the production process could be improved.

3   The term 'production' applies to any business process that adds value. Banks provide services such as processing cheques, providing bank accounts, providing advice and lending. These services are part of the bank's production process.

Progress check C

1   A retail outlet provides the customer with the products that the customer wants in a convenient location. It adds value by choosing an appropriate range of products and providing the convenient location as well as expertise/advice.

2   The total costs are $30, the value added is $30, so the value to the customer is $60.

Progress check D

1   The process of promotion can increase the desire of consumers to purchase the particular model of car. The promotion can emphasise the special features of the car and its image, both of which could increase its desirability. Increased desire provides the opportunity for the producer to increase the price. Provided that the promotion costs are less than the increase in price then value added will have increased.

2   New software could give the laptop greater flexibility and the ability to undertake different tasks. If these tasks are what the customer wants, then value will have been added as the customer will be prepared to pay more for the laptop.

Progress check E

1   Effectiveness of a school could be measured by examination results. Efficiency could be measured by comparing the costs with the costs at a similar school.

2   Running the capital equipment for longer hours, more efficient management of the production system.

3   If teachers worked longer hours, then more students could be taught. If classes were larger, more students could be taught. Both ways would increase the output of teachers.

4   Teachers would neither want longer hours nor larger classes as both would involve them in more work.

5   Capital intensive methods rely more on capital items such as machinery, robots etc. and so less labour would be needed than with a labour intensive system. Employees would be concerned that the might lose their jobs.

Additional exam-style questions

1   Added value is defined as the increase in value a business adds from one stage of production to the next. If a business buys a dress from the manufacturer for $10 and sells it for $30 it has added $20 (ignoring other costs).

2   A labour intensive business is one that relies more on people (labour) than it does on machines (capital). An example of a labour intensive business is a hair dressing business which, apart from the building, relies almost totally on the hairdressers.

3   a   • Competitive nature of the computer industry.

   • Need to keep costs down in order to compete.

   • Methods to keep costs down: cheaper materials, cheaper overheads, improved efficiency (discussion of various methods in each category).

   • Conclusion as to why improving efficiency is better than other methods and hence its importance.

   b   • Discuss the process of manufacturing computers.

   • Discuss features of labour intensive production systems and their relevance to computer manufacture.

   • Discuss features of capital intensive production systems and their relevance to computer manufacture.

   • Balance the features of the two systems to conclude which is the most appropriate.

Chapter 23

Progress check A

1 Preparing input resources and managing resources and systems to meet expected demand.

2 Expand facilities, buy raw materials, recruit employees, seek finance, plan production schedules.

3 Changes in consumer tastes/demand, changes in technology, competitors' behaviour.

Progress check B

1 Hand-made pottery, exclusive fashion dresses, ships.

2 Economies of scale, higher volumes of production, standard products.

3 Manufacturing cars is a complex process with many stages of production, each stage depending on previous stages. Cars are often of a standard basic design. Flow production is suited to these features as well as high volumes.

4 These days customers demand a range of features. Car manufacturers compete in terms of options available, e.g. engine sizes, upholstery satnav and music systems. By using mass customisation a high volume of cars of basic design can be produced with a large range of features.

5 Personal computers are often made to the user's specification using a basic choice of features, eg storage, memory, software. These can be made using mass production with variations brought about by mass customisation.

Progress check C

1 Main feature is nearness to customers. Also, transportation is important as well as a suitable site.

2 Lower costs including property and wages. Also, English is generally spoken in India.

3 Nearness to potential customers, ease of getting to the theatre.

4 Will not need retail outlets, can locate somewhere that reduces costs.

5 Principally because of the large market and to be able to compete effectively with USA businesses.

6 Outsourcing is transferring a business function, such as HR, to another company. It is only offshoring if that company is based in another country.

Progress check D

1 The more customers and branches a bank has the greater range of services the business can offer and the greater degree of professionalism they can employ. It would be easier to buy bigger and better computer systems.

2 The larger the business the greater the opportunity for employing the best managers. In addition, the business could employ more specialist managers, e.g. HRM managers.

3 The larger the operation the more services could be offered. Larger company may allow for cheaper deals buying buses.

4 If there is only one supplier of electricity it means that the business is going to be very large. This can lead to communication issues. There will be a large work force and this may be difficult to manage. Lack of competition will be an issue.

Progress check E

1 Because Amazon is an international, online bookshop it will have very complex operations involving managing customer orders, managing stocks, managing relationships with suppliers, managing accounts. All of this information will need to be shared between branches and warehouses around the world. ERP is a tool that helps in planning and managing such activities in a coordinated way.

2 Manufacturing car engines is a complex process involving assembly components from a variety of suppliers and ensuring equipment and labour are available when needed. SCM will analyse the detailed flows in the supply chain to minimise problems and maximise efficiency.

3 ERP is the use of computer software to manage information flows in order to increase efficiency. Lean production is an approach to operating a business that seeks to minimise waste throughout the business. It relies mainly on the role of employees rather than the flows of information.

4 JIT relies on reliability of suppliers. ERP analyses supply chains and manages them to ensure the greatest efficiency. This contributes towards meeting the requirements of JIT.

Additional exam-style questions

1 a CAM is the use of computers and software to control and manage a production process such as through the use of robots and computerised machine tools.

 b Job production allows for customised production. It can also help to achieve high quality.

 c Mass customisation is a form of mass/flow production that enables products to be adjusted to customers' specifications.

2 a Advantages:

 • Allows the business to produce a wide range of computers with different specifications.

 • Helps to ensure that the computers meet customer needs.

 • Allows production flexibility.

 Disadvantages:

 • Needs expensive investment in robots, computers and other equipment needed for mass customisation.

 • Production line is more complex and so more likely to go wrong, and difficult to find faults.

 b The answer to this question would depend on which country the student resides in. However, a typical answer would include a discussion of the likely needs of a car manufacturer within the context of the country, e.g.:

 • the need for a skilled workforce
 • the availability of a suitable location (cost, nearness to market, nearness to resources)
 • the local market and other market issues
 • training needs
 • wages
 • industrial relations
 • laws and regulations
 • competition.

 The student should analyse these factors in relation to their own country and develop an argument as to which are the most important.

3 a A director is a senior manager with important decision-making authority, usually in control of a functional business department. A Managing Director is the most senior director.

 b Quality is important as HE produces health equipment. A product that did not reach high quality standards could endanger patients' lives and put future orders from government hospitals at risk. It would also damage HE's reputation.

Chapter 24
Progress check A

1 Shoes made/delivered in batches, customers need choices, variety of shoe sizes need to be available.

2 A fast-food outlet provides a service in which the manufacturing process takes as short a time as possible – as long as it takes to cook the meal which is likely to be as short as minutes. A construction company may take several months to take a new building from start to completion and their output will all be 'work in progress' throughout that period.

3 A soup manufacturer may require vegetables, meat, liquids, flavourings, tins, labels, a source of heat, cooking vessels and utensils.

4 Ice creams, winter coats, air conditioners.

Progress check B

1 Opportunity cost of the oil, storage facilities, insurance.

2 In the above example, the money tied up in holding inventory of petrol could have been used for buying more equipment for refining.

3 Maximum levels for milk could be determined by:

 • the short life of milk (often 1 day)
 • the level of demand
 • the storage available (chilled).

4 Maximum level for newspapers determined by:

 • space available
 • demand
 • number of types of newspapers available (titles)
 • how many sold yesterday
 • competition.

Progress check C

1 JIT requires a large investment and a 'well-oiled' supply chain, neither of which would apply to a small family business.

2 Reliable suppliers, constant demand.

3 It might be if the demand were predictable.

4 No, there are many examples of businesses that wisely keep buffer inventories. For example, medical equipment for emergencies or where the costs of a stock out are high.

Additional exam-style questions

1 a Buffer inventory is the level of inventory of a product held by a business in order to be able to cope with unexpected changes in levels of demand for the product.

b Lower storage costs, less likelihood of products becoming out-of-date.

c The time it takes between ordering additional inventory and the new supplies arriving.

2 Advantages:

• It can be difficult to predict the demand for a book so there will be a need for buffer inventory.

• Books are produced using batch production so there is a need to hold inventories.

• It takes time to print a new edition of a book.

Disadvantages:

• Costs of holding inventories.

• Many books have a short 'life' so the publisher might be left with many unsold books.

• Many books have frequent new editions.

• Inventories often held by retailers rather than publishers.

3 Define JIT first.

Explain the circumstances with regard to product, customer and the need to hold inventory.

• Assess Product A against the JIT criteria (conclude that about the right level of inventory is being held). JIT possible.

• Assess Product B against the JIT criteria. Currently far too much inventory. Once this is run down could be ideal if costs of running out are not too high.

• Assess Product C. Does not really seem suitable.

• Assess Product D. Unsuitable.

Conclude: Mixed picture, ultimate decision depends on costs of running out of inventories. If disastrous then JIT not suitable.

Chapter 25
Progress check A

1 50/75 × 100 = 67%

2 $500/50 = $10

3 If utilisation is 80 per cent, 60 rooms would be filled. Average overheads would be $500/60 = $8.33

4 Increased capacity utilisation = more customers = greater revenue. In addition, average fixed costs would decrease either increasing profits or allowing for reduced prices.

5 Cell phones need to be made with precision. As capacity utilisation increases there is more scope for error. Machines working under pressure may fail or become inaccurate. Quality may suffer.

Progress check B

1 People getting tired, higher stress. More machine error, less flexibility.

2 Advantages: creates more capacity, removes need for building own new capacity.

Disadvantages: loss of control, communication issues.

3 Short-term problems can be tolerated so 'doing nothing and putting up with it' is an option. Long-term problems require a solution.

Progress check C

1 Greetings cards are highly seasonal so there will be quiet times of the year. In addition, demand might fluctuate due to competitors' behaviour.

2 With six plants it may be easiest to close one of them down, however, it depends whether they all make the same vehicles. If not, it would be best to reduce production at those plants that produce the most affected cars.

3 Perhaps if the new products are fashionable. It depends on why there is excess capacity. If the problem is price or lack of customers, then new products may have little impact.

4   Marketing might be used to change customer behaviour – to encourage repeat purchases, to stimulate new demand, to reinforce brands. This may increase sales which could reduce overcapacity.

Progress check D

1   Depends on size of school and budget but HRM is not a core activity/skill of a school so could be better run by an outsourced agency.

2   It may be difficult to outsource reporting as editorial control might be lost.

3   Reduced costs, can focus on core activities (although this might be regarded as looking after customers!).

4   Mainly due to lower costs, could be due to skills' shortages or greater availability of skills elsewhere.

Additional exam-style questions

1   Reasons for outsourcing:

- It is small, so it may be difficult to find the skills and resources for its own HRM.

- It is a manufacturing company so its skills and focus/priorities may not include HRM.

- It cannot afford to get HRM issues wrong – dissatisfied employees, unfair dismissals and so on.

- Better to get job done by experts.

However:

- Likely to be expensive.

- How easy is it to find a suitable outsourced business?

- What if things go wrong? How easy is it to control quality?

2   Problems likely to be faced:

- Possible redundancies: How much would it cost? What would be the effect on the rest of the workforce? Could employees be redeployed?

- Reorganising the workforce: Resistance to change? Are skills transferable?

- Deciding whether to keep unused equipment: Might TTC want to use them in the future? Could it be sold? Will it deteriorate if unused?

- Disruption while the change takes place: How much? How long? Where?

- Dealing with some loss of flexibility: Did the line produce only one product? What about the other production lines?

Recommendation based in balanced arguments.

Chapter 26
Progress check A

1   Lean production involves reducing waste. High levels of inventories can waste resources, e.g. opportunity costs. JIT reduces levels of inventories hence reducing waste.

2   Could be let out as meeting rooms. Could be used for paid for holiday activities.

3   Although cars follow a basic design there are changes in fashion and new technologies and increased design options can make it necessary to keep production as flexible as possible. This can be achieved through flexible specialism.

4   Main features of cell production: employees in teams, teams are semi-autonomous, teams manage their own processes.

Progress check B

1   A major change in technology will be a large one-off change that will require careful and detailed planning. Kaizen is a philosophy of continuous change and presumes an evolving situation.

2   As the situation improves it will get closer to the 'ideal' so room for improvement will be less – there will be decreasing returns to scale.

3   Kaizen means continuous improvement in a heuristic manner. Employees should be given the responsibility of changing their own jobs, and the process should be bottom up.

4   Synergy, better coordination, improved motivation.

Progress check C

1   Quality control takes place at the end of a process and checks the results of the process. Quality assurance reviews the whole process and changes the process to make sure that agreed standards are met at all stages.

2   Safety is paramount for an aircraft manufacturer so zero defect is essential. Mistakes could ruin the business.

3 Expectations will depend on income, fashion, preferences which will vary from person to person.

4 Sampling only looks at a fixed proportion of the finished product. Even if there are zero defects in this sample it does not guarantee zero defects overall.

5 The primary sector produces raw materials. Businesses/people buying these raw materials will expect a particular level of quality. The tertiary sector provides paid for services. People buying services will expect good quality services.

Progress check D

1 ISO9000 is recognition that a business has achieved a given standard. It does not guarantee that the business will maintain that standard.

2 Comparison with other businesses is focusing on what currently exists. Innovation implies something new and different.

3 Quality circles involve empowerment. This is one of the ideas of Herzberg's motivators.

4 Benchmarking involves getting information from competitors who may not want to reveal information that might affect their competitive advantage.

Additional exam-style questions

1 The change will involve:

- investment
- finance which could upset shareholders (reduced dividend) or increase gearing (increased borrowing)
- changes to working practices – will employees accept this?
- management of change problems
- training needs
- management and coordination.

2 JIT will reduce waste, could reduce costs, releases working capital, increases efficiency and capacity utilisation. Fashions may change so reduces potential for obsolescence.

But toy sales are often seasonal – need for buffer stocks? Likely to be made in batches? What volumes are involved? Is it worth the change if storage is not an issue?

Chapter 27
Progress check A

1 Projects need planning as they can be complex, need resources at specific times and need to be completed in a known time frame.

2 Projects need monitoring because the individual activities that make up a project can be subject to uncertainty including delays.

Progress check B

1 Customers depend on bank systems. They need to be sure that the IT system is easy to use and does the job it is supposed to do, and is safe and secure.

2 Customers will usually look at the past performance of a building firm before contracting them to do work. Bad publicity on an existing project may discourage them from using that business.

3 The customer will have plans for the completion of the resulting facility. There may be penalty clauses for late completion. Contractors will want to move on to a new project.

4 Inadequate resources could include insufficient skilled labour or materials such as concrete, tarmac.

Progress check C

1 EST is the earliest time an activity can begin taking into account all the preceding activities.

2 It is useful to know the project duration for monitoring and planning purposes.

3 Delay in critical activities will delay the overall project. Delay in non-critical activities may not delay the overall project. It is therefore important to try to avoid delaying the overall project. This can best be achieved by monitoring the critical activities.

4 Critical activities always have zero floats.

5 Free float involves delays to the next activity, total float involves delays to the overall project.

Progress check D

1 Two benefits include: better planning, exploring 'what ifs?'

2 Two limitations include: the data is often estimated, delays can be unforeseen.

3 CPA is simply a management tool that helps managers. It is the quality of management that is important not the tools. The critical path is that sequence of activities in a project such that any delay in any of these activities would delay the overall length of the project as a whole.

4 CPA does not guarantee success because it is only a planning tool. The management has to manage resources effectively and monitor progress to ensure completion of the project. There has to be no unforeseen delays.

5 Building a house, launching a new product, building a new IT system.

6 Dummy activities are needed to ensure the correctness of the logic in a diagram. While without dummy activities it would be easy to show C follows A and B; and D follows A and B; but it is not possible to show C following A and B but D following only A. This can only be shown with the use of dummy activities.

7 No, it would be difficult to estimate what needs to be done and how long it will take – revision tends to evolve.

Additional exam-style questions

1 • Discussion of minimum project duration – 16 weeks. This is only just before the rainy season and this might be a matter for concern. Are there durations that can be reduced/looked at again to make it even more 'safe'?

• Discussion of which activities are on the critical path A, D, E, H, I and what this means for resource allocation and hiring contractors.

• Discussion of the nature of the time estimates – how they could differ from those used. The benefits of then doing 'what if' analysis and making contingency plans based on that.

• Discussion of the usefulness of floats – monitoring, reallocating resources, determining priorities.

• How accurate are the estimated durations? If similar projects have not been undertaken before, this could be open to considerable misjudgement.

• How good is the management? It is going to be difficult managing all the various subcontractors – this is a farm, not building contractors. Would it be worth employing a project manager?

• Draw together strands of argument to conclude that it is potentially an invaluable tool but it does depend on whether the farm has the skills to use it effectively and even the best CPA cannot guarantee a successful project.

Chapter 28
Progress check A

1 Start-up capital for equipment etc. Working capital for commencing day-to-day operations.

2 Capital expenditure is spending on fixed assets such as equipment, machinery, vehicles etc. Working capital is the finance needed for day-to-day operations – buying inventories, paying wages and so on.

3 The business environment cannot be predicted with certainty. Consumers may behave differently than anticipated, there may be an economic downturn, competition could increase unexpectedly. Money needs to be set aside so that unexpected adverse events can be catered for.

4 Machinery, buildings.

Progress check B

1 Short-term finance is finance that is provided for a period of up to a year. Long-term finance is provided for a period of longer than a year.

2 Assets are usually owned in order to be productive. If they are productive it would not be wise to sell them as it would adversely affect the operations of the business. The only assets that could be sold are unused assets. However, sometimes assets are sold and then leased back in order to raise finance.

3 Overdrafts are the most expensive form of borrowing. There is no contract with an overdraft and the lender can demand their money back at short notice.

4 If a business can extend its trade credit period then the money that would otherwise be due to be paid now can be delayed, leaving that money within the business to be used, stopping the need to find that money from elsewhere.

5 Using retained profits does not involve interest payments. The 'cost' is the foregone dividends paid to owners. If owners are happy to leave their money within the business it is probably because they expect to make greater returns in the future.

6 Leasing equipment appears as a cost in the income statement rather than as an increase in assets in the statement of financial position. There may be tax benefits from leasing. Instead of a large capital outlay it will involve much smaller regular payments. The leaser will be responsible for any problems with the equipment.

Progress check C

1 Partnerships are usually unincorporated businesses and cannot issue shares.

2 A public limited company could:
- issue new shares
- get a long-term bank loan
- sell debentures.

3 A sole trader could get improved trade credit and an overdraft.

4 Long-term loans will alter the balance between loan capital and equity and will, therefore, change the risk to shareholders. Loans have to be repaid even if profits are not being made.

Additional exam-style questions

1 a Revenue expenditure is money spent on day-to-day items such as inventories, wages in order to earn an income. It contrasts with capital expenditure.

b External sources of finance are sources outside of the business such as loans, issuing new shares.

c In order to operate effectively, businesses need a continuous flow of money that starts with paying for inputs such as wages etc., and finishes with earning an income from the sale of the finished product. The money that flows around the business is known as working capital.

d A business selling electronic goods will have a medium to high income per customer. If the products are sold on credit the customers will owe the business significant amounts of money. A debt factoring business would be prepared to buy those debts, at a discount, providing a source of finance for the electronics company.

2 a A sole trader will have limited potential sources of finance. A hairdresser will need to buy equipment and raw materials as well as probably renting/buying premises. The finance needs will not be great and could possibly be provided from the owner's personal finance or from bank loans.

b Advantages of loans for a plc:
- A loan is a fixed contract so there is more certainty/predictability than other sources.
- There is no loss of shareholder control.
- Wide variety of different types of loan available.

Disadvantages include:
- Can be expensive.
- Increases gearing/risk.
- Penalties can be high if loan not paid back on time.
- Some loans require collateral.

Chapter 29
Progress check A

1 Fixed costs are costs that do not vary with the level of output of a product or service such as repayment of a loan used to purchase a building. Indirect costs are costs that are not directly related to a specific activity within a business, for example, a headteacher's salary is an indirect cost in relation to running a Business class at your school.

2 If a business has a special order for a product to be supplied to a customer packaged in the customers' own design – for example an 'own brand' product for a supermarket, the cost of changing the machinery that produced the packaging would be a direct cost in relation to that order, however it would be a 'one-off' fixed cost.

3 The manager of the shop will want to monitor the performance of the shop, identify ways of saving costs, calculate profits for the shop.

4 The cost of heating a school would probably be fixed but if there were more students then additional rooms might become classrooms so the heating cost would go up as the number of students increased.

5 Total cost for a month = \$5 000 + (100 × \$100) = \$5 000 + \$10 000 = \$15 000.
Average cost = \$15 000/100 = \$150.
Marginal cost is \$100.

Progress check B

1 Margin of safety is the difference between the current level of production and the break-even level of production, assuming that production is greater than the break-even level.

2 The break-even level is the dividing point between making a loss (below break-even production) and making a profit (above the break-even level). Below break-even there will be insufficient income to cover fixed costs.

3 b/e = $10 000/($20 − $10) = 1 000 books.

4 The margin of safety will be 100 students.

5 Good for 'what if' questions, helps inform decisions.

6 Only as good as the data. Assumes linear costs.

Additional exam-style questions

1 Variable costs are costs that are directly related to the level of output of a process. Direct costs are costs that are directly associated with the process and could be fixed or variable.

2 The headteacher's salary is likely to be a fixed cost. The costs of admin staff are likely to be fixed in the short term.

3 A good answer is likely to be along the lines of:

Supporting the statement:

- Several pricing strategies are based entirely on the market including penetration, skimming, competitive, price discrimination.

- There are other factors such as brand image, newness of the product, nature of the market that are more important.

- Prices are likely to change due to economic conditions.

Opposing the statement:

- Some strategies such as cost plus are dependent on costs.

- Even for market related prices the business needs to be sure that there is sufficient income to cover costs.

Final statement to balance the two arguments.

Chapter 30
Progress check A

1 i   GP = 30 990 − 17 088 = $19 902 million

   ii OP = 13 902 − 11 671 = $8 231 million

   iii Retained profit = 2 231 − 1 040 − 800 = $391 million

2 In normal circumstances this would be very disappointing, however retained profit has fallen from $4.9 billion to $0.4 billion. In normal circumstances this would be disappointing however there may be some unusual factors such as adverse trading conditions, unusual tax payments, changes to dividend policies.

Progress check B

1 The brand name 'Metro Cola' is an intangible asset and is the biggest asset the business has.

2 Many customers will be warehouses and supermarkets so that the transactions are B2B. It is usual in such transactions to offer trade credit.

3 They should not be worried. The level of loans is small compared with the annual turnover, current assets, fixed assets and share capital.

4 i   already done.

   ii current assets (inventories) up, current liabilities (short-term loans) up

   iii Intangible assets down, long-term loans down.

Progress check C

1 CR = CA/CL = 12 714/13 169 = 0.97

2 ATR = (CA − inventories)/CL = (12 714 − 2 298)/13 169 = 0.80

3 Both are below the 'normal' levels (1.5–2 and 1 respectively). However, Metro Cola is a very large business and would be able to operate effectively at these levels. What is more important is the trend, which we do not know.

Progress check D

1 GPM = 13 902/30 990 × 100 = 45%

2 NPM = 2 231/30 990 × 100 = 7%

3   Pepsi Cola is in the same line of business so a comparison would be useful as it would help identify competitiveness issues and possibly best practice. Pepsi's gross profit margin in 2015 was around 55 per cent and its profit margin was around 13 per cent, so Metro is performing less well as far as profit is concerned. However, Pepsi is a large multinational with a wide and diverse range of products, so comparisons may not be meaningful. Ford is in a totally different industry so a comparison would not be useful unless Metro Cola was thinking of diversifying, so comparison is not so useful. For interest, Ford's gross profit margin was around 12 per cent in 2015 and its profit margin was around seven per cent.

Additional exam-style questions

1   An asset, in relation to a business, is an item that is owned by the business. It could be physical such as property or intangible such as a brand name.

2   Operating profit is the profit that is made by a business relating directly to its day-to-day operations. It is calculated by deducting cost of goods sold and relevant expenses from sales.

3   Food retailers generally sell directly to the public and receive their income from sales almost immediately – whether their sales are for cash or on a credit card. In addition, inventories are likely to be low because many foods are perishable. This means current assets are likely to be small. In contrast, they will almost certainly buy the foods from producers on credit. This will mean significant current liabilities relative to current assets and hence low levels of liquidity.

4   Discussion is likely to revolve around:

- Managers: For decisions, monitor progress, set budgets, measure performance, compare. However, detail may not be enough and accounts may be out-of-date.

- Suppliers: Is company safe to supply on credit? Is it able to repay debts? However, may be more interested in the future rather than the past.

- Government: How much tax due? How well is the industry/economy doing? However, much of the detail in the accounts may not be relevant.

- Customers: Will the business survive? – important for spare parts, repairs etc. However, customers likely to be more influenced by marketing, fashion etc. unless it is B2B.

- Banks: Is business secure enough to lend to? Is it safe to give an overdraft? Critical in the banks' decisions.

- Workers: Are jobs/wages secure? Could the business afford wage increases? Negotiating strength may be a more important issue.

- Shareholders: What are the business prospects? How has it performed? More interested in the future than the past.

Conclusion likely to be that accounts are important but there are other key pieces of information and that the accounts may not be sufficiently up-to-date.

5   Outline: liquidity ratios can help to identify possible liquidity problems and so reduce the risk of liquidation. They can help in the management of working capital including inventory control as well as managing debtors and creditors and also cash.

Inventory control is unlikely to be a major issue for a fresh fruit business in relation to the fruit (which is perishable) but there may be issues relating to inventories of materials such as packaging and other items needed for day-to-day operations. Unlike manufacturing businesses there is unlikely to be inventories of raw materials, work in progress or finished products for any significant period of time – the fruit will be turned over in days rather than weeks or months.

Most businesses risk creditors/debtors getting out of control and this is likely to be the case for this business.

Because the business deals in fresh fruit liquidity may not be as much of an issue as for, say, a traditional manufacturing business but poor liquidity could still put at risk the future of the business.

Chapter 31
Progress check A

1   There are many difficulties in setting up a new business as there are many uncertainties. However, difficulties can be made more manageable by careful planning. Cash-flow forecasts are a very useful planning tool and can help identify potential problems. If the owner of the business needs external investments, then cash-flow forecasts will be essential to show to potential investors.

2. Cash-flow forecasts involve attempting to predict the future. The future is uncertain so assumptions need to be made about the unknown outcome of future events.

3. By identifying potential future cash-flow problems it is possible to identify means of reducing their scale and also ways of solving possible cash-flow shortages.

4. A taxi firm needs to buy fuel. If oil prices change then eventually there will be changes in fuel prices. The taxi firm will have to pay for this fuel so cash outflows will change, changing the closing balance and so on.

5. Although income from sales may be more than the costs of those sales (hence making an operating profit), the business may have failed to manage its cash well leading to a cash-flow problem. For example, too much may have been spent on inventories of raw materials which will be a drain on cash but will not produce inflows until sometime in the future.

Progress check B

1. 'Opening balance' describes the cash available at the beginning of a time period.

2. By buying the premises there will be an immediate large cash outflow, reducing the closing balance. There will be no further outflows related to the purchase of the property. If instead the property were leased there will be regular smaller payments occurring in a number of time periods so there will be a larger closing balance in the first period, declining from then onwards.

Progress check C

1. Poor credit control means that customers are delaying paying for their goods purchased on credit. This means that cash inflows are arriving later than they should. This means that net cash flow is smaller than it otherwise would be.

2. Farms are very susceptible to weather, market prices are often unpredictable, there may be breakdowns in essential farm machinery.

3. Some purchases of cars are essential (e.g. when one car is beyond repair and a car is essential to the owner). However, many purchases can be considered discretionary. At times of recession some people will be forced to reduce their discretionary expenditure as they will have lower incomes. This means that sometimes the purchase

of a new car can be delayed, sometimes a cheaper car can be bought.

Progress check D

1. A steel manufacture will sell most of its product (steel) to other businesses such as car manufacturers, building firms, ship builders. These customers are likely to buy steel on credit. That means that trade receivables (debtors) are likely to be relatively large. Selling these debts to the firm to a debt factor transfers the money owed to the steel manufacturer to the debt factor in return for payment by the debt factor. This payment will be a cash inflow.

2. Giving more credit to customers means that customers will pay later than they otherwise would. These delays in payment reduce cash inflows and so reduce the net cash flow.

3. It would worsen the cash flow of the business as more cash will need to be found to pay suppliers more quickly.

4. Overtrading means buying supplies on too much credit. Although this increases net cash flows (by delaying cash outflows) it is storing up problems for when the debt eventually has to be paid.

Progress check E

1. Working capital is an amount of finance available to a business at a particular time for day-to-day finance. It might be held in a non-cash form such as inventories. Cash flow is the net amount of money flowing into a business over a particular period of time.

2. Car retailers work in a very competitive market. Cars are very expensive items and the vast majority of customers cannot buy a car for cash – they need to borrow. A car retailer that does not offer credit will be less attractive to customers, and so less competitive than one that does offer credit.

3. Excess cash means holding more cash than is needed for day-to-day operations.

   The cash could be used for:
   - paying off any overdrafts or other flexible loans
   - making capital improvements
   - increased marketing.

4. - Debt factors can be expensive.
   - It might send out panic signals to customers/competitors.

Additional exam-style questions

1 Forecasting cash flows involves predicting cash inflows (usually from sales) and cash outflows (mainly for expenses) for a future time period. Anything to do with the future involves uncertainties so cash flows cannot be predicted with any certainty.

2 Each individual item sold may be profitable but some of the sales may be on credit. So a business may have to incur all of the costs long before it receives payment. This means that cash outflows will be greater than cash inflows.

3 Purchase of raw materials, payment of wages.

4 a New businesses will need to know how much finance will be required in the early days of the business, before cash inflows are being produced by sales. It is likely that some of this finance will have to come from external sources and banks, and other investors will want to see cash-flow forecasts.

b There are two aspects to cash-flow problems. Inflows may be insufficient, outflows may be too much. Selling more cars may produce more inflows but the effect will only be immediate if these cars are sold for cash. By making and selling more cars the manufacturer is likely to incur more cash outflows through, for example, purchases of raw materials, payment of wages. Cash-flow problems will only be reduced if the new inflows exceed the new outflows, which is unlikely until the original problems have been solved.

5 a How realistic is the cash-flow forecast? Is Mike likely to be able to repay any loan? Does Mike have any security? Does Mike have a good credit rating/record? Where will Mike find the extra $800 needed in month 2? Is six months realistic?

b Any chance that sales could be increased or brought forward? Could Mike inject more of his own capital? Could there be cheaper start-up costs? Can operating costs be reduced? What are the overheads? Can they be reduced? Can the taxi be leased rather than bought?

Chapter 32
Progress check A

1 A profit centre is a part of a business for which both revenues and costs can be identified. A cost centre is part of a business for which costs can be identified but there are no revenues, e.g. a HRM department.

2 The concept of profit applies to a business as a whole not an individual product. Most firms produce many products. Many costs in a business will not be associated with an individual product, for example the costs of the accounts department should be shared by all products not just one. For this reason any individual product will make a contribution to the business as a whole rather than making a profit itself.

3 Costs can be monitored, targets can be set.

4 Allocating overheads, identifying and measuring direct costs.

Progress check B

1 Full costing attempts decision making based on all costs including indirect costs which have to be arbitrarily allocated. Contribution costing bases decisions on direct costs so that there is no arbitrary allocation.

2 Profit = sales revenue − all costs = $15k − $18k = −$3k.

Contribution = Sales revenue − direct costs = $15k − $13k = + $2k.

The profit centre is making a positive contribution. Provided the overheads are being covered by the total contribution in the business it cannot be said that the centre is performing poorly.

3 The main use of contribution is that it avoids the distortions created by arbitrary allocations of indirect costs that pertain to other costing methods.

4 Full costing applied to individual models of car will mean that decisions are based on the arbitrary allocation of indirect costs. Decisions will depend on the allocation rather than the merits of the individual model of car.

5 It would depend on whether the overheads of the supermarket are covered by the sum of all the individual contributions. The department may attract customers who then spend in other departments.

Progress check C

1 The quantitative contribution calculations do not take account of capacity, marketing or HRM issues and these will all be important in a decision.

2 The decision may have an impact on other products. Customers may be very unhappy if a product is discontinued. Sometimes 'loss leaders' are valuable to a business.

3 Contribution = revenue – direct costs
Revenue = 100 × $75 000 = $7.5m
Direct costs = ([100 × $60 000] + $50 000)
= $6.05m
Contribution = $7.5m – $6.05m = $1.45m

It makes a large positive contribution.

However, what will other customers think? Will they know?

Is there enough spare capacity to make these extra lorries?

Depending on the answers to these questions the firm probably should accept the offer.

4 The direct costs at off-peak times are very low – the system is running well below capacity and trains and staff would probably be idle but still be a cost to the railway company.

Additional exam-style question

1 **a** Contribution for Midgets = $440m – $(200+90+120)m = $440m – $410m = $30m

Since most other products make a contribution it is likely that overheads are paid for by these contributions leaving an overall profit.

b Two approaches:

• Increase revenues. How? Will there be associated increased costs, e.g. marketing?

• Reduce direct costs. May be very difficult to reduce wage costs. Material costs could be reduced through cheaper suppliers or using less ingredients but would customers like 'inferior' chocolates? May be scope for reducing direct overheads through

efficiencies, but would this have an impact on other chocolate products?

Chapter 33
Progress check A

1 Forecasts are what we think may happen in the future. A budget is a plan of what we want to happen in the future.

2 The budget will be useful for ordering raw materials and other supplies, ensuring there is sufficient labour and machinery, and that production targets are realistic in terms of the market. For a shoe manufacturer the budget will need to accurately forecast production of various types of shoe. There will have to be enough leather and other materials.

3 A budget will have to take account of the expected number of operations, staff needed, patients treated and so on. By comparing outcomes with budget data the hospital will be able to see whether it achieved its planned levels of activity. If not, then lessons could be learned.

4 A delegated budget involves people at many levels in the preparation of the budget. People who have been involved in planning for their own targets are far more likely to take notice of those targets than targets that have been prepared 'remotely'. Because of this proximity to the planning employees will be more likely to want to achieve the targets, hence improving motivation.

Progress check B

1 It helps identify potential problems, for example the need for additional finance. A budget may be needed by potential investors. Without a budget they may be reluctant to lend/invest. It could help in deciding on levels of raw materials to purchase – too much could be a waste of money, insufficient could lead to production slow downs.

2 It could help in the monitoring of progress, productivity. Retail outlets depend on their staff and budgets would provide targets and a mechanism for monitoring. Budgets could help identify potential problems, for example product lines that do not sell well. It could help understand the outcome of marketing efforts such as two for the price of one.

3 People who work in schools are good at what they are qualified for, such as teaching, managing, cooking

school dinners and so on. Most people involved will have little financial experience and will have had little experience setting budgets. Training will be needed for these people to be able to set realistic budgets.

4 Often in large organisations there is competition between departments for funding. Often the sum of individual budgets is larger than the available budget so departments will often overstate so that when their budget is cut back it will be closer to the budget that they actually want.

Progress check C

1 An adverse cost variance means that actual costs are higher than budgeted costs and profit will be adversely affected. A favourable cost variance has the opposite effect.

2 A favourable revenue variance means that actual revenue is above budget and profit will rise (assuming no adverse cost variance). An adverse revenue variance will have the opposite effect.

3 Variance analysis allows managers to identify the major difference between actual and budgeted data and take appropriate action.

4 The manager of a hotel would be able to see which areas of the business are performing well and which need improvements. Areas such as the restaurant, housekeeping, reception, bar, administration, bookings could all be separate cost centres. They could then be monitored. This could help identify training needs, pay rises, need for new equipment and so on. A hotel relies on good customer service so it is very important to identify the areas that are not performing well. Variance analysis would also help the business improve its budgeting.

Additional exam-style questions

1 a The variances are:

	Variance ($)
Food sales	55 000 − 50 000 = +5 000 (F)
Other sales	3 000 − 4 000 = −1 000 (A)
Wages	20 000 − 16 000 = +4 000 (A)
Other variable costs	10 000 − 8 000 = +2 000 (A)
Overheads	12 000 − 9 000 = +3 000 (A)
Profits	16 000 − 21 000 = −5 000

Only food sales is favourable.

They are certainly useful for monitoring purposes and to systemise forward planning. But there are limits to the extent to which they can be used to improve business performance. More research would need to be done before satisfactory methods for improvement could be identified but at least a potential problem is clear.

b Actions could include:

- Further increases in food sales, but how? Reduced prices may not produce extra revenue, increased marketing might increase other costs. Competition issues?

- Increase other sales. What are they? How could they be increased?

- Reduce wages. But a café is based on customer service so is this wise? Are there inefficiencies that can be addressed?

- Reduce other variable costs. Probably food and beverage so is it wise to buy cheaper materials or reduce the quantities sold?

- Reduce overheads. Likely to be rates, rent, electricity which may be difficult to reduce.

So is the problem one of poor budgeting? Worth reviewing.

2 It is unlikely that all areas of a school are performing equally well. Setting a budget for the whole school will prevent differences between parts of the school from being identified. A school has a range of functions which are completely different – from providing food in the school canteen to management services and administration support. Each subject area is likely to have different cost structures – from capital intensive subjects like IT to other subjects such as languages that require fewer capital resources. An additional problem is that the budget is 'top down'. This will not help with motivation issues and the governors may not be the best people to produce budgets. However, it is important to have high levels of motivation at a school because students need to learn in a creative and enthusiastic environment. On the other hand, teachers and other people in education may not be good at preparing budgets. There may be competition between departments for funds which could lead to setting budgets too high. In addition it will be very difficult to allocate overheads, such as the headteacher's salary to individual subject areas.

However, with good management and training these difficulties could be overcome and each department having 'ownership' of the budget may help both the realism of the budget and the commitment of the staff to achieving the budget.

Chapter 34

Progress check A

1 Several items on the accounts will transfer over from the end of year levels to start the new year. So for example, the fixed assets at the end of the year remain the same, inventories remain the same at the beginning of the new year.

Progress check B

1 Depreciation reduces the value of an asset. It represents a using up of the resources of a business and so represents an expense. By applying depreciation, it will increase expenses in the income statement thereby reducing retained profit, if nothing else changes, which then transfers to a reduction in shareholders' funds.

2 As stated above, depreciation is regarded as an expense which appears in the income statement.

3 The lorry will be recorded as a non-current asset and the loan as a non-current liability. As the lorry is depreciated, expenses will increase each year by the amount of annual depreciation and this will reduce profit. The value of the lorry on the statement of financial position will fall each year by the value of annual depreciation. The loan will be reduced as it is paid back.

Progress check C

1 Fixed assets need to be depreciated because the business is eventually going to have to replace them (unless they are buildings). The depreciation represents the reduction in worth of the asset as well as the amount the business should account for in preparing to eventually replace the asset.

2 For example a lorry might last for 20 years before it needs to be scrapped (its actual life) but a business might want its lorries to look smart and modern, and be reliable as it only keeps them for two years (useful life) before it sells them.

3 Depreciation is a non-cash expense which appears as a deduction in the income statement.

4 The only item that appears as an expense in relation to an asset is depreciation. The amount paid for an asset will be balanced by any reduction in other assets such as cash or increases in liabilities such as loans or share issues.

5 Depreciation is $(30\ 000 - 5\ 000)/5 = \$5\ 000$ per year.

Additional exam-style questions

1 Inventories are likely to be mainly the products on the shelves of the supermarket and these will have a short life. Therefore, their 'cost' and worth is likely to be the replacement cost. Valuing them at the sale price may be regarded as risky. Typically, a supermarket may keep its equipment for two years or so, thus it makes sense to depreciate over two years. Usually buildings hold their value so that market prices may reflect the current worth of the building, although to guard against property price falls it might make more sense to value at cost.

2 Fixed assets such as machinery and vehicles are difficult to value because there needs to be a decision made about the level of depreciation. Current assets such as inventories require decisions about how to estimate the net realisable value – markets might be continuously changing the market value of such assets. In addition, some intangible assets, e.g. trademarks, brand names are largely matters of opinion – what someone might be prepared to pay for them This might suggest that the accounts, particularly the statement of financial position are not very useful. However, there are factors that lessen these difficulties. One of the main uses of accounts is to compare one time period with another. Provided assets are treated consistently over time periods these comparisons can be made and remain useful. Further, tax laws of many countries provide narrow boundaries for assets and inventories within which businesses have to operate. Thirdly, there are 'checks and balances' to ensure a fair representation of business behaviour: auditors, the professional competence of accountants and shareholders and other suppliers of finance who will want to see a 'proper' and fair picture.

Chapter 35

Progress check A

1   Liquidity ratios tell the manager about the ability of the business to survive in the short term. For a shoe shop poor liquidity is likely to arise from poor inventory management (too many shoes) and poor cash management – having to borrow for day-to-day operations.

2   Supermarkets are usually very significant buyers of produce from food and other manufacturers and farmers. This means that they can negotiate favourable credit terms. So trade payables are likely to be high. In contrast, the supermarket receives instant payment from customers – even if they pay on credit card they will receive instant cash – so that payables are likely to be relatively small. In addition, there will be a very high inventory turnover meaning that inventories are small relative to sales. With the two major current assets being low and the major current liability being large the ratios will be small.

3   Profitability ratios can be improved by increasing revenues or decreasing costs. Revenues could be increased either by increasing sales (although it might be expensive in terms of marketing costs) or by increasing prices (but if the meals are elastic then revenues might even fall). Cost could be decreased through cheaper ingredients, lower wages or improved efficiency. Poorer ingredients might affect sales and customer perceptions, lower wages might lead to poorer service.

4   High gearing implies high risk. A business will have high gearing if it has high debt relative to equity. High debt means high commitment to repaying both interest and capital whatever the circumstances facing the business. If the business cannot afford the necessary repayments the business could be forced into liquidation. The bank may then not get back any finance it has lent to the business.

5   The price/earnings ratio will go up. This is because the takeover threat would increase the share price but earnings would remain the same. Since the price earnings ratio is: current share price/earnings per share the ratio will increase.

Progress check B

1   The car manufacturer will want to benchmark itself against the competitor. It may also want to analyse how the competitor business is performing and to help identify its strengths and weaknesses.

2   Accounts are fairly complex and performance is not always obvious. Ratios help to summarise/analyse the accounts into key areas such as profitability, liquidity and so on, so that quick comparisons can be made between businesses that may be of very different sizes.

3   One example is that on the income statement you can find a figure for 'profit'. However, there is no indication as to whether the figure is satisfactory or not. That can only be determined by looking at the size of the business (e.g. from assets in the statement of financial position) or comparing with other businesses (e.g. by using ratios). The answer is not obvious simply looking at the accounts.

4   Ratios give a simple summary of a business that is easy for making comparisons.

Progress check C

1   a   2016 first:

GPM = $100/800 \times 100 = 12.5\%$ and $70/700 \times 100 = 10\%$

NPM = $30/800 \times 100 = 3.75\%$ and $20/700 \times 100 = 2.86\%$

ROCE = $30/400 \times 100 = 7.5\%$ and $20/400 \times 100 = 5\%$

Profitability for all three ratios is falling. Net profit margins of around three per cent are quite small so the business must be concerned. The fall in NPM is greater suggesting expenses are not fully under control. Sales are falling. Is this due to lower sales volumes or lower prices?

b   CR = $120/80 = 1.5$ and $130/130 = 1$

ATR = $(120 - 60)/80 = 60/80 = 0.75$ and $(130-80)/130 = 50/80 = 0.38$

Days sales in receivables = $40 \times 365/800 = 18.25$ days and $30 \times 365/700 = 15.64$ days

Stock turnover = $(800 - 100)/60 = 11.7$ and $(700 - 70)/80 = 7.88$

Generally, the business's liquidity is falling. In 2015 the current ratio is at a generally accepted level but the acid test ratio is down a bit. By 2016 CR and ATR have fallen to levels which are generally regarded as risky. Receivables show no cause for concern, but stock turnover is falling suggesting poor stock control.

c   Gearing = 100/400 = 0.25% and 120/400 = 30%. Although it is increasing it is below 50 per cent so there is no suggestion of long-term risk to a lender.

d   p/e = 6.00/(30m/80m) = 16 and 3.00/(20/85) = 12.75. The share price is falling faster than earnings suggesting lack of confidence in the future.

2   An increasing gearing ratio means that the business debts are rising relative to equity. Debts involve commitments to repaying the loan and interest repayments. This is in contrast to equity when dividends do not have to be paid when profits are poor. Greater debt means that it may be difficult to meet commitments when profits are poor, increasing the risk of the business getting into financial difficulty.

3   A manufacturing business is likely to use large quantities of raw materials. These are likely to be bought on credit. If it uses a batch production system it is likely to have large levels of inventories. Often manufacturing businesses sell on credit. Since value has been added receivables will be larger than payables. This means that current assets will be larger than liabilities so a current ratio of 1.5 or above will be suitable. In contrast a large retail outlet will sell its products for cash whereas it can probably get good credit terms for its purchases. Inventories can be small relative to sales. In this instance current liabilities can be smaller than current assets with a current ratio less than one.

4   Usually a sale involves selling items at a price below market prices. Depending on how inventories are valued the selling price might be less than that used for stock valuation. This means that the rise in cash held by the business (receipts from the sale of the inventories) may be less than the reduction in inventories. This means that the current ratio will fall. If that cash is then used to pay off short-term debt the ratio will change again.

Additional exam-style questions

1   Stakeholders can include:

- Managers: useful for taking operational decisions. Pay could be based on business performance.

- Employees: want to know about job security, possible future pay rises.

- Owners: want to know how their business is performing, want to know what income they can expect, base decisions on the information, make comparisons with competitors.

- Government: want to be able to determine taxes.

- Suppliers: want to be sure they will get paid.

Discussion in the answer should balance these needs.

2   High gearing means dependence on debt rather than equity. This means that the business is committed to debt and interest repayment which is riskier than discretionary dividends paid to equity holders which at a time of poor performance can be withheld. Whether or not this is a good idea depends on:

- the character of the owners, who may be risk takers or risk averse

- the nature of the business – some industries are inevitably riskier

- the age of the business – new businesses are inevitably going to have to take greater risks than established businesses.

Chapter 36
Progress check A

1   Staff uniforms would normally be considered as revenue expenditure – part of day-to-day operations and therefore not an investment. There is no clearly discernible return on the spending.

2   New offices, new computer systems, design and launch of a new piece of software.

3   'Annual net cash flow' in relation to a piece of machinery refers to the difference, each year, between the incomes generated as a result of buying the machinery and the costs associated with operating it.

4   Net cash flows for an oil refinery will depend on the incomes generated by it and the costs of operating including the raw materials. Crude oil processes are subjected to some considerable uncertainty. This means that prices for refined products will also be subject to fluctuation. As a result both incomes and costs are uncertain, the two components of net cash flows.

Progress check B

1 Computer systems generally have short useful lives and are likely to be replaced in less than four years. So a four-year payback is not quick enough.

2 To repay a possible loan, to recognise that it is a competitive market, to reflect rapid advancements in technology.

3 If the business has borrowed to build the new factory the lenders will want reassurance that the loan can be repaid. A shorter payback would help to provide that reassurance.

4 ARR does not take any account of the time value of money. When opportunity costs are considered the project may not look so attractive.

5 It would be better to put the money into the bank to earn interest.

Progress check C

1 To take account of opportunity costs, risk.

2 Prevailing interest rates, returns achieved on similar projects.

3 Because it represents the opportunity cost of spending on a product. Below that rate it would be better to save rather than spend on a project.

Progress check D

1 That after taking account of the time value of money the project is worth undertaking as it gives a positive return.

2 It will reduce the NPV as the discounted cash flow in year 5 will now be less.

3 One of the key features of the discount rate is that it represents uncertainty about the future. If the future becomes less certain then it should be discounted more. This means that the discount rate should increase.

4 There may be an expectation that the prevailing interest rate might rise. Other projects within the business may achieve higher rates of return.

Progress check E

1 Project B. The IRR is the return at which the NPV is zero. Because the IRR is higher for project B, it has zero NPV at 20% and will certainly have a positive NPV at 10% because the future benefits will be discounted less at 10%. Whereas project A has zero NPV at 10% but will have a negative NPV at 20% because the future benefits will be discounted more.

2 The IRR would increase because a higher discount rate is now needed to reduce NPV to zero.

Progress check F

1 The local community is an important stakeholder and can exert influence on governments and local authorities if they are not happy. In addition, it is an important consideration if the business subscribes to corporate social responsibility.

2 A newspaper relies on the loyalty of its readership and this could be put at risk as a consequence of such a change. It would also need to take account of the impact of the change on its employees, an important part of the business.

3 Are the staff trained? Will they need training? Would the new software make working easier/better? What problems will arise during the changeover? Are the right facilities available?

Additional exam-style questions

1 It is certainly the case that the future cannot be predicted with any certainty. However, it is often possible to make forecasts of the future based on reasonable assumptions. Using these assumptions, it is possible to appraise projects based on a 'reasonable' view of what may happen in the future. Moreover, it is possible to explore the impact of the assumptions chosen by varying these assumptions and re-appraising the project. This is known as 'what if' analysis. 'What if' analysis not only explores the impact of varying assumptions but it can also give the analysts a good idea of the level of risk involved in a project. This type of analysis together with careful choice of assumptions and analysis of a project is better than simply guessing. Another issue is that it would be unwise to base a decision about a project simply on the strength of an investment appraisal. Other factors, most particularly risk, should be considered. In addition, it is a good technique for comparing competing projects using common assumptions for all of the appraisals. Most business ventures involve risk and ruling out investment appraisal because the future is unknown implies that risk is never worth undertaking. This risk averse approach would rule out any kind of investment.

So investment appraisal is a valuable tool in an uncertain world and so is not a waste of time.

2   It is always very wise to consider factors other than an investment appraisal and in this instance it is particularly important. Spending on a marketing campaign is a particularly uncertain investment partly because it is often unclear how customers/ potential customers might react to marketing and partly because the success of the marketing is highly dependent on the behaviour of competitors and on trends in consumer behaviour influenced by external factors, both outside of the control of the business. Directors would need to consider whether the business can afford the five per cent, how it is going to be spent on marketing, whether the marketing is likely to be successful, how competitors might respond and whether there are better investments that the business could make. Impact on other areas of the business would also be an important consideration. The greatest factor would arise from determining why the business is losing market share. If it is because the product is no longer suitable for consumers, then increased marketing may not be successful.

Chapter 37
Progress check A

1   This is an objective – it is specific, measurable and time limited. It needs a strategy (at least one) to try to ensure that the objective is reached. This long-term plan or strategy could be to 'start selling our products online with a dynamic website giving the business a differentiated online presence'.

2   Strategy: it is an outline plan of action. Perhaps the corporate objective was to gain a technological advance over competitors.

3   Use marketing mix more effectively, e.g. use a wider range of channels of distribution or develop an e-commerce strategy for existing products.

4   Strategy: use the new product to break in to foreign markets for the first time.

Tactics: establish a distribution network in the foreign country and use advertisements that reflect local tastes and culture.

5   Tactical: they are largely confined to marketing department and they would be quite easy to reverse.

Progress check B

1   Needs to analyse business environment, e.g. strength of competitors.

Must make the final strategic choice about the new products carefully.

Needs to implement necessary changes, e.g. to workforce levels or training, effectively and with support of employees.

2   Major internal change is often required as a result of a new strategy, e.g. to the structure of the organisation, workforce numbers or skill levels. Implementing the strategy will require careful management of change. Opposition of the employees will be unlikely to lead to success of the strategy.

3   To assess success. Has the strategy achieved the original objective? If it has, where do we go from here? If it has not, why not and what changes to the strategy are needed?

Progress check C

1   Need to delayer the organisational structure to reduce costs and be more flexible to change, e.g. less centralised.

2   To give delegated authority to managers who will operate in these other countries. This should allow the necessary changes to be made to ensure that the business's products, marketing strategies and employment practices fit in with local cultures and legal constraints.

3   For example, low cost airlines aim for the lowest fares for passengers. They achieve this by cutting costs, e.g. no free food/drinks on board; no special lounges at airports etc.

Business class passengers will be offered services that airlines claim are the best in the industry, e.g. aircraft seats that fold completely flat for sleep during the flight.

Additional exam-style question

1   a   Competitive advantage means being able to compete effectively against rivals. This is difficult to achieve in a market, such as T-shirts and other forms of non-exclusive clothing, which has few barriers to entry.

By having a competitive advantage TeePrint could gain sales and profit – important for this business as it plans to expand into other products.

New competitors are entering the market in the home market. TeePrint needs to respond or it might be either taken over or just lose sales and profit as the MNC will almost certainly have cost advantages. Differentiation and effective branding of fashionable clothes ranges might be the only way for TeePrint to gain a competitive advantage. This might give higher profit margins – but this might be difficult as it may not be within its core competence to develop these new ranges and brand image.

Chapter 38
Progress check A

1   It is an important form of strategic analysis that focuses on the internal features of a business that might influence which future strategies it could adopt (strengths and weaknesses). It also identifies the opportunities/risks that exist external to the business in the market it operates in. This analysis will influence which strategies are considered for the future operations of the business.

2   No, probably too expensive. It might be advised to consider those opportunities that take advantage of its core competencies.

3   Student's own answer.

4   It is a subjective form of analysis – and opinions differ, e.g. about the main strengths and weaknesses of an organisation.

Progress check B

1   Different political systems with different policies towards business; different legal constraints on business.

2   External shocks such as rise in oil prices or trade restrictions by a major trading partner could be introduced and these will impact on most businesses. These are sometimes very difficult to forecast for.

3   Mean/median age of population; cultural diversity of the population; average family size.

4   Mobile phone developments – positive for consumers but negative for those mobile phone businesses that do not invest enough in R and D.

Driverless cars and trucks – positive for businesses with big transport bills but bad for drivers and their trade unions.

Drone photography – negative for aircraft operating businesses that take aerial pictures.

Progress check C

1   Student's own answer.

2   Gain market research information to help devise an adapted marketing mix which better fits in with consumer expectations.

3   Dogs – low market share in a low growth market.

4   Constant product development – extension strategies. Reducing prices will only work for a limited time period.

Progress check D

1   Industry of student's own choice. One supplier goes out of business, supplier takes a patent out for an important component and is therefore the only supplier.

2   More supplying businesses enter the market; buyer takes over another 'buying' business and its orders for supplies increase in size.

3   Branding – cost of competing with existing businesses 'established brand names; cost of capital equipment required' e.g. steel production.

4   Lack of a differentiated product so easier for other firms to copy; increased competition between businesses by making it easier for customers to switch, e.g. between electricity providers.

5   The number of competitors; the size of competitors, e.g. if they are roughly equal size the competition will be more intense; if products are undifferentiated; slow growth rate of the market.

6   These wind turbines could be used to provide power to a range of products that require electricity to be generated especially in areas not connected to the traditional electricity supply.

Additional exam-style question

1   b   Explain both models – using diagrams, perhaps, but making clear reference to TPC and the two options in the case of both models.

Explain the potential usefulness of both models **in this case**. Assess the limitations of both models in this case.

Justify their use – but with caution. Suggest and justify other techniques of strategic analysis too which would be useful in this case, e.g. SWOT and PEST.

Chapter 39

Progress check A

1 New markets mean different consumers (or industrial customers) who may have different tastes and requirements to those the business is used to providing for. One example is starting to sell food products to another country for the first time. It would be risky to do this without research into the culture, religious beliefs and consumer tastes in that country.

2 New product development is risky because it might be impossible to actually develop the product required, e.g. cure for a common cold, or a clever invention is not always accepted by the market – no demand for it.

3 The bank could buy a construction company that builds houses – this is in a completely different market to banking services.

4 Promotions – to attract new customers; price discounts – to encourage consumers to buy more; opening more stores – to widen market coverage.

Progress check B

1 Driving: lower costs increasing competitiveness; may be closer to some markets – easier transport.

Restraining: concerns over product quality; impact on existing workers and threat of job losses.

2 Driving: lower costs increasing competitiveness [8]; may be closer to some markets – easier transport [3].

Restraining: concerns over product quality [9]; impact on existing workers and threat of job losses [4].

3 Encourage some existing workers who might lose their jobs to relocate to low-cost country to take control of quality assurance in the new manufacturing facility. Apply for government grant in the country being relocated to – this makes the potential gain greater and therefore raises the value of a major 'driving force'.

Progress check C

Decision tree layout and solution:

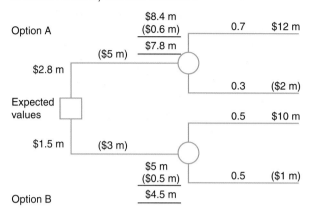

Progress check D

1 Economic outcome/pay-off X probability

2 No past experience makes determining likely 'probabilities of events occurring' very uncertain.

3 Decision by a clothing manufacturer to launch a range of exclusive fashion clothing for men.

Additional exam-style question

1 **b** Student's own answer – use decision tree results, data from Table 39.2 and other information.

Chapter 40

Progress check A

1 Lack of planning suggests that the entrepreneur has not thought out the major factors needed for the business to succeed – this will add to investor's risks. The entrepreneur needs to include in the Business Plan detail about the market they are entering, the way the product/service will be provided and marketed, the amount of finance needed, the most suitable location – and several other important factors – before investors will consider putting capital into the new venture.

2 It is like setting up a new business – research must be undertaken, budgets set, resources prepared, finance obtained etc. – so planning will be essential for success.

Progress check B

1 Yes, all businesses need a plan to follow so that decisions can be judged against the plan to see if they are consistent with it – but flexible planning is essential to allow unforeseen events to be taken into account.

2 All departments need to be working together for the plan to succeed, e.g. a strategy to export products for the first time will need integrated planning between operations, marketing, HR and finance.

3 E.g. depreciation of your country's currency allows the business to lower the foreign currency price of its exports – but any imported materials and components will be more expensive.

Progress check C

1 R and D needs creative thinkers who are not afraid of making mistakes – hence the importance of entrepreneurial culture. Government departments have to have all similar tasks performed in the same (bureaucratic) way – hence task culture.

2 Yes, potential culture clash is a major reason why takeovers/mergers often fail. A consistent culture will require cultural change – which will have to be managed very sensitively and effectively.

3 New vision/mission statements; new CEO or at least some change in senior directors; new incentive system for senior managers with less emphasis on production targets at all cost; ethical code and employee training based around it.

Progress check D

1 Managing is making sure the resources are ready; leading is about giving a vision and making others want to follow.

2 Population growth; economic growth.

3 Privatisation; major change of government.

4 Explain need for change; communication with stakeholders; explaining impact on employees and steps to be taken to reduce the negative effects; employee (may be student) involvement in some decision making, e.g. design of classrooms; project champion.

Progress check E

1 Keeping the business open and operating during a crisis.

2 Some shocks are 'out of the blue' and cannot be predicted.

3 Shows the business is taking steps to ensure their safety and continuity of operations following a crisis. For example, having alternative accommodation available following a fire so the business can restart trading quickly.

4 Major fire: employees know how to evacuate building and raise alarm; senior managers are available for press/media communication; resources in place to reduce risks for residents/employees/customers; alternative premises are made ready to allow business to continue; those injured are quickly compensated.

Additional exam-style question

1 b Define contingency planning. AC seemed to respond well to the crisis caused by the inflammable material – there was clear evidence of a plan of action and this was carried out effectively. Owing to this the impact on sales was small. So contingency planning has been very important.

A bad reputation for handling crises – especially when they concern consumer safety – could have a damaging impact on future sales and success. This is particularly true when the market segment aimed for is higher income groups with 'quality fashion clothing'.

Safety of new equipment will also be important – and an accident in the factory could upset production plans as well as cause concern amongst the workers – who may be worried about the effect on them of AC's changes. Contingency planning will help to reassure workers that AC's directors/managers are concerned about worker welfare.

But: contingency planning can be expensive – can AC afford it with falling profitability? Other factors will determine AC's success too – retail competition might drive down prices and profit margins further; failure to introduce strategic changes effectively will certainly put AC's future success at risk.

So, contingency planning important – but costly and not the only factor determining AC's future success.

Index

Note: The letters '*f*', and '*t*' following locators refer to figures, and tables respectively